STORIES BEHIND
WORDS

STORIES BEHIND
WORDS

*The origins and histories
of 285 English words*

BY

PETER R. LIMBURG

THE

H. W. WILSON COMPANY

1986

Library of Congress Cataloging in Publication Data

Limburg, Peter R.
   Stories behind words

   Includes index.
    1. English language—Etymology.   I. Title.
PE1574.L46 1985   422 85-26398
ISBN 0-8242-0718-1

To my wife,

Maggie,

and my children,

Richard,

Karin,

David,

and

Ellen,

who always hoped I would amount to something.

CONTENTS

TO THE READER

Words are endlessly fascinating. Why do they mean what they mean, and how did they acquire their meanings? (In the simplest terms, a word means what it means because people agree that it does, but that still leaves a lot of questions unanswered.) Meanings are constantly, if slowly, changing, which is one reason why so many people feel that Shakespeare's English is really a foreign language. Take the word *presently*, for example. Everyone knows that it means "by-and-by." But in Shakespeare's day everyone knew that it meant "right away." Or consider *clever*, which once meant "dextrous" or "nimble," and now means "nimble-minded." In the 19th century, *clever* did extra duty as a synonym for "handsome" and "good-natured." In the slang of the 1940s, when I was a teen-ager, *terrific* was a word of the highest praise. But to my parents it meant "terrifically bad," which caused numerous family quarrels.

Words' meanings change because words mean different things to different people. Every person reacts slightly differently to words, since we are all unique individuals. And we are often careless in the way we use them. As Humpty-Dumpty put it so neatly in Lewis Carroll's *Through the Looking Glass*, "When I use a word, it means just what I choose it to mean—neither more nor less."

To The Reader

Advertisers, politicians, and con men of every kind try daily to manipulate us with skillfully crafted verbiage. In this world where we are constantly being manipulated with words, it is useful to keep in mind that the word is not the thing, any more than a map is the countryside it represents, or a picture the object it depicts. If you doubt this, try eating a luscious peach from a still-life painting, or a juicy steak from a color ad in a magazine. Yet, without words, we would not be truly human. Other animals can communicate in a limited way by scent, sound, gesture, and body language. But only man can speak and, by speech, achieve all that we have achieved.

Words can also give us an excursion through human history, reflecting man's infinitely varied customs. *Silk*, for instance, takes us back to ancient China, where the secret of turning a certain caterpillar's cocoons into soft, lustrous cloth was first discovered, and into the attempts of moralistic Roman senators to ban the use of silk in the Roman Empire, as well as the reason why so many American cities have a Mulberry Street (visionary entrepreneurs planted mulberry trees to start a native silk industry). There is drama and tragedy attached to many a word, too, as in the story of Madame Pompadour, whom we know for the popular hairdo named for her. But she was a king's mistress who virtually ruled France, and her anger at some nasty poems written about her led to a general war and changed the map of Europe. *Cardigan* takes us to the Crimean War and the shocking story of how a feud between two aristocratic brothers-in-law led to the tragedy of the Light Brigade.

To explore the history of every word is, of course, impossible. But here is a selection of some I think are particularly interesting. I hope you will have as much fun reading about them as I did writing this book.

MOOD
and
CHARACTER

Arrogant the word arouses instinctive dislike and resentment. Dictionaries define it in various ways, such as "making exorbitant claims of rank or importance" and "aggressively conceited." Another way of describing an arrogant person is that he expects others to defer to him as a matter of right, and gets angry if they don't. Yet *arrogant* originally meant no more than claiming something for oneself. One of the meanings of its Latin original, the verb *arrogare*, is "to ask for." Apparently arrogant people asked for too much too often, so that the word gradually took on its present meaning.

I referred to the arrogant person as "he," and in fact arrogance seems to be more of a male than a female characteristic. In some cultures, male arrogance is actually honored, and in others tolerated as if it were a law of nature. It may have to do with the fact that male animals in so many species compete for females, food, and other good things of life, and often the one that behaves in the most dominant fashion can intimidate other males without a fight. Jane Goodall, the noted student of primate behavior, found this pattern among the chimpanzees and baboons she studied in Africa. However, there is a big difference between ape and human arrogance. Among the chimps, the male who has just won a dominance contest consoles the loser with a pat or a hug. Among humans, the winner

1

can seldom let well enough alone, but continues to punish and humiliate the loser. Perhaps we could learn something from the chimps!

To Badger

To badger someone is to torment him without respite. To capture the flavor of the expression, one must go back to its origins in the cruel "sport" of badger-baiting. In this once-popular diversion, a badger was placed in an artificial burrow and dogs were set on him. To keep the badger from escaping, a chain was passed through a hole in his tail and secured by a stout stake driven down through the closed end of the burrow. Infuriated by the pain, the badger usually managed to inflict terrible mutilations on the dogs before he succumbed. Even so, the tenacious badger often had to be knocked on the head to put him out of his misery.

The badger is one of the giants of the weasel family. A prodigious digger, it has immensely strong forelegs armed with formidable claws. It also has powerful jaws, strong teeth (one old source claims they can splinter iron), and a thick, loose skin that is difficult for an attacker to get a grip on. It is also very tenacious of life. These qualities all made it a suitable object of solicitude for the sadistic "sportsmen" of days gone by. The term "to badger" dates back to the late 18th century.

Of course, "to badger" is not the only animal-related term of this kind. Very close in its meaning is "to hound" someone, keeping after him like a hound on the track of its quarry. The same is true of "dogging the footsteps" of a person. The dog, indeed, does yeoman service in our language as a symbol of all kinds of qualities, from fidelity to savagery. The Vietnam War brought to temporary prominence the Chinese insult "running dog," a phrase that Chinese leaders applied assiduously to the United States. Young American radicals and protesters were fond of flinging this bit of invective about, but most of them probably did not understand why it was such an insult in Chinese terms. To the Chinese, the dog is not running to its master but running away—and for the best of reasons. It is not considered a pet, but an item of food.

The dog's relative, the wolf, has contributed to many terms, all pejorative. To "wolf down" your food means to gobble it with gluttonous haste, as a wolf devours its prey. (In nature there are good reasons for this. One is that the wolf must try to get its share before the other members of the pack eat it up; another is that adult wolves bring back food for the pups in their stomachs. When they return to the den, they regurgitate most of what they have swallowed.) A wolf is also a male human who behaves in a predatory fashion toward females. Need more be said?

Man—at least European and Near Eastern man—seems to loathe the wolf more than any other predator. Yet, scientists believe, man and wolf coexisted fairly peaceably during the long centuries of prehistory when man was a wandering hunter and gatherer of wild plants. Wolves even followed human hunting bands and scavenged the leftover scraps of meat and bone. In time, some were tamed and became ancestors of our domestic dogs. But then man began to settle down and raise livestock: sheep, goats, cattle, and swine. All of these offered tempting meals to the wild wolves. Thus it was that the wolf became man's enemy and a symbol for everything evil.

"Chicken out" dates from the World War II period, but the chicken as a symbol of timidity has a long if not glorious history. "Chickenhearted" was in use not long after 1600. This is strange considering that man has pitted fighting cocks against each other for at least three thousand years, and the gamecock remains a symbol of fighting spirit.

"To parrot"—to repeat someone else's words mechanically without necessarily understanding them—dates back at least to 1581. It is a realistic description of a real parrot's "conversation," since the bird repeats words without knowing what they mean. No doubt the parrot (for parrots are intelligent birds) learns that there is a connection between "Polly want a cracker!" and getting a snack. But parrots do not make up sentences or phrases of their own. It may be that they regard the phrases humans teach them as a kind of song, and birds' songs are pretty well stereotyped in most species.

The parrot used to be known as the popinjay (from the Old French name *papegai*), now a name applied to people who are very vain of their appearance. The word *parrot* is thought to be a corruption of another French name, *Perrot*, roughly equivalent to "Petey," which was probably a common name for pet parrots.

To "eat crow" means to humble oneself, probably because the crow was regarded as an ignoble bird. (Young crows, however, are said to make good eating.) Englishmen in Queen Elizabeth's time had an expression, "I have a crow to pluck with you," meaning the same as the modern "I have a bone to pick with you." Man has always regarded the crow as a pest and used its name pejoratively. No one has ever written lyrical poems to crows as Keats did to the nightingale, or Shelley to the skylark. On the other hand, the crow's larger cousin, the raven, became the focal character in Poe's celebrated poem.

The cat was long burdened with a bad reputation in Christian lands—even worse than the crow's because cats were connected with witches and devil-worship. Early on they became symbols of slyness, malice, and cruelty. But the word *catty*, in the sense of "sly and spiteful" dates only from the 1880s. It is still in use, though often replaced nowadays by the formerly tabooed "bitchy." The tomcat—the male of the species—is renowned for his supposedly insatiable sexual appetite, and so "tomcatting" refers to human males who overindulge in the pleasures of sex.

To *cow* someone is to overawe him, to intimidate him into submission. One might think that it refers to the ease with which cows can be dominated. But the word has nothing to do with cattle. It is derived from an Old Norse word, *kuga*, meaning "to tyrannize over."

Coward, similarly, has nothing to do with bovine lack of courage. (Cows, in fact, can be pretty fierce under certain conditions.) It comes from the Old French *coart* (from *coe*, "tail," plus *-ard*, "one who overdoes things"), and traces its ancestry to the Latin word for tail, *cauda*. Scholars have disputed endlessly over the precise connotations of the tail—whether it refers to an animal's turning tail (fleeing an enemy) or a dog's tucking its tail between its legs in submission. Most Americans have heard of the Cowardly Lion in the Oz books, but that amiable beast has a little-known ancestor in European heraldry. On coats of arms, the cowardly lion was drawn with his tail between his legs. Why a symbol of cowardice should be placed on the insignia of an aristocracy whose claims were based on martial valor and fierceness I have no idea, unless perhaps it was a whim of the noble authorities who approved coats of arms.

Bully, strangely enough, originally meant a sweetheart or lover. The authorities trace it back to a Dutch word, *boel* (pronounced "bool"), that entered the English language in the 1530s when King Henry VIII was in his prime. At first applied to either sex, it came to be used for men only. By the early 1700s the word had taken a sinister turn, now meaning a pimp. A quarter-century later it meant a hired thug. Some time after that "bully" took on its current meaning. But when Theodore Roosevelt exclaimed "Bully!" as one of his highest terms of approbation, he was using an adjectival form of the word that dates back at least to 1681 and was revived in the mid-19th century.

We shall wind up this essay with two more terms: to *weasel out* and to *skunk*. Weaseling out means evading an obligation through some trumped-up excuse. The allusion is to the weasel's legendary slyness and cunning in evading capture. *Weasel words*, an expression attributed to Theodore Roosevelt, are words that take the meaning out of a seemingly plausible statement, the way a weasel sucks eggs through a tiny, barely visible hole. The skunk, a member of the weasel family, was a natural choice to describe a mean-spirited, generally detestable person—a real stinker. *To skunk* an opponent in a game of cards, in sports, or any other kind of contest means that you win without his scoring a single point. In other words, his skill —or perhaps his luck—stinks.

Blue   For a beautiful color, blue carries a heavy freight of negative connotations: Blue Monday, the cheerless start of the work week, Blue Laws, the repressive legislation enacted by the Bluenoses; and, of course, the Blues, that miserable state of depression and dejection made famous by Negro singers. Why this should be is rather mystifying, for a blue sky is undeniably more cheerful to look at than a gray one, and in some cultures blue is the symbol of hope. Blue is the color that decorates the edges of the prayer shawls that Orthodox Jews wear; blue is the color of the Virgin Mary's mantle for Roman Catholics. To the Mongols, blue was sacred because it was the color of a clear, peaceful sky, free of threatening storm clouds.

How, then, did the blues get their name? It seems that back around 1740 the English coined a phrase, "the blue devils," meaning low spirits or deep depression. Like many another useful expression, this one was shared with the colonial cousins across the Atlantic. Early in the 19th century, Americans abbreviated it to "the blues." The name was easily transferred to the vigorous laments that Negro singers and musicians composed toward the end of the century.

Blue

"Blue" must be part of dozens of expressions, ranging from sentimental to obscene. "True blue" dates back at least to 1500, when someone decided, and others agreed, that blue was the color of loyalty and constancy. It was also taken as an emblem by the stern Scottish Presbyterians during the English Civil War. (The King's party chose the lively, dashing red for their color.) A "blue funk," a somewhat obsolete term for panic, dates back to the 1840s and may have originated as British boarding-school slang.

Then there are the famous "bluestockings." Around 1750 a little group of upper-class Englishwomen—and a few men—began to meet regularly for a very eccentric purpose. Instead of playing cards and shredding reputations, they discussed literary works. Worse yet, they dressed plainly, ostentatiously disregarding fashion. One of the group even went so far as to wear blue worsted stockings instead of the customary black silk. (They were plainly visible, for the offender was a man, and men wore knee-breeches.) Fashionable society sneered at the eccentric little band as "bluestockings," and the name stuck, long outliving its originals.

The word *blue* itself comes from an old Germanic word, *blaewoz*. Variations of this turn up in many European languages, such as the French *bleu*, the German *blau*, the Italian *blu*, and Swedish *blå*. But it won't mean anything to a Spanish speaker, who says *azul*, nor to a Russian, who would retort *siniy*.

Of the many other expressions in which colors appear, consider the puzzling phrase "in a brown study." In the early 1500s brown meant "gloomy" as well as the color brown. So a person in a brown study was wrapped in gloomy thoughts. Now it simply means being absorbed in thought.

A "black mood" needs no explanation, but it refers back to the ancient Greek theory of the body's being composed of four substances called "humors." These were blood, phlegm, yellow bile, and black bile. Blood was considered hot and wet; phlegm, cold and wet; yellow bile, hot and dry; and black bile, cold and dry. An excess of black bile was supposed to plunge a person into deep melancholy (indeed, *melancholy* comes from the Greek *melas*, black, and *chole*, bile), or the blues. Today, however, a black mood simply means being in a rotten temper.

We turn *green* with envy; a coward is *yellow*; an overdose of colorful writing results in *purple* prose—all figurative expressions. But there is one color-related expression with a basis in reality: *seeing red* when we are beside ourselves with rage. In an extreme state of anger, the eyes can become suffused with blood so that the angry person actually sees the world through a reddish haze.

Conceited

Call a person conceited, and everyone knows what you mean—but before the early 1600s your hearers would have been puzzled. From the time that the word *conceit* entered the English language (as an import from France, probably with the Norman invasion in 1066) until the end of Elizabeth I's reign it meant an idea, a concept, or an opinion. Even as late as 1806 Noah Webster, the father of American lexicography, defined conceit as "a fancy, idea, fondness, pride."

This was not unnatural, since *conceit* stems from the Latin verb *concipio*, which meant "to grasp," "to conceive," and several other things depending on context. Thus, conceit was something you conceived. At one time, *conceit* even doubled as a verb, as in: "I conceit that a rich reward awaits the lucky winner."

But loose usage and change inexorably crept in, and by 1588 one could say of a self-infatuated rival, "He hath a great conceit of himself," and "self-conceit" was a noun in common use. A mere couple of decades later, "conceit" had taken on its modern meaning, at least in some contexts. Gradually the older meanings faded away, until they are now at best quaint conceits.

The closest synonym for "conceited" in English is "vain," which comes from the Latin *vanus*, meaning "empty." When the Biblical prophet Ecclesiastes lamented, "Vanity of vanities . . . all is vanity," he was not talking about men's or women's concern about their clothes or hair or jewelry. He was announcing to his readers that the world is all a big nothing. This meaning lingers on in such phrases as "He tried in vain . . ." and "a vain search." The word did not take on its modern meaning until the end of the 1600s. (The OED gives 1692 as the date of the first recorded use.)

How, then, did the word acquire its modern sense? It seems that the Romans had a phrase for it, *vana gloria*, meaning "empty glory," or empty, boastful pride. In English this became "vainglory," with "vainglorious" as the adjectival form. From here it was a simple step to chop off the "glorious," leaving plain "vain." (This began around the end of the 17th century.) Interestingly, to Romans the word *gloriosus* meant "boastful" as well as "glorious." Perhaps those stuffy old orators were better psychologists than we give them credit for being.

Mythology and folklore furnish us with many examples of vanity, from the legendary Narcissus, who was so in love with himself that he fell into a pool and drowned while trying to kiss his own reflection, to the peacock, which was accused of having grown its beautiful, iridescent tail to distract attention from its ugly red feet. But an English wit, Sir Max Beerbohm, gave us perhaps the best distinction between vanity and conceit. Said he: "To say that a man is vain means merely that he is pleased with the effect he produces on other people. A conceited man is pleased with the effect he produces on himself."

9

Cranky
The story of the word *cranky* leads through many twists and bends of the etymological path—appropriately so, for *cranky* traces its ancestry to a Germanic root that meant something bent or crooked. The name of that venerable mechanical device, the crank, is derived from the same source.

Apparently *cranky* in its modern sense of "peevish" or "ill-tempered" was first used in 18th-century British dialect. It also meant "out of order" or "sickly." This may have been influenced by a Dutch and German word brought in by merchants and seamen: *krank*, meaning "sick." This imported word, again, is connected to the ancestral root and once meant "twisted by illness."

In an earlier day *crank* had some surprisingly different meanings. In the late 16th century, for instance, it could mean a fanciful turn of speech, as in the "quips and cranks" that professional entertainers spouted on command. In thieves' slang of the same period, a crank or counterfeit crank was a beggar who feigned illness or deformity. Originally it seems to have meant one who threw simulated epileptic fits, as "crank" was a low-life slang term for epilepsy. In the 17th century, *crank* had a brief fling in standard English in the unexpected sense of "lusty" or "vigorous."

Sailing buffs may be familiar with the terms "a crank sailer," a phrase as arcane as "yare." The term refers not to a crew member who is a bad sport, but to a sailing ship (or sailboat in these more modest days). It means, not a ship that peevishly refuses to respond to the rudder, but one that is prone to capsizing. The term comes from a Dutch word, *krengd*, which refers to a ship turned on its side (as in the operation of careening, although language experts have hinted no connection).

Cranky and *crank* also have a long-standing meaning of "crotchety" or "eccentric," full of whims, which goes back at least as far as the late 16th century. The poet Milton used it in this sense in *L'Allegro*, while around the beginning of this century baseball fans were called "baseball cranks." That is not strange, since *fan* (in the sense of a devotee) is just a short form of *fanatic*.

Most dictionary definitions of *cranky* use the word *cross* or *cross-tempered*, and there we have another story. One of the many meanings of *cross* was something that lies across another, thus, by extension, blocking the way or opposing. For example, "Aaron Burr and Alexander Hamilton were at cross purposes." So a cross-tempered (or simply cross) person was one who disliked whatever other people did and got into a bad temper over it.

Crazy "Crazy" originally re-
ferred to a cracked piece of crockery rather than the human mind. The modern use was born as a metaphor. Etymologists have traced "crazy" back to an Old Norse word, *krasa*, which meant, roughly, "to bash into little bits."

In the Middle Ages, people in England were using the word "craze" to mean shatter, batter, or crack. By the end of the 15th century they were using it figuratively to mean "to cause harm to the health" or "to render insane." It is not certain when someone tacked a *-y* to the end to make "crazy," but it appeared in the written language in the 1570s. By the early 1600s it had taken on the meaning of "insane." But it kept its older meanings for a surprisingly long time. Thus Noah Webster defined "crazy" in his original dictionary of 1806 as "broken, weak, feeble, sickly, maddish."

"Cracked" as a colloquial form of "crazy" also goes back a long time, at least to about 1600. Originally it seems to have been "crack-brained" or "crack-skulled." When referring to others as "cracked" or "crazed," people seem to have identified the head—and the brain inside it—with a clay pot. This imagery must go back at least to the Romans, for the French word for "head," *tête*, comes from *testa*, one of the Latin words for a clay pot. (This word has no connection with *testicle*, which many etymologists believe is derived from the Latin *testis*, a witness, from the ancient custom of men's taking oaths on their testicles, the seat of their manhood. The testicle is literally a "little witness.")

Insane is also a Latin contribution, coming from *in-*, "not," plus *sanus*, "sound" or "healthy." Students of bygone days had pounded into them the hoary Latin maxim *mens sana in corpore sano*, "a healthy mind in a healthy body," though they usually had quite different ideas from their schoolmasters about how to attain these praiseworthy goals.

Insane came into English about the mid-1500s. A far older word for the same condition is *mad*, which dates back to the earliest days of the English language. Language scholars have traced it back even further, to a hypothetical Indo-European root, *mei*, meaning "to change." Certainly a mad person is changed from his normal state. *Mad* in its current American sense of "angry" is a shortened form of "mad with rage."

Madmen—and madwomen—have been treated in very different ways by different societies. In some, they have been tolerated as having been afflicted by a divine power; in others they have been regarded as possessed by devils and treated with utmost cruelty to drive the devils out. In Europe and the Americas they were often tormented by cruel children and adults, being regarded as fair game. Often, too, their families simply locked them up in a garret and refused to let them out, concealing their disgrace. Of course, madness is a relative concept. The extreme self-torment and religious visions of many of the early Christian saints would surely classify them as highly neurotic, if not clinically insane, today, but to their contemporaries it made them holy.

Gentle

"Tough but gentle" used to be the slogan of a popular facial tissue, whose advertising symbol was a thuggish-looking male smiling sweetly as he cradled a beaming baby. The meaning was clear, but the original meaning of "gentle" had nothing to do with the tender care the tough man was lavishing on the infant. In the 13th century "gentle" had very little to do with behavior and much to do with accidents of birth, for a "gentle" person belonged to a family of rank and position.

The word "gentle" goes back to the Romans and their social organization. In the Roman scheme of things, every aristocrat belonged to a clan called a *gens*—traditionally, there were supposed to be three hundred such *gentes*. *Gens* is derived from the verb *genere*, "to beget" or "to bear," with the idea of a common ancestry. The common folk—the plebeians—had no *gens* of their own, although they could become hangers-on of one aristocratic clan or another.

At any rate, the adjective denoting one who belonged to a *gens* was *gentilis*, a high-born or noble person. After the breakup of the Roman Empire, this word became *gentil* in Old French, and the Normans carried it to England. (The Old English equivalent was *aethele*, but that fell out of use when the Normans imposed their brand of French as the language of the ruling classes. It survives only in the woman's name Ethel.) By the 13th century the modern form *gentle* could be heard, and even seen in written form (by the few who could read). A frequent use was in the phrase "of gentle birth," meaning that the person in question had aristocratic parents.

But along the way *gentle* picked up some new meanings. Even in the 13th century it had the connotation of courteous or generous. Two centuries later people could describe animals as gentle, meaning domesticated or tame. And, since *gentle* also described the ideal of behavior for the gentry, it came to imply mildness or softness and consideration for others, its meaning today.

Gentle also had a few strange offspring, now obsolete. When Izaak Walton wrote his fisherman's classic *The Compleat Angler* in 1653, one of his favorite fish baits was "gentles"—meaning maggots. The *Oxford English Dictionary* explains this as a special sense of "soft," which maggots certainly are. Another was the expression "gentle reader." This did not imply that the reader was mild-mannered and considerate, but rather that he was one of the gentry, a rather unsubtle form of flattery.

Another word that *gens* begat was *generous*, which in its original Latin form meant noble, well-born, or, in the case of property, producing well. It carried the same meanings in England until the 17th century, when it began to take on its modern meaning of "free in giving," as befitted a nobleman.

Gentile, in the sense of someone who is not Jewish, comes from *gens* in the sense of "tribe" or "nation." In Old Testament times, Jews distinguished themselves from all other peoples, whom they called "the nations"—in Hebrew, *goyim*. When the Jewish Scriptures were translated into Latin, the translators used the corresponding Latin term. Early Christians sometimes used "gentile" as an epithet for pagans, but today the word means only a non-Jew—except to Mormons, to whom it means a non-Mormon. A Mormon community is the only place in the world where a Jew is classed as a Gentile.

Genteel comes from the French *gentil*, which nowadays carries the meaning of "nice." "Ah, *que vous êtes gentil*," a Frenchman will say when you do him a good turn. But originally it meant "befitting a person of quality." As far back as the 14th century, Chaucer used *gentil* in *The Canterbury Tales*. In fact, he used it pretty freely, and sometimes sarcastically. Thousands of former college students remember Chaucer's "verray parfit gentil knight" if they remember nothing else; but Chaucer also described the rascally Summoner as "a gentil harlot." A few hundred years later, *genteel* came to imply polished manners, but in our more democratic days it connotes an excess of etiquette, an overdone, affected politeness.

"When Adam delved and Eve span, Who was then the gentleman?" cried 14th-century English peasants as they rebelled against their overlords. The answer was not, as we might suppose, Adam, for a gentleman then was a member of the lower levels of the aristocracy, not important enough to be a noble but still too exalted to perform manual labor. A gentleman was also entitled to bear weapons, a privilege denied to common folk.

No gentleman felt really secure unless he had a coat of arms, and by Shakespeare's era the granting of coats of arms was a well-established business. The applicant satisfied the heralds (the authorities in charge of creating and bestowing coats of arms) that he could support himself without manual labor, that he had a certain amount of education or had performed military service, and could afford to outfit himself with armor if called to war. He then—most important—paid a fee and received his coat of arms. He was also entitled to be called "Master." A contemporary writer noted gleefully that "the prince do lose nothing by it, the gentleman being so much subject to taxes and public payments as is the yeoman or husbandman." Furthermore, "with the government of the commonwealth he medleth little." Commoners could, by using their connections, sometimes get themselves transformed into gentlemen. Shakespeare himself did so.

But the idea of gentleman-as-exalted-rank changed and softened as society grew less rigid. By the mid-19th century, even in stuffy England, a gentleman was defined not by his ancestry or his wealth, but by his standards of behavior.

Happy

"This happy breed of men," John of Gaunt termed his fellow Englishmen in a rhapsodic passage in Shakespeare's *Richard II*. What Shakespeare meant to say was not that Englishmen were forever smiling and contented, but that they were fortunate to be English. For *happy* comes from *hap*, an Old Norse root meaning "chance." *Happen* comes from the same root. Originally *hap* was neutral; it could mean either good fortune or bad fortune. It gradually came to connote good luck rather than bad, and then to mean "lucky" or "fortunate." The word *mishap* had to be coined to indicate bad luck. Only in the the early 1500s did *happy* begin to mean what it does today, and the older meaning held sway for a couple of centuries more. (Even as late as 1806, Noah Webster defined *happy* as "fortunate," and the old meaning lingers on in expressions like "a happy choice.") The slang meaning of "drunk" did not appear until a few years before the American Revolution. It refers, of course, to a drinker's jovial frame of mind in the early states of his drinking, before he gets mean and nasty.

The phrase "the pursuit of happiness," linked with life and liberty in the preamble to our Declaration of Independence, has been interpreted in a great variety of ways. But it is likely that the framers of the Declaration meant nothing more than the right of ordinary people to better themselves without government interference, which was not the case under the rigid social systems of Britain and the other countries of 18th-century Europe.

Gay in its original sense meant joyous, lively, or lighthearted. It comes from the Old French word *gai*, whose origin remains a mystery. It appeared in English by the 13th century, and immediately began to take on new shades of meaning. By the next century, it also meant bright-colored; two centuries later it had acquired connotations of dissipation and immorality. In 18th-century English criminal lingo, the "gaying instrument" was the penis. But it was not until our own century, probably in the 1920s, that "gay" became a synonym for "homosexual." Why this word was chosen in preference to others is an enigma, but we seem to be stuck with it for the foreseeable future.

Merry in Anglo-Saxon times meant "pleasing" or "agreeable," as in the original "Merry England." In the 1300s it acquired the meaning of "lively and cheerful," which it has kept to this day. It also has a slightly disreputable secondary meaning of "slightly tipsy," which it got in the 1500s. Strangely enough, language scholars believe that *merry* comes from an Indo-European root meaning "short," the idea being that merriment makes the time seem short.

Heckle

Heckle has no connection with *heck*, that cautious 19th-century euphemism for Hell. It is instead derived from the fiendish process to which man subjects the flax plant in order to extract from it the fiber that is spun into linen. In the old days, this was all done by hand. The harvested flax stalks were laid in water to rot, or ret (a favorite crossword-puzzle word), in order to soften them up and loosen the fibers from the woody cores. The retted stalks were next beaten with a sharp-edged paddle called a swingle—a brutal series of karate-like chops—to break up the woody cores and loosen them further. Then came the heckling. A burly workman would seize a bundle of flax stems and dash them down with all his might upon the heckle, a stout board set with long, sharp spikes pointing upwards. He would slowly work the flax through this iron comb from one end to the other, combing out woody fragments and aligning the flax fibers. Then he would do it over again from the other end. The process was repeated several times with finer and finer heckles until the flax was ready for bleaching and spinning.

In the sense of tormenting a speaker or performer, *heckle* dates from the early 1800s, when rude Britons subjected politicians to a barrage of embarrassing questions. This usage may also have been influenced by *hector*, which as early as the mid-1600s meant "to bully." (This was a sarcastic comparison of swaggering bullies to the noble Hector of Troy, whose exploits were popularized with the revival of classical learning.) Hector's name was also used in a mild oath, "By Hector!", which was often abbreviated to "By heck!" And that brings us full circle.

Humble

Humble is one of the many Latin-derived words that found a home for themselves in English. It dates back to the 13th century, having probably come in with the Norman conquerors, who themselves were anything but humble. But then, humble people would never go out and conquer someone else's nation in the first place. *Humble* comes ultimately from the Latin *humilis*, which in turn comes from *humus*, "soil." It literally means "not far above the ground," or "low," like a stunted tree that lacks the strength to grow tall, or a hapless servant flinging himself on the ground to appease his master's wrath. *Humus* has an intriguing, distant linkage with *homo*, the Latin word for "man." As a matter of fact, many cultures have a creation myth in which a divine being creates mankind from dirt, but that is another story.

The meaning of *humble* has not changed since it first appeared in 13th-century English. Then, as now, it meant having a low opinion of oneself (or of one's rights). Soon another meaning was added: of lowly social position. As a verb, *to humble* has been used from the 14th century and is still going strong, perhaps a testimony to the persistence of some of humankind's nastier traits.

Humility was little esteemed in the ancient world—it was generally regarded as the mark of an inferior person. Jewish prophets like Isaiah preached humility as a virtue, but their message had no effect beyond the Jewish community. It was another Jewish preacher, Jesus of Nazareth, who gave humility a leading place among the virtues, and the triumph of Christianity gave humility an officially recognized position. Even then, humility was honored more in the abstract than in practice. As the character Prince Mordred in *Camelot* sneered, "It's not the earth the meek inherit, it's the dirt." People the world over seem more interested in applying humiliation to their brethren than in taking a dose of it themselves. During the 18th and 19th centuries it was customary to sign letters "Your Humble Servant." But did they mean it? Not on your life!

"Eating humble pie" is, or course, one way of expressing humiliation, but this picturesque expression actually originated as a 19th-century pun. In medieval English there was a word, *numbles*, which meant the edible portions of an animal's entrails, particularly of a deer or other game animal. *Numbles* was an Old French version of a Latin word for "little loin," one of the many culinary euphemisms man has used to disguise the less appealing kinds of food. A pie was traditionally made of the numbles of game animals after a hunt. Authorities cannot agree on whether it was a prized delicacy or something that was given to the servants while their masters feasted on the better cuts. In any case, "a numble pie" gradually became "an umble pie." Since the old-fashioned pronunciation of *humble* was *umble*, it gave punsters a prime opportunity to pounce. With this inside joke, your humble author ends this essay.

Humor

When we say that so-and-so is in a good or a bad humor we are unwittingly referring to an ancient and unscientific medical doctrine. Hippocrates, still revered as the father of medicine, held the theory that the body was composed of four fluids (*humors*, in the Latin translation): blood, phlegm, choler (yellow bile), and melancholy (black bile). Good health depended on these four humors being in proper balance. If there were too much or too little of any one of them, sickness would result.

The four humors also became associated with personality traits. The sanguine person, influenced by the hot, moist blood, was cheerful and optimistic. The phlegmatic person, dominated by cold, moist phlegm, was even-tempered, stodgy, and dull, not reacting much to events. The choleric person, ruled by the hot, dry bile, was hot-tempered, quick to take offense, and usually angry about something or other. The melancholy soul, governed by the so-called black bile (a wholly imaginary substance that was thought to be cold and dry), was sad, brooding, and depressed.

Humor in the sense of a personality trait dates from the late 15th century. People began to use it in the sense of a temporary mood in the first quarter of the 16th century, while King Henry VIII was chafing over the failure of his first wife, Catherine of Aragon, to give him a son. *To humor* a person (in other words, to cater to his humor of the moment) dates from the reign of Queen Elizabeth I; Shakespeare used it in his plays. *Humorous* in the sense of "funny" or "amusing" was a relative late-comer to the language, dating from about 1680.

The old humor theory of medicine is long discredited, but its ghost lives on in our language.

Jealous

Many a murder is committed by a jealous spouse or lover, and there are few people who have not felt the pangs of jealousy at one time or another. But most would be surprised to learn that the word *jealous* is derived from the Greek word for zeal, *zelos*. A jealous person is thus one who guards his or her spouse or sweetheart with excessive zeal. Of course, jealousy spreads far wider than love or sex. One can be jealous of a job, of prerogatives, of fame, of power. We often use "jealous" and "envious" interchangeably, but there is a difference. Envy has to do with resenting the good fortune of someone else; jealousy has to do with the fear that someone else is going to steal something from you.

Shakespeare called jealousy a "green-eyed monster," and English speakers still associate jealousy (and envy too) with green. But Germans go pale with jealousy. Swedes become "black-sick," and their slang term for "jealous" is "sooty."

Nice

"Nice guys finish last," sneered Leo Durocher, a baseball player and coach who was known for his boorish behavior. Leo the Lip obviously equated "nice" with "stupid," and thereby reverted to the original meaning of "nice" even as he outraged the moral sensibilities of decent folk. *Nice* comes, in fact, from the Old French *nice*, meaning "silly," from the Latin *nescius*, "ignorant." The *Oxford Dictionary of English Etymology* traces it back to the 13th century, when it meant "stupid" or "foolish." But the word then underwent a wild series of changes, first to "wanton," then to "shy," then to "fastidious," "precise," or "critical." In the 18th century it began to take on its modern senses of "agreeable," "pleasing," or "kind and considerate to others."

Some of the old meanings hung on for centuries. As late as 1806, Noah Webster, the father of American lexicography, defined *nice* as "exact, refined, squeamish, finical, fine." Even today we refer to a very fine distinction between things as a "nice distinction." And we still talk about the niceties of protocol or the niceties of behavior, meaning the fine points.

Outrageous

Contrary to what one might expect, *outrageous* does not come from *rage*, but from an Old French word, *ultrage*, which meant more or less "going too far." (*Ultrage* came from the Latin word *ultra*, "beyond.") In medieval times, an outrage was anything from lack of moderation to deeds or words that passed beyond accepted bounds. It could also mean violent or disorderly conduct, passionate behavior, or insolence. By the mid-1500s, about the time Bloody Mary mounted the throne of England, *outrage* carried the meaning of a violent injury to others. Perhaps a decade before the American Revolution, it had acquired its modern sense of a gross injury to personal feelings or social principles.

Although *outrageous* is not derived from *rage*, its meaning has certainly been influenced by it. It seems to imply actions or words so offensive that they put the victim into a state of anger so extreme that "rage" isn't a strong enough name for it. And, since *rage* itself is derived from a late Latin word for rabies, this may tell us something.

Sarcastic

"Hey, here comes Mr. America!" someone yells as a fat, unathletic youth waddles up to a group at the beach. "You have stated that with your customary brilliance," you may remark when your opponent in a discussion makes a particularly stupid statement. We have all been the object of such sarcastic remarks, or dealt them out ourselves on occasion. We think of remarks like these as biting or cutting, and thereby hangs a verbally gory tale.

Sarcastic, in fact, comes ultimately from the Greek verb *sarkazein*, which meant "to tear flesh with one's teeth," like an angry dog. In the mouths of the Greeks, it took on the figurative meaning of "to speak bitterly." *Sarkasmos*—sarcasm—was the kind of thing one said when engaged in verbally tearing someone else's flesh. The ancient Greeks, for whom oratory was one of the main forms of public entertainment, must have raised sarcasm to the level of an art, for they also had a word for a sarcastic speaker, *sarkastos*. The adjective formed from this term was, of course, *sarkastikos*, which needs no further explanation.

The root of all these terms is the Greek *sarx*, "flesh," which also turns up in the imposing word *sarcophagus*. It seems that the Greeks believed that a certain kind of stone had the property of consuming the flesh of corpses, and they named it *sarkophagos*, or "flesh-eating." (*Sarcophagus* with a *c* and a *u* is the Latin form.) Sarkophagos stone was used for making burial chests, the idea presumably being that it would quickly get rid of all the corruptible portion of the dead person's body, leaving only the pure and incorruptible essence. The name of the stone came to be applied to the coffin itself, and then from coffins of stone to those of wood or other materials. Finally, *sarcophagus* came to mean any large and elaborate coffin, especially one that was designed to stand out in the open, where its rich and ornate carvings could be admired, rather than being buried away in the ground.

A word that is closely allied in meaning to *sarcastic* is *sardonic*, which in the original Greek referred to bitter or scornful laughter and the facial expression, lips drawn back in a snarl, which usually accompanies it (like the expression on the face of someone who retorts "Ha, ha! Ve-ry fun-ny!" to an insult). This word was used as early as the time of Homer (8th or 9th century B.C.) and was originally spelled *sardanios*. Later, but still in antiquity, scholars guessed that Homer was really referring to a kind of plant that grew on the island of Sardinia and whose juice was so acrid that it made one draw back one's lips in agony as one spit it out. The spelling was then changed to *sardonios* (in Latin *sardonicus*), meaning "Sardinian."

Snob
A snob, as we all know too well, seeks to ingratiate himself with those of greater prestige or wealth in the belief that he will thereby acquire social status himself. He also looks down on those beneath him on the social ladder, and often on his peers as well, for without someone to look down on, where is his superiority? Yet, despite the snobbish person's efforts to be borne upward to higher social strata by association with the great—like a kind of sociological hot-air balloon—the word *snob* itself is of distressingly humble origin.

Originally it was an uncouth dialect word for a shoemaker or cobbler, or sometimes the cobbler's young apprentice. Then, in the late 18th century, aristocratic English students at Cambridge University took up the term and applied it to the townspeople, on whom they naturally looked down as menials whose principal function was to take care of their aristocratic needs and desires. Next, it came to mean anyone of the lower orders. Finally, shortly before the middle of the 19th century, it took on its current meaning.

This is one of the rare cases in which a change in a word's meaning can be accurately pinpointed, for it was due principally to a series of articles in the English magazine *Punch*, beginning February 28, 1846. The series was entitled *The Snobs of England*, and the author was none other than William Makepeace Thackeray, himself a Cambridge dropout.

Thackeray had a strain of snobbery in his own makeup—after all, he was descended from substantial gentry—but he loathed pretense and unfairness, and snobbery is quintessentially unfair and pretentious. Also, his biographers point out, Thackeray had a personal ax to grind. He was deep-down angry because the reading public was lapping up inferior novels by authors with noble titles and snubbing far better works by non-titled professional writers. And he struck back with his biting series of satires once a week for a full year. By the end of the series, he had succeeded in offending members of almost every social group in Britain—but he also increased the circulation of *Punch*, and in the process firmly established *snob* in the English language.

Sophisticated

For most of its history this word, now a term of high praise, was an insult and an accusation. As far back as the 14th century, when it first appeared in English, it meant "adulterated." It was used especially in connection with the spice trade, in which it was not unknown for dealers to mix the costly spices imported from the Far East with cheap local ingredients. Down the centuries, *sophisticated* kept its damning meaning, growing worse with use. In the late 16th century, for instance, it also meant "to corrupt, pervert, or mislead." In the mid-18th century the great Samuel Johnson thundered that *to sophisticate* was "to corrupt with something spurious." Even in the early 19th century, Noah Webster defined it only as "to adulterate." The current meanings of "worldly wise," "knowing one's way about," "not naive," and so on are relatively recent, as is the latest catchword, "sophisticated technology," meaning highly developed and complex technology.

This word of protean meanings traces its ancestry back to the sophists of ancient Greece, a class of intellectuals-for-hire who flourished for a time beginning in the mid-5th century B.C. *Sophist* comes from *sophos*, meaning "wise" or "clever," and can be translated either as "wise man" or "wise guy," depending on your opinion of them. The sophists began harmlessly enough as purveyors of higher education to whoever could afford to pay for it. They were bitterly opposed by the Philosophers, or "lovers of wisdom," led by Plato. The philosophers claimed to be searching for the ultimate truth; the sophists said that the ultimate truth was unattainable and chose success in life as their goal. Plato despised the sophists for charging a fee for dispensing wisdom. But then Plato, an archsnob from an aristocratic family, disdained anybody who had to work for a living. Plato also outlined a rigidly authoritarian state as his ideal republic, whereas the sophists took a libertarian tack. It may well have been Plato who first used "sophist" as a term of reproach.

At any rate, from general education the sophists eventually came to specialize in rhetoric and disputation. The Greeks were a litigious people, but they had no professional lawyers. Each citizen with a grievance pleaded his own lawsuit in court, so that there was a booming market for specialists who could teach a citizen how to construct ingenious arguments and couch them in elegant rhetoric, for thus was the administration of justice swayed. But the sophists outsmarted themselves in the end. With winning lawsuits as their only goal, they constructed arguments of such ingenious deviousness that people stopped trusting them, and "sophistry" became a synonym for clever trickery. With this sort of image, it was no wonder that "to sophisticate" came to mean "to adulterate." The real wonder is how a term of reproach was converted into a compliment.

Supercilious

Many a mammal, from baboons to buffaloes, raises its eyebrows as a threat or warning signal. In a number of human cultures, raised eyebrows express contempt or disapproval. This was the case among the ancient Romans, whose word *superciliosus* meant exactly the same as our modern supercilious. The word derived from *supercilium*, *"eyebrow,"* which literally meant "above the eyelid." Eyebrows raised and looking down his nose, the supercilious person surveys the world with haughty contempt while unconsciously displaying the paler skin of his eyelids in the ancient baboon gesture of mild threat.

Haughty is a key concept in defining "supercilious." It comes from the Middle English *haught*, "high," an adaptation of the French *haut*, which in turn traces back to the Latin *altus*. Thus a haughty person is literally high and mighty. In the early 1500s it came to mean proud or arrogant, high in one's own consideration. Late in that same century it strangely enough took on a complimentary connotation of exalted or high-minded, but soon enough it fell back into its old meaning.

One who practiced haughtiness in a highly visible form was the cavalier, literally a horseman. From his lofty perch atop his steed, the cavalier could look down on the common rabble with as much aristocratic disdain as he wished. No one, in those days of rank and privilege, would have dared object. *Cavalier* entered the English language sometime before 1560 as an import from France and Italy. Actually, the Spanish form was in use even before then, and the English considered the Spaniards particularly arrogant. As an adjective, *cavalier* originally meant "gallant," a quality deemed peculiarly appropriate to the aristocracy. Then (about 1655) it took on the meaning of "offhand," "casual," "free and easy," as still befitted the aristocracy's concept of itself as nobly spontaneous, un-

27

like the plodding peasantry and plotting bourgeoisie. Not until the mid-1700s did it take on the meaning of haughtiness and disdain that it has retained to this day. The decline of the old military and land-owning aristocracy probably had much to do with this linguistic change, along with the slow germination of the idea that God had created all men equal.

But even in its heyday of complimentary use, *cavalier* had its dark side. In *Henry IV*, Part 2 (written about 1598) Shakespeare has the comic character Justice Shallow drink to the thuggish roisterer Bardolph—one of Falstaff's disreputable retinue—and "all the cavaleros about London," implying that a cavalier was no better than a petty criminal—and maybe not so petty at that. In the English Civil War in the mid-1600s, "cavalier" was applied as an uncomplimentary epithet to the Royalist side, with reference to the arrogant behavior of the King's hangers-on. There was much reason in this, for the mounted man has traditionally lorded it over the man on foot, with corresponding resentment on the other side. Yet, paradoxically, the word *cavalier* stems from the Latin word *caballus*, meaning a plain and simple packhorse. Thus, this word has evolved from the prosaic to the high-flown to the reproachful.

Taken Aback
In the days of square-rigged sailing ships, it sometimes happened that the wind would suddenly shift from behind or from the side of the ship to directly ahead. The sudden gust would blow the sails back against the mast and drive the ship backward, out of control. Seamen called this being *taken aback*. In bad weather, being taken aback could force the stern of the ship under the waves and sink it. Eventually this vivid figure of speech was applied to people and their reactions to some unexpected event that leaves them surprised, confused, and disconcerted.

Two other nautical terms that have floated into the general language are *half-seas over* and *three sheets to the wind*, both meaning "drunk." "Half-seas over" actually implies that the drinker is not quite completely drunk, and calls up the image of a ship with its deck awash with waves of beer or gin, but not quite submerged. "Three sheets to the wind" refers not to laundry drying on a clothesline but to the ropes that are attached to the lower corners of a sail to control it. Normally the sheets are fastened to cleats on the ship's gunwales to hold the sail steady, but if they come loose in a strong wind, the ship is in serious trouble, with sails flapping out of control and the ship losing steerage way. Thus, a person who has three sheets to the wind is just about falling-down drunk.

Tease
Like *heckle* and *tenterhooks*, *tease* comes to us from the medieval textile industry. Actually, it refers to a process that goes back to very ancient times: separating the tangled fibers of wool, flax, or other materials so that they could be spun into thread and then woven into cloth. This had to be done with small, careful, picking movements so as not to make the tangle tighter or break the fibers. Once the cloth was woven, it was teased in another way. Its surface was combed with the burrs of the teasel plant, which are about as spiky and uncomfortable to the skin as you can imagine. This process raised a soft, fluffy nap on the cloth. The teasel plant looks a good deal like a thistle, though the two are not related, and teasels were formerly raised on a large scale until the late 19th century, when a mechanical device that used wire brushes took their place.

The word *tease* itself comes from the Old English *taesan*, "to pull apart." This plus the actual teasing operation suggested the figurative meaning of tormenting a person playfully or maliciously, which is what *tease* calls to mind today. From this come such modern derivatives as "tease," designating a flirtatious girl who does not deliver what she promises, "teasing" hair to make the hairdo look full and fluffy, and "teaser," a device used by writers, film-makers, and producers of TV commercials to arouse the audience's interest.

On Tenterhooks
"The bank really kept me on tenterhooks waiting for that loan to be approved."

"I was on tenterhooks until the biopsy turned out negative."

Reader, can you gather from these examples that "on tenterhooks" means "in unbearable suspense?" This is no more than appropriate, for the phrase is a very literal metaphor derived from the medieval cloth-making trade.

After woolen cloth had been woven on the cumbersome hand looms, it tended to be uneven: some parts were more tightly woven than others, there were gaps in the weave, and the cloth would not hang properly when made into garments. To even it out, the cloth was put through a process called fulling. The cloth was placed in a large tub filled with water and fuller's earth or lye. (Sometimes soapy plant juices or stale urine were used instead.) Then a workman trampled the cloth about with his bare feet. When the cloth had been trampled enough, it was washed and then stretched on a large, heavy frame called a *tenter*.

The tenter had a heavy crossbeam on each end, set with large, sharp hooks. The ends of the cloth were stuck onto the tenterhooks, and workers heaved on ropes to pull the tenter beams as far apart as they could go without tearing the cloth apart. Then the ropes were made fast to pegs in the ground, and the cloth was left to stretch for several hours. Had a person actually been stretched on a tenter, his torment would have been extreme—a combination of crucifixion and that favorite medieval torture appliance, the rack.

The tenter and the tent that soldiers and campers use both owe their names to the same root: the Latin verb *tendere*, "to stretch." So do "extend" and "tense." Anyone extended on a tenter would have ample reason to be tense!

Thrifty

Frugal, saving of money and old pieces of string, reluctant to spend—that is what *thrifty* means in everyday speech. Now and then it appears in self-consciously archaic books on gardening in quite a different sense, and those who look it up in the dictionary find that here it means "thriving, vigorous, in good health." And this is exactly what *thrifty* meant when it was born as an English word, for it comes from *thrive*, which itself is an English version of an Old Norse word, *thrifask*, meaning "to do well, to prosper, to succeed," and all the other things that thriving implies.

Thrifty in the sense of "in a thriving condition" dates back to the 13th century. Chaucer, in the 14th century, used it metaphorically to mean "respectable" or "worthy." It took another two centuries, however, for *thrifty* to take on its current meaning. The idea was probably that one who saved his wealth and spent it carefully would thrive and become better off, whereas one who spent it as fast as he made it would remain poor. At this time the Catholic Church exalted poverty—though very few Catholics practiced it by choice—and preached that getting rich was worldly and sinful (although the Church was always happy to receive large gifts from wealthy men who were worried about their souls). Then the early Protestant theologian John Calvin taught that prosperity was a sign of God's grace. As Calvinistic ideas spread, thrift became not just an unpleasant necessity but a positive virtue.

31

Nowadays, installment buying and credit cards have made thrift unpopular, and inflation has penalized it. But no doubt it will be rewarded again some day.

Thrilled

"I'm really thrilled to be here with you all tonight!" If you had made this rather banal statement at the Battle of Hastings in 1066, your hearers would have thought you were wounded by an enemy weapon. For *thrill* was once the Old English word *thyrlian*, meaning "to pierce" or "to perforate," or, less elegantly, "to make a hole in." *Thyrlian* came from another word, *thyrel*, "hole," which in turn was derived from *thurh*, the grandparent of "through." Thus *thrill* is related to *through* and *thorough*.

In Middle English, which developed after the Normans conquered England, *thyrlian* became *thirl* and then *thrill*. (*Thirl* lingers on in our word *nostril*, which used to be called *nosethirl*, or "nose hole." Those who had to study Chaucer's *Canterbury Tales* probably remember that the Miller's "nosethirles blake were and wide." Wide nostrils were then regarded as lower-class and a sign of a bestial nature. But this is leading us off on a false scent.)

Thrill retained its meaning of "to pierce" until shortly before 1600, when it for no logical reason at all acquired a secondary meaning of being affected (or affecting someone else) by a wave of emotion. Then it also came to mean trembling or quivering with emotion, as in the line "My heart with rapture thrills" in *My Country, 'Tis of Thee*. Later yet, it came to mean simply "very excited" or "very happy." *Thrilling* as an adjective seems to have been first used around 1760, when the American Colonies were embroiled in the French and Indian War and many people were thrilled (in the old sense) by arrows and bullets. *Thriller*, to describe a book or play, was first used in print in 1886 and was considered dreadfully slangy. At that point in Queen Victoria's reign anything thrilling was itself somewhat disreputable.

Tribulations
How often have we heard and read the phrase "trials and tribulations?" Most of us can guess from context that it means some kind of harrowing ordeal or at the very least an unpleasant experience. Like many a time-worn expression, it has lost real meaning. But originally it was a vivid and graphic description, for *tribulations* comes from the Roman *tribulum*, a kind of sledge used for threshing grain.

The tribulum was built of heavy timbers set with sharp-edged flints on the bottom side. Back and forth across the hard stone threshing floor it went, slowly dragged by a struggling donkey, until the friction and pressure of the sledge separated the inedible chaff from the kernels of the grain spread out on the floor. Often the tribulum was loaded with big stones to increase its weight and bear down harder on the grain. So a person who suffered tribulations was, metaphorically at least, crushed and torn like the grain beneath the threshing sledge.

Donkeys were preferred for this work because their dung, being in the form of round, solid pellets, was relatively easy to separate from the grain. Oxen, on the other hand, excrete a liquid mass that spreads out and soaks into the grain, spoiling a great deal of it. Horses were too expensive to use for this kind of work. Owned only by the aristocracy and the rich, they were used for riding and to draw chariots. It would have been quite in character for the Romans to use slaves to drag the tribulum, except that slaves were not strong enough to move it. Also, a slave was more costly to feed than a donkey.

Trial apparently comes from a medieval Latin word, *triare*, which meant to sift or to pick out, a process of separation. Thus, in the administration of justice, the trial was the process of sifting out the truth from everything else that was said. But even before trial took on this meaning, it had another: to test the purity, strength, or fitness of materials or persons. This meaning lingers on in the expression "trying gold."

"Trials and tribulations" was first used in a religious sense, as far back as the 1300s. At that time, gold was tried by melting it in a fiery crucible and by dousing it with strong acids. If the gold came out of the trial with its weight and luster unchanged, it was pure. Again, a graphic metaphor for the suffering of the soul being tested by God.

We spoke earlier of a harrowing ordeal. A harrow, for those who are not familiar with farm equipment, is a spike-toothed piece of heavy equipment that is dragged over a field after plowing to break up clods and smooth the soil. (The disc harrow is a modern invention.) Being harrowed was therefore as bad as being tribulated.

The ordeal was an old custom of trying a suspected criminal by subjecting him to some form of torture, such as plunging his hand into boiling water or holding a red-hot iron. If the accused person were innocent, God was supposed to protect him from harm. If not, he would suffer pain and injury. Naturally, most people who were put to the ordeal were found guilty.

Many people consider "trials and tribulations" a trite expression. *Trite* is another word that has lost most of its original meaning. Nowadays it carries the meaning of stale or overused to the point of being boring. But it comes from a Latin verb that means "to rub." So a trite expression has had its meaning worn away by constant usage, like the features on an old coin worn out by constant handling.

DEMOCRACY
and
ARISTOCRACY

Alderman

Anyone who thinks of an alderman as a beer-bellied, blowsy machine politician is in for a big surprise, for in the beginning *alderman* was a title given to a few select persons at the top of the ruling class. *Alderman* comes from the Old English word *ealdorman*, literally "old man," from *ald*, "old," plus *man*. But *ealdorman* did not mean just any oldster: it carried the significance of "chief" or "prince." (The habit of identifying old age with high rank is a pretty common one. The senators of ancient Rome and the sheikhs of Arab lands, for example, were and are literally "old men," of which more under Senator.)

Although *alderman* began in this exalted fashion, a century after the Norman Conquest it had spread to include almost anyone of noble or high rank. The title of alderman was given to magistrates and to the chief officers of guilds, who were commoners. In Anglo-Saxon times there was an *aldermannus totius Angliae*, or Alderman of All England (all government work was conducted in Latin, the language of the Church, because most of the people who could read and write were clerics). This official was apparently the chief justice of the realm. Then there was a whole series of successively lower aldermen: the king's alderman, who was a judge of cases involving the Crown; the county alderman, or chief magistrate of the county; and so on down the ladder to aldermen of the city, town, castle, and hundred. (The hundred was a subdivision of the county and one of the smallest administrative units in England.)

While in Britain an alderman is a magistrate, in the United States he is a municipal legislator. In the 19th and 20th centuries, aldermen often earned themselves a bad name for corruption and graft. But, corrupt or not, aldermen have usually had a high opinion of their importance, causing lesser folk to poke irreverent fun at them. Thus, from the late 19th century to the beginning of World War II, "alderman" was slang for a big belly, since so many aldermen sported them. (Obesity was once a badge of status, since only the rich and powerful could afford to eat enough to get fat.) In Britain, a big crowbar used by thieves was called an alderman. Also from Britain comes the expression "voting for the alderman," meaning to be drunk. But the most picturesque (again from Britain) is "alderman in chains," which flourished from the late 1700s to the early 1900s. It meant a roast turkey garnished with chains of sausage links, which presumably represented the golden chains of office that aldermen wore. However, anyone familiar with the history of Tammany Hall and other American political machines might well conclude that the alderman was wearing prisoner's chains, having been caught out in some particularly flagrant act of corruption.

Aristocracy

In almost every human society, certain individuals establish themselves in power. Sometimes they manage this by natural qualities of leadership, sometimes by force and guile. Sometimes they conquer another nation. In any case, once they are in power they invent a rationale for it by saying that they are the best fitted to rule. The ancient Greeks called this *aristocracy*, from *aristos*, "best," and *kratia*, "rule."

Aristrocracy

It may have been Plato, the famous 5th-century B.C. philosopher of Athens, who coined the word *aristokratia*. At any rate, he used it in his influential treatise *The Republic*. To Plato, the ideal society was governed by a group of the best citizens, wise, unselfish, without personal ambition or lust for power, and devoted to the public good. Of course, the "best" citizens would come from the leading families, whose high rank in itself proved their fitness to rule (at least to Plato and those who agreed with him). As for the common people, nature itself had fitted them only to obey their betters. Unfortunately, in reality the aristocrats rarely practiced the Platonic virtues. They were interested not so much in the public good as in having power and showing it. However, Plato, himself of the aristocratic class, chose to overlook these defects.

Aristocrats also had a habit of making their aristocratic status hereditary (did they not deserve this, since they were the best?). The stupidest, most cowardly child of an aristocrat was also an aristocrat by right of birth and thus entitled to lord it over those of lower rank. By the same token, it was very difficult for a commoner, no matter how talented or how brave in war, to become an aristocrat. Even when a ruler rewarded an outstanding commoner by raising him to the aristocracy, those who had made it already usually snubbed him.

Naturally, the common people felt that a hereditary aristocracy was unfair. Yet at the same time they perceived that some people were better fitted to rule than others, as they were wiser, fairer, and less apt to settle disagreements with a sword or gun. Thomas Jefferson, an enlightened Virginia aristocrat, proposed an "aristocracy of virtue" to be composed of citizens of all ranks, chosen on the basis of their individual merits. Jefferson's great rival and enemy, Alexander Hamilton, preferred a hereditary aristocracy even if the aristocrats had to defer to republican sentiment by not using titles. A psychologist might suspect that this was a case of overcompensation on Hamilton's part, since Hamilton was not only low-born but illegitimate. The struggle between these ideologies still goes on. The trouble is that it is the aristocrats themselves who decide who is the best. And, human nature being what it is, they choose themselves.

Baron To most Americans, there is something slightly sinister about the word *baron*. It suggests an arrogant, titled foreigner with a waxed mustache, haughtily ordering the common folk about and ready to debauch their womenfolk at any opportunity. Historically speaking, there is much to justify this prejudice, but originally *baron* was simply another word for "man." It is one of the words the Normans brought to England after 1066. In its original Old French form it was *barun* or *baron*, which was derived from a late Latin word, *baro*, a man or warrior. Some medieval scholars theorized fancifully that *baro* was derived from the Greek word *barys*, "heavy," because a baron was heavily armed or pulled a lot of weight in the affairs of the realm—or, as we might say today, was a real heavyweight. Others less flatteringly derived it from a Latin homophone meaning "simpleton." But in fact its real origin is unknown.

Apparently, *baro* first meant merely a male person, then a fighting man, then a man of importance, a great man. (In medieval society, most people attained importance by their martial prowess.) The Norman conquerors took *baron* a step further and applied it to those men who were granted land by the king or a very powerful noble in return for military or other service. The baronial applicant first had to go through the ceremony of homage to the king or nobleman (see VASSAL), which made him the king's or nobleman's "man." He now stood on the lowest level of the nobility.

The Norman kings and great nobles created a great many

barons to reward their followers and ensure their loyalty. Before very long, the barons were divided into two grades: the greater barons, who held large grants of land, and the lesser barons, who might hold only a few farms. The greater barons were men of consequence and were entitled to be summoned to the parliaments that the King called when he wanted to raise money. The lesser barons were gradually squeezed out of the peerage.

Baron was not used as a title until 1387. Until then, barons were titled *Dominus* (Lord) or *Chevalier* (Knight). In the later Middle Ages, *baron* was used as a general title of respect, like "colonel" in Kentucky, and even applied to Jesus and the saints.

The title of *baronet*, or "little baron," was invented by King James I in 1611. James created this title to raise money by selling it to ambitious members of the gentry. A baronet ranked between a baron and a knight. To avoid cheapening the title by overproduction, James promised to limit the number of baronets to 200. James also planned to grant baronetcies in Nova Scotia as an inducement to rich men to sponsor settlements there. He died before he could put this plan into effect, but his son, Charles I, carried it out with enthusiasm. Charles also created so many new baronetcies in England that the price dropped from 1095 pounds to a mere 350 pounds or less. The title soon became a mere honorific.

On the European mainland, *baron* was first used as a title in France, in the 12th century; it referred to large noble landholders. It remained an important title until the reign of Louis XIV, who cheapened it by creating barons wholesale. The title was abolished, along with all others, by the French Revolution. Napoleon restored it in 1808, but cunningly severed the title from all political power.

Baron was introduced to the various German and Austrian lands (which then included large parts of central and eastern

Europe) in the 17th century in imitation of the French. But since every son of a baron was also entitled to call himself Baron, the title soon lost all significance except to mark the bearer as a member of the aristocracy. And in class-ridden Europe, that in itself was a big advantage.

The original barons were, as we have said, fighting men, and they were a hard and brutal lot. In the Middle Ages, certain barons on the European mainland who controlled important trade routes would exact exorbitant tolls from merchants passing through their domains. They became known, naturally enough, as "robber barons." This epithet was revived in the United States in the post-Civil War era to describe a number of businessmen who enriched themselves by corrupt means such as swindling their stockholders and bribing state legislatures to grant them favors. "Baron" was also used to describe the most powerful men of a given industry, for example, "steel baron" or "oil baron." Today we also have "labor barons" for the heads of the most powerful unions. It is perhaps ironic that these representatives of the common man should be dubbed with an aristocratic title, but men like the late Teamsters' Union chieftain Jimmy Hoffa were just as ruthless practitioners of force and violence as the original Norman barons.

Caucus

John Smith, the man that Pocahontas befriended, learned a word from the Indians of eastern Virginia that he rendered as *caw-caw-aasough*. They somehow got him to understand that it meant one who talks, an adviser, one who urges. Today, the caw-caw-aasough is our word *caucus*, a term that has always reminded me of some huge, ungainly, long-extinct bird, squawking raucously as it stalks its prey through the primeval forest. However, the caucus is far from extinct; it is still alive and flourishing among the fauna of our political jungle. Along the way, it has changed from a lone adviser to a meeting of the members of a political party—or of a wing of that party, to continue the avian metaphor.

Smith probably learned his version of *caucus* in 1607 or 1608, but the word probably did not come into common use until about a century and a half later, when it was used as an up-to-date, American term for a private meeting of party leaders to decide which candidates and which issues to offer the voters. Since then, its meaning has been democratized, although caucuses have often been run in very autocratic fashion by powerful bosses who brooked no opposition.

Noah Webster, in 1806, defined *caucus* as "a cant name of secret meetings for electioneering purposes," but he was a man of strong and often crotchety biases. Caucuses are about as good or as bad as the people who make them up, and, although they often push a special interest, that interest does not always prevail. Presidential candidates were formerly picked by caucuses; now they are chosen at conventions. The quality of the candidates has not improved notably since the change.

Congress
The United States Congress dates back to 1789, when the old and ineffectual Confederation became the United States. But the word *congress* itself dates back to the 16th century. *Congress* is derived from the Latin verb *congredi*, "to go together" or "to meet," and its first use in English, in 1528, was to describe an ecclesiastical meeting. Toward the end of the 16th century it picked up a clashing meaning: sexual union; then in the 1620s it was also used for social relations.

Its first use in the political sense was in 1636, for a meeting of delegates called by the Pope to negotiate an end to the Thirty Years' War. This congress failed to solve the problem, and another one followed in 1647. Some of the delegates to the latter congress objected to the word on the grounds that it was coarse and inappropriate (the sexual connotation was already firmly established after a mere twenty years or so!), but they stayed on nevertheless and eventually worked out the Peace of Westphalia in 1648—one of the important dates of European history.

In Europe, the word *congress* was used mainly for meetings of diplomats who convened at the behest of their governments to settle the fate of nations (today we would call it a "summit conference"). In the United States, however, *Congress*, with a capital C, refers to the supreme legislative body of the land. The first Continental Congress was held in 1774, when delegates from the thirteen colonies met to consider how to solve the growing conflict between the colonies and Britain. When the colonies, after much hesitation, declared their independence, the Congress became the overall ruling body of the weakly united states. The states considered themselves independent, sovereign nations that had joined together for the common purpose of the struggle for independence from Britain, and they were not about to defy the British Crown only to become the subjects of some American Caesar, no sirree! It was to emphasize their sovereign nature that they called the Congress a congress—a gathering of emissaries from sovereign nations—rather than a Parliament.

The original Congress had little real power and was often unable to raise enough money to pay the Revolutionary soldiers. After peace was declared, the thirteen ex-colonies formed the Confederation of the United States. It was an unfortunate experiment. Each state, jealous of its sovereign importance, had its own currency (and would not accept the currency of neighboring states except at a heavy discount) and levied its own tariffs. Some even played at running their own foreign policies. Vermont (not yet a state because both New York and New Hampshire had claims on its territory) was flirting with the British; certain politicians in the Kentucky territory were playing the same game with the Spanish, who had taken over the vast Louisiana Territory from France. Europe's leaders sneered at the bumptious Americans and waited for the new republic to break up. However, wiser heads among the Americans prevailed, and the present Constitution was adopted by a narrow margin in 1788, going into effect in 1789. Since then, Congress has been at work more or less continuously, with time out for recesses and campaigning.

Since about the middle of the 19th century, *congress* has also been used as a title for meetings of scientists, scholars, and other experts who gather, ostensibly to read papers. The real action takes place in the coffee shops, bars, and obscure corners of convention hotels, where the experts intrigue for new and better jobs or try to establish helpful connections. In this sense, *congress* has returned to something like its original meaning, a meeting of persons or an interview.

Convention
A word of slippery versatility, *convention* can be a political gathering, an international agreement, or an established usage. All are derived from the Latin *conventio*, a meeting or agreement, which comes from *convenire*, to come together.

In English, *convention* can be traced back to the 15th century, when it meant simply a formal assembly. It could also, as among the Romans, mean an agreement. In the English political scheme, it took on a special, somewhat revolutionary meaning: an assembly of the Houses of Parliament without being summoned by the Sovereign. This did not exactly make crowns tremble on the heads of tyrants, but it was an assertion of power on the part of the commoners, as well as the nobility, and thus a challenge to royal dominance. It was not always used that way, however. It was a Parliamentary convention in

1660 that abolished Cromwell's commonwealth and invited Charles II back to the throne; but another convention twenty-eight years later made up for this by deposing the untrustworthy King James II.

In the United States, as far back as Colonial times, a convention has always been a meeting of delegates or members of a group for some particular purpose. Many professional and social groups also hold conventions, and sometimes these can be pretty rowdy. Conventions of the American Legion and other veterans' groups, for instance, were notorious for drunkenness, crude tricks played on bystanders, and a general acting-out of petty nastiness that would never have been tolerated in the members' home communities.

This violation of social conventions leads us to another meaning of *convention*. In the sense of "an established custom," *convention* has been around since the late 18th century. This sort of convention is not established by law. It is simply something that is generally accepted, something that members of society can agree about. Conventions usually develop because they are useful in some way, but after a time they often become restrictive and oppressive. A conventional person is one who lets conventions do his thinking and feeling for him, and rarely if ever ventures an independent opinion. Still, social conventions tend to rule our lives because they are convenient (a word that also comes from the Latin *convenire*). The most rarefied sense of *convention*, an international agreement, dates from the 15th century. It used to be equivalent to "treaty," but was downgraded to a less important level in the 19th century. Good examples are the Geneva Conventions, which govern the treatment of prisoners of war. The Geneva Conventions were concluded in 1864 and 1865. Could the world's nations be induced to sign them today? One wonders.

Count

While *Baron* conjures up (for me, at least) the image of a brutal fighting man, *Count* strikes me as slick, suave, and sophisticated, an aristocrat with a splendid uniform, a waxed mustache, and oodles of old-world charm mixed with his *hauteur*. He probably has his eye out for a wealthy American heiress to take advantage of, too. In fact, the count began as an official hanger-on of the Roman emperors—the word comes from the Latin *comes*, which originally meant "fellow-traveler" and then came to signify "companion" or "associate." It was the Emperor Hadrian (A.D. 117–138) who invented the position of count. Hadrian, an energetic administrator, traveled almost constantly around his empire to observe things for himself. With him he took a chosen group of senators as his traveling companions and administrative assistants. He called them his *comites* (the plural of *comes*). In time, *comes* became a recognized title for high state officials.

The position of count survived the breakup of the Roman Empire. In France, the early Frankish kings employed a number of counts. These counts were not hereditary nobles but high-ranking royal servants. Some accompanied the king and saw to it that his orders were carried out. Others held specific offices, such as the *Comes Palatii* (Count of the Palace, or Palatine Count), and the *Comes Stabuli* (Count of the Stables). Still other counts administered local districts in the king's name. They were administrators, military commanders, judges, prosecutors, and enforcers of the king's peace all in one.

At this time, counts were appointed by the king from all classes of free men, noble or common. Even freed slaves were sometimes made counts. The king not only made the counts but could remove them at his pleasure, which served as a certain restraint on the counts' behavior. This began to change under the great Charlemagne and his successors in the 8th and 9th centuries. Only the big landowners were appointed to countships. As the feudal system developed, the countships became hereditary. Meanwhile, the counts had been taking advantage of the weakness of the kings to become more and more independent. By the 13th century, some of them were virtually sovereigns in their own domains—and by business-like marriages some of them managed to amass huge parcels of real estate. Certain counts were equal in rank to dukes and were in actuality more powerful—that is, they controlled more fighting men.

In Old French, *comes* became *conte*, and the Normans took the title with them to England. Anglified Normans mispronounced it until it became *counte*. Thus the word entered the English language. However, all British historians of language and of politics insist strenuously that it was never an English title—just a foreign, un-English equivalent of the English *Earl*.

Throughout Continental Europe, the countship followed pretty much the same pattern as in France. In Germany, the counts were able to grab power more quickly than they could in France. The position of count became hereditary there as early as the 9th century. As the number of counts increased, they became divided into different classes according to their importance. At one time in Germany there were four or five different grades of count.

Perhaps resentful of their counts' power and anxious to dilute it, the kings of France began selling countships in the 16th century. The old-line counts resented this policy, but the lesser nobles and rich commoners who bought the titles liked it fine. Rulers in all regions followed suit; in Italy, which then had hordes of petty local sovereigns, new counts were almost cranked out en masse. The French Revolution did away with countships in France and the areas that the revolutionary armies overran, but Napoleon reinstated the title when he became Emperor in 1804. To the disgust of all aficionados of nobility, he sold even more countships. These titles remained in force even after the bad little Corsican was packed off into his final exile.

By the mid-19th century, there were a great many impoverished counts in Europe who where quite happy to lend their aristocratic titles to wealthy heiresses among the common folk. In the decades just after the American Civil War, many a newly rich man sought to legitimize his possibly ill-gained wealth by acquiring a titled son-in-law. It became a recognized custom among the plutocracy to make trips to the fashionable places of Europe to acquire these social ornaments. Democratically minded Americans poked fun at it; some fulminated against it; but it went on anyway, as if to demonstrate how little attraction the simple, republican ideals of the American Revolution held for the generations that followed.

A *county* was originally the area that a count ruled. The Normans brought the word to England and used it as an equivalent for the Anglo-Saxon *shire*. Counties were established as units of government in Britain's North American colonies as soon as the population grew large enough. In the Northeast, which was relatively densely settled, the towns became the most important units of local government; elsewhere the county was the center of power, and the county seat, with its courthouse, was where the action was. Before the days of railroads, a county's size was generally limited by the necessity of having the county seat within a day's travel of the most distant resident. As transportation improved, the counties could become larger. In some of the Western states there are counties as big as the whole state of Rhode Island, and several that are larger than Rhode Island and New Jersey together.

Today the county's role has shrunk as the states and the Federal government have taken over many functions. In fact, Rhode Island and Connecticut have done away with their counties. But in most of the United States, the county court-house, the county sheriff and his troopers, the county highway department—and the county taxes—remind us of the days when the counts rode high.

Democracy *Democracy* liter-

ally means "rule of the people." Like its antithesis, aristocracy, it comes to us from the Greeks, from the words *demos*, "the people," and *kratia*, "rule." Now, ancient Greece was not one country: it was divided into a host of angrily independent little states that consisted of a city and the surrounding farmland. And the kind of democracy that was practiced in the city-states of ancient Greece was far different from our own. To begin with, not everyone qualified as one of the "people." Only male citizens qualified for this privilege, and citizenship went by descent. Resident foreigners were not citizens and had no legal rights, no matter how long they had lived there. Women and slaves, of course, did not count either. Even in Athens, the great example of Greek democracy, well over half the adult population was disenfranchised.

Every citizen was expected to take an active part in the political life of the city-state. It was his duty to attend the assemblies faithfully and vote on whatever issues came up. He was also expected to be able to fill any public office for which his fellow citizens chose him. Naturally, this kind of direct democracy can work only when the number of citizens is low —Plato decreed that the ideal number was 5,040. (He arrived at this figure partly for administrative convenience—5,040 can be divided by every number up to 10—and partly because he believed in the mystical qualities of numbers.) Even so, Greek democracy broke down as the citizens' selfish interests and desire for power outweighed their public spirit.

A series of conquests, by Sparta, Philip of Macedon, and

Rome, crushed the remnants of democracy in Greece. With that, democracy vanished from the scene for centuries. It did not revive until the 17th century A.D., cautiously expressed in the writings of a few philosophers. On a practical level, it took the "new world" of America to give democracy a chance to develop. In the frontier conditions of the new land, a man's native ability was more important than his rank, and the idea slowly grew that one man was perhaps as good as another. This was reinforced by the fact that most of the colonists sprang from very humble stock indeed: farmers, craftsmen, servants, even petty criminals. Even so, at the time of the American Revolution democracy was considered a very radical and dangerous idea, and no respectable man would call himself a democrat. It would have been as unpopular as declaring oneself a Communist today, for to most people "democracy" called up the image of mob rule. Plain farmers and craftsmen didn't like that idea any better than the great landowners and wealthy merchants. Thus it was a daring action for Thomas Jefferson and his supporters to name their new political party the Democratic Republican Party in 1791. One of their reasons was that they suspected the opposition Federalist Party of harboring secret ambitions to impose a monarchy and hereditary aristocracy on the United States. (In 1828 the "Republican" was dropped from the party's name, and it became the Democratic Party.)

Long after the American Revolution the states imposed property qualifications for voters. Even after all white males had won the right to vote, women and Negroes remained disenfranchised. The first state to grant women the right to vote was Wyoming; on the national level women did not gain the vote until 1919. Negroes also gained the vote slowly. In the South they were barred by various discriminatory laws until the great civil rights movement of the 1960s. Some western states barred Orientals from citizenship until after World War II. But despite these injustices the democratic ideal survived.

Whereas democracy may be defined on paper as "rule of the people," in practice it is more difficult to pin down. A democracy does not have to be a republic: Great Britain and the Scandinavian countries, for example, are democracies and have kings. There are many countries that call themselves republics that have very undemocratic societies. Probably Abraham Lincoln's phrase, "government of the people, by the people, for the people," sums it up best.

In the Communist lexicon, "democracy" means carrying out the will of the people—as defined by the elite Communist Party—and is achieved by collective ownership of means of production by the people (actually by the state in the name of the people). Such things as freedom of speech, freedom to travel or to change your job without getting permission from the authorities, or having a choice between candidates at elections are, to the Communist, just window-dressing, if not lack of discipline bordering on anarchy. This disagreement on the meaning of "democracy" is a basic source of misunderstanding between the Communist bloc and the Western bloc.

Democracy is not perfect, and it is no guarantee of an ideal society. Many people become disillusioned with its shortcomings. Nevertheless, as Winston Churchill once said, it is the worst of all forms of government—until you have tried the others.

Despot
Say "despot" and everyone thinks instantly of a tyrannical ruler, a dictator. Yet in its original Greek form, *despotes*, it meant no more than the head of a household or the master of slaves. Actually, the head of a family in the ancient Greco-Roman world did rule despotically as we understand the word. He had absolute authority over his wife and children, could punish them as he pleased, and could even kill them if they incurred his displeasure. It is

true that, due to the pressure of public opinion, this seldom happened, but the right remained and was upheld by conservative legislators.

The Greeks also used *despotes* as a title of respect for various gods and to denote the absolute rulers of peoples whom the Greeks regarded as unfree. Such a ruler, as the Greeks saw it, treated his subjects as strictly as a Greek patriarch would treat his family. Later, in the Byzantine Empire, "despot" was used as a title for the Emperors and other high dignitaries such as bishops and patriarchs of the Church. It apparently meant something like "Lord and Master" and was no more than a routine piece of flattery with no menacing connotations.

The modern, unfavorable sense of "despot" was popularized in the later 18th century by French Revolutionary writers. It gave them a powerful weapon in their struggle against the oppressive Old Regime of king, church, and nobles. As is often the case in revolutions, the revolutionary leaders themselves fell into despotic ways, but that is another story.

Tyrant is often used as a synonym for "despot." It, too, has a Greek origin. The Greek word was *tyrannos*, which meant one who had seized power, a usurper. Although "tyrant" calls up images of cruel, unjust, and authoritarian rulers, the tyrants of ancient Greece were not actually all that bad. Usually they came to power as champions of the common people against the oppressions of the aristocrats, and a few were legally elected by the people instead of taking power in a coup. One tyrant, Peisistratos of Athens, ruled so well that afterwards people looked back on his reign as a golden age. However, the tyrants dealt harshly with the aristocrats, and that was their etymological downfall—for the histories were written by the aristocrats, and they spared no pains to give their enemies a bad name. Nevertheless, anyone who qualifies as a tyrant today is definitely a Bad Guy.

Dictator In times of crisis,
such as a war that was going badly, the ancient Romans would
appoint an official with absolute power to take charge of the
state. They called this man a *dictator*, from the verb *dictare*,
"to say often," or "to repeat," or, by inference, "to command."
(Our words "dictate" and "dictation," as in "Miss Damm,
please take a letter to the Police Commissioner," come from
the same root. One can just imagine some patrician Roman es-
sayist repeating a phrase over and over to the slave who did the
actual writing down of his immortal words.)

The aristocratic Senators who ruled the Roman Republic
were chary of entrusting so much power to a single man—they
still had unpleasant memories of their kings—so they limited
his power to six months. According to tradition, the Senate appointed the first dictator in 501 B.C. The last dictator was Julius Caesar, who manipulated and intimidated a reluctant
Senate into making him dictator a number of times: in 49 B.C.,
48 B.C., and 46 B.C. for a ten-year term (by now the original
six-month limit was disregarded). But Caesar soon improved
on this arrangement: in February, 44 B.C., little more than a
month before he was assassinated, he was made dictator for
life. In the tumultuous time that followed Caesar's death, his
friend and ally Mark Antony convinced the Senate to pass a
law abolishing the office of the dictatorship.

One of the most admired of Rome's dictators was Lucius
Quinctius Cincinnatus, who was born about 519 B.C. An impoverished aristocrat who lived on a small farm and actually
did his own farm chores, Cincinnatus was called to the dictatorship twice. According to the uplifting legends that Roman
historians spun about him, Cincinnatus was busy plowing his
fields when each summons came. With admirable Roman
gravity, he left the plow, brushed the dust off his clothes, and
hastened to the battlefield to take command of the faltering

troops. The victory won, he returned to his farm and his simple, austere life. After the American Revolution, a number of Washington's officers formed the Order of the Cincinnati, inspired by the traditions of Cincinnatus' republican simplicity and unselfish devotion to his country. They conveniently overlooked the historical fact that Cincinnatus had been a fierce opponent of the rights of common folk. Or perhaps they secretly sympathized, for America has always had a goodly number of persons who will stoutly maintain that they are as good as anyone else, but will not concede that anyone else is as good as they.

A man of quite a different stamp was the highly unpleasant dictator named Sulla, who set an example of sadism and vindictiveness for all the dictators who followed him. Sulla, a brilliant military leader, had himself proclaimed dictator in 81 B.C. after emerging the victor in a bloodthirsty civil war. Sulla celebrated his triumph by publishing a list of all his enemies (mainly those who had supported the rights of the common people) and having them hunted down and executed. He also confiscated their property as a further lesson to everyone. Many Romans feared that Caesar would become another Sulla, and this may have been one of the reasons for his assassination.

After Caesar's death there were no more dictators, although emperors, kings, emirs, sultans, rajahs, and shoguns carried on the same grand old absolutist tradition. The revival of dictatorship really dates from the end of the 18th century, when a conspiracy overthrew the French Republic and declared Napoleon First Consul, with virtually absolute powers. This was in 1799; soon Napoleon used his popularity to have himself declared First Consul for Life, and in 1804 he crowned himself Emperor. Few people except the aristocrats opposed him, for the middle and lower classes believed him to be a man of the people. As Emperor, Napoleon brooked no dissent; so we may call him the first modern dictator.

Dictator

In the 19th century, many a dictator came to power in the newly independent nations of Latin America. However, they did not call themselves dictators. Like Napoleon at first, they preserved democratic titles and called themselves "president." But they acted like dictators all the same, and their spiritual heirs are still going strong, despite occasional lapses into democracy by some countries.

The period between World Wars I and II was the golden age of dictators in Europe. Beginning with Lenin in Russia, there followed Mussolini in Italy, Hitler in Germany, Pilsudski in Poland, Salazar in Portugal, Franco in Spain. Even minor nations like Austria, Hungary, and Lithuania fell to native dictators before the Germans or the Russians swallowed them up. The defeat of the Axis powers in World War II led many people to hope that the world was at last ready for democracy, or at least some kind of constitutional government that respected the rights of the governed. But as one former European colony after another gained independence, most of them fell under the rule of dictators who were either military men or civilians backed by the military.

It is interesting that modern dictators do not use that title. Hitler called himself simply *Der Fuehrer* (The Leader), although he also held the title of *Reichskanzler* (Chancellor of the Realm). Stalin ruled for years as General Secretary of the Communist Party until he promoted himself to Generalissimo and Field Marshal during the war. Juan Peron, the fascist dictator of Argentina, followed Latin American tradition and called himself President. The minor-league but vicious dictator of the Dominican Republic, Rafael Trujillo, basked in the warmth of the title "El Benefactor."

Dictators may call themselves by whatever title they please; they may espouse a right-wing or a left-wing ideology; they may be a single charismatic leader like Hitler or a junta like the colonels who took over Greece in the 1960s. But dictatorships share certain common characteristics. They permit only one political party (although sometimes they maintain a completely powerless minority party or two for show); only one official ideology is permitted; dissent is severely punished. Order is maintained by the secret police and a network of informers, and the whole structure is maintained by terror, torture, and murder.

Duke

"Put up your dukes!" used to be a challenge that no red-blooded American male could ignore. The dukes in question were one's fists, but the peculiar and apparently all-American metaphor was actually borrowed from Cockney rhyming slang of the early 1870s. In that colorful British lingo, "Duke of Yorks" stood for "forks," that is, fingers and by extension hands or fists.

This still leaves the question of how the original Duke of York—or any other Duke—came by his title. Once more the search leads us back to the Romans. That military-minded people had a title, *dux*, which signified a military leader, more or less equivalent to a general. (The word was derived from the verb *ducere*, "to lead.") During the later years of the Roman Empire, there was a *dux* in charge of the defense of every frontier province in Europe. The Frankish kings who took over the old Roman province of Gaul continued the office of *dux*. As Latin, Gaulish, and Frankish German merged into the French language, *dux* eventually became *duc*, from which our English word is derived.

The Roman or Frankish *dux* held no land, and his office was not hereditary. However, the German tribes east of the Rhine had their own equivalent of the *dux*. This was a war leader called the *herizogo* (literally, army leader) who was chosen to take over temporarily from the regular king in case of war. Since the German tribes were at war a good deal of the time, the *herizogi* sometimes took over their tribes permanently. Charlemagne crushed the power of these German tribal dukes, but less than a century later his descendants could no longer control the territory he had conquered, and the German dukes bounced back stronger than ever. These dukes were kings in all but name, and their powers and their lands passed on to their descendants. Thus the classic dukedom of Western Europe was born.

In France there were also powerful dukes. One of them was William, Duke of Normandy, the same treacherous nobleman who led the Norman conquest of England in 1066. However, William stepped up a rank by making himself king of England, and the title of duke was not used in England until 1337, when Edward III declared his seven-year-old son Duke of Cornwall. The next duke was not created until fourteen years later. For a long time, the English dukedoms were limited to the royal family, but eventually the kings gave the title to a few powerful nobles whose support they needed. But there is still a social distinction today in Britain between "royal" and "non-royal" dukes.

In the Austrian and Russian empires, some nobles considered themselves too important and distinguished to be mere dukes. Thus, the titles of Archduke (Austrian) and Grand Duke (Russian) were invented. The question of who outranked whom at court gatherings or in marriages between ducal families of different nations became the foundation of a whole branch of study with ramifications as tangled and as thorny as the stems of a bramble patch.

There are still dukes around today, but they have none of their former power. Only one country is now ruled by a duke: the Grand Duchy of Luxemburg, which is smaller than the state of Rhode Island. It's enough to make a red-blooded nobleman cry "Put up your dukes!"

Earl

According to Scandinavian mythology, the god Heimdall once paid a visit to mortal men to improve the breed. In pursuit of this procreative mission, he copulated conscientiously with three women. The first bore him a dark-skinned, ugly son named Thraell, whose descendants became the thralls, or slaves, who were low men on the Scandinavian social ladder. The second woman produced a handsome, ruddy-faced son named Karl, who became the ancestor of the free men. The third bore a blond-haired son named Jarl, with eyes that glittered like a snake's. Jarl became the founding father of the aristocracy. With this self-serving myth the aristocrats and their hired bards explained the origin of the social classes among the Northmen.

Now, the word *jarl* actually meant no more than a man of high rank, a leader in his community, and it had a cousin in Old English, *eorl*, which later became *earl*. The *eorl* could be a nobleman, but the word could also mean a warrior or a brave man—outstanding warriors tended to gravitate to the top, no matter what their other qualities were. In Anglo-Saxon times it was chiefly a title of respect with no connection to vast estates.

It was King Canute, a Dane, who introduced *eorl* to English as an official title. Canute entrusted local government to subordinates who used *jarl* as a title, and the English quickly converted this to *eorl*. The *eorls'* job was to govern the shires for Canute, who did not have time to attend to each one personally, especially since he was also King of Denmark. The *eorls* replaced the former governors of the shires, who had been called *ealdormen*, or aldermen. As a matter of fact, the Anglo-Saxon ealdormen had been busily intriguing with the Danes for years; so they had only themselves to blame if they were replaced. The office of *eorl* was not hereditary, and an *eorl* could be dismissed by the king.

The *eorls* continued to govern England for about a century

and a half, until the Norman Conquest turned Anglo-Saxon-Danish society upside down. The Normans brought with them a version of Roman government which they had learned from the French, and under the Normans the *eorls* became the equivalent of French counts. As the feudal system developed, earldoms became hereditary, like other noble ranks. This made it very difficult for the king to get rid of an earl he disliked, and the earls, feisty in their security, often gave the kings a great deal of trouble. Until 1337, when Edward III introduced the title of duke, an earldom was the highest rank in the English peerage. Today it is only the third-highest, but it still impresses a lot of people. The title of Earl does not exist outside the British Commonwealth. An earl's wife is called not Earless but Countess; why I do not know.

While *eorl*/earl retained its high status, the contemporary word *ceorl* sank lamentably. In Anglo-Saxon times a *ceorl* was a free man, but after the Norman Conquest most *ceorls* lost their freedom and were reduced to the position of serfs. And with that *ceorl*, later *churl*, became a term of contempt. By the time Chaucer wrote *The Canterbury Tales*, "churlish" implied a surly, discourteous, brutal person. And so it still does.

Emperor
An *Emperor* is the supreme ruler of a group of nations, a super-king who may have other kings as his subjects. *Emperor* comes from the Old French version of *imperator*, the title of the Roman emperors. *Imperator* was at first a title of honor given to victorious generals; it literally means "commander." When Augustus Caesar took supreme power in the Roman state, he had the Senate declare him *imperator* instead of *rex*, or king, because the title of *rex* would have been too offensive to Romans. (He also took the title of *princeps civitatis*, or "first citizen.") But Augustus and his successors were so powerful that *imperator* soon came

to mean an absolute ruler. At the same time, Rome's possessions were so vast, and so many kings around the Mediterranean had come under Roman rule, that it took on the meaning of a king of kings. There used to be a number of emperors in the world. They ruled China, India, Russia, Turkey, the Austro-Hungarian Empire, and earlier realms that broke up or were conquered, like the Holy Roman Empire and the Byzantine Empire. There were the Aztec Empire in Mexico and the Inca Empire in Peru, both short-lived because they fell to the Spanish conquistadors. Spain and Portugal once had mighty empires. The only emperor reigning nowadays, however, is the Emperor of Japan.

The Emperor Augustus was the nephew of Julius Caesar, and his family name was originally Octavius. Shortly before his death, Julius Caesar, who had no legitimate sons, adopted Octavius as his son and heir, conferring on him the name of Caesar. After Augustus, all the other Roman Emperors down through Hadrian (reigned A.D. 117–38) took the title of Caesar, even though they were no longer related even distantly to the original Julius Caesar. (The last of the Caesarean line was the mentally unstable Nero, who committed suicide in A.D. 68 to avoid being captured by rebels.) From this imperial title of Caesar, which was pronounced KY-SAR in Latin, we get the German word *Kaiser*. (Some linguistic historians believe that *Caesar* was the first Latin word to be adopted into the Germanic languages.) When Christian missionaries carried Greco-Roman civilization into the Slavic lands, the Slavs turned *Caesar* into *Tsar*, for by that time the *k*- sound of Caesar was probably pronounced as *ts* before certain vowels. In English, *tsar* is sometimes spelled *Czar*, following the Polish rules of spelling. This is unfortunate, because non-Poles tend to pronounce it as "Zar," which is wrong.

In the late 19th century, "czar" became a synonym for an autocratic and despotic ruler of any kind. The long-time

59

Speaker of the House, Thomas Reed, a Republican from Maine, earned the name of Czar Reed for the tight discipline he enforced. In the early 20th century, when professional baseball was rocked by scandal, the major leagues appointed a commissioner to keep them straight. He was known as the Baseball Czar, a title which lasted until after World War II, when anything Russian was no longer popular.

Lord and Lady

Lord was once nothing more than the head of a household or a man who had servants. The name comes from the Anglo-Saxon *hlaford* or *hlafweard*, meaning "keeper of the loaf." (*Hlaf* meant "loaf" and *weard* was "guardian" or "keeper.") A servant, incidentally, was a "loaf-eater," or *hlafaete*, since most of his pay was in the form of food, and bread was the chief item in the diet.

Lady comes from the Anglo-Saxon *hlafdige*, "loaf-kneader," and originally meant the mistress of a household. Around the 14th century, *hlaford* became simplified to *lord*, and *hlafdige* was shortened to *lady* or *leddy*.

When the Anglo-Saxons were converted to Christianity, *Lord* was applied as a title of honor to God and Jesus, and the Virgin Mary became *Our Lady*. (The common British swearword "bloody" is supposed to be a contraction of "by Our Lady," which would have made it quite blasphemous.) In this, the Anglo-Saxons were only following the lead of the Romans, who used the title *dominus* (master of the house) for God and Jesus, and *domina* for Mary. In the Old Testament, the Hebrew equivalent is *adon* or *adonai* (*my Lord*), which was used to avoid pronouncing the true name of God, which was so sacred that it could not be used even in prayer.

On the secular level, *lord* gradually took on the meaning of a man of rank, a nobleman, or a feudal superior. It was a loose sort of synonym for *baron* and other ranks below the king.

Under the feudal system, almost all of the land belonged to the king, who granted the use of it to various nobles and church dignitaries in return for service. They, in turn, parceled out their portions of land to their subordinates, and so on down the line. Thus, *landlord*, the lord of the land, came to mean anyone who controlled land or buildings, even though he might not own them himself. Many a modern tenant feels that his landlord conducts himself as despotically as a feudal lord.

Free by law and custom from many of the restraints that common folk had to obey, lords earned a reputation for arrogant and uncontrolled behavior. What the commoners thought of all this we can still see in such expressions as "drunk as a lord" and "lording it over." In the old days, foul-mouthed people swore like a lord, though today they swear like a stevedore.

The lady fared somewhat better in this respect. During the Middle Ages, *lady* became the female equivalent of lord, but the slow growth of democratic ideas spread its meaning to a woman of good breeding or culture. Today, of course, it is simply a politer way of saying "woman," although certain extreme feminists object to this. Perhaps they object because "lady" implies behavior that feminists disapprove of.

King

In the 1950s the deposed Egyptian King Farouk is supposed to have said, "By the end of this century there will be only five kings left in the world: the kings of spades, hearts, diamonds, and clubs—and the King of England." Whether or not Farouk was right, the institution of kingship is very ancient. In many early societies, the king was both ruler and priest. He embodied the spirit of growing vegetation, especially of the crops on which the people depended. He was also believed to control the fertility and the well-being of the livestock and of the people themselves. In fact, he was often considered a god in his own right. But kings

61

grew old and weak, and their subjects believed that then they could no longer bring good luck to the people. So the king was killed with an appropriately solemn ritual, and a new one was crowned. In some societies, like that of ancient Ireland, the king was killed every year. In others, the king served a fixed term, such as twelve years, a powerful magical number. As society developed, kings were able to do away with this custom and live as long as they could hold the throne against rivals or enemy kings. In the beginning, a king was a village headman, but, beginning with the Egyptian Pharaohs, some kings grew very powerful indeed.

Our word *king* comes from an old Teutonic root, *kuningaz*, which was very close to the root for "kin" and meant something like "scion of the kindred." Everyone understood, of course, that the kindred was a noble one that the people respected. When the Angles and Saxons began to push into England in the 5th century A.D., they were ruled by tribal chiefs called *cyning* or *cyng*. The *cyng*-ship, or kingship, did not pass automatically from father to son, as it did later. Instead, the *cyng* was chosen from a royal clan called the *cynn* (our word *kin*). These royal clans traced their ancestry to the god Woden, still hanging on to the idea that a king was superior to mortal men. (The Japanese had a similar idea. Their emperor was supposed to be entirely divine, while other Japanese contained less and less divine essence as they descended the social scale. Even the most lowly of Japanese, however, contained a tiny spark of divinity, while non-Japanese had none.)

Many of our words dealing with royalty—including *royalty* itself—come from the Latin word for king, *rex*. This word was derived from the verb *regere*, "to guide," and the early Roman kings guided their subjects so oppressively that *rex* became a bad word under the Roman Republic.

During the Middle Ages in Europe, kings were essentially the strongest of the nobles, with nothing else special about them. They often ruled insecurely, threatened by other nobles with ambitions to sit on the throne or by relatives who thought they had a better claim. Often the nobles were strong enough to defy the king's wishes. Naturally, the kings wanted to get the upper hand over their unruly nobles; so the doctrine of the divine right of kings was developed. This theory, which reached its high point in the 17th century, held that the king held his throne by the grace of God and that he was therefore God's representative on Earth. To defy the King was to defy God and invite a terrible retribution. The nobles resented this doctrine bitterly, even while they gave lip service to it. But the middle classes and the peasants supported it enthusiastically, for they saw the king as their protector against the violent and rapacious nobles. The nobles saw their liberties diminished, but the commoners had no liberties to speak of in any case, and they were happy to see the nobles taken down a peg.

Beginning with the victory of the Puritans in the English Civil War in the mid-1600s, kings gradually had their powers whittled away. The surviving kings and queens perform only ceremonial functions, and the business of government is carried out by elected officials who can be changed at election time if they do a bad job. A majority of the people of those countries that still have royal families seem satisfied with this arrangement, for the human animal seems to crave someone to look up to—especially if that person is no longer a threat to their freedoms and their purses.

Knight
The knight in armor is a symbol of gallantry and nobility, at least in the Western world. So it may come as a surprise to learn that the word *knight* itself once meant nothing more than "servant." Its original Old English form was *cniht*, and it has a German cousin, *Knecht*, which still does mean "servant." In its very earliest

use, *cniht* meant "boy" or "young man." Next, it meant a serving-boy, then any male servant. At last, in the 11th century, it came to mean an armed servant or military follower of some person of importance. Such knights were known as "the king's knight" or "the bishop's knight," and so on, depending on whom they served. In time, the qualifier was dropped, and *knight* then meant a member of the professional warrior class.

The Anglo-Saxon knights (then confusingly called *thegnas*, or thanes) always fought on foot. The Norman conquerors introduced a new factor by mounting all their knights on horseback, which gave them a great advantage in battle. The Normans called their knights *chevaliers*, Old French for "horsemen." This term was derived from the medieval Latin word *caballarius*, from *caballus*, a late Latin word for "horse." The Spanish term *caballero* and the Italian *cavagliere* come from the same root. Indeed, knighthood and horses have always gone together—except in Anglo-Saxon England. After the Norman Conquest, Anglo-Saxon scribes translated *chevalier* by the word *ridere*, which by amputation of the last *e* becomes *rider*. Knights were also called "riders" in the other Germanic languages, *Ritter* in German, *riddare* in Swedish, and so on.

The Middle Ages were the great era of knighthood, and from the beginning knights were classed above the common people, although they were not necessarily of noble birth. Some knights were feudal tenants who held their land on condition of performing military service for their superior and providing their own horse and armor. But land was limited; so many knights simply hired on as members of the private fighting force of a nobleman who owned a castle. It was difficult for a commoner to become a knight, but it was not unknown for an especially brave common soldier to be knighted after a battle. Even troubadours were sometimes knighted for their outstanding performances.

Knight

A knight's training began when he was seven or eight years old and sent off to be a page at the castle of a knight or nobleman who was on good terms with his father. For seven or eight years he waited on his master and mistress and picked up the basics of etiquette, hunting and falconry, and the handling of weapons. At some point in his teens, the page became a squire, or knight's attendant. He devoted more and more of his time to military skills and physical training until he was considered ready for active duty. Then he took his sword to the castle priest to be blessed and entered the world of real (as opposed to practice) combat. He might remain with his old master, but more likely attached himself to another knight.

The word *squire* literally means "shield-bearer" (it is a short form of *esquire*, which comes from *écuyer*, a French perversion of the Latin term *scutiger*, from *scutum*, "shield," and *gerere*, "to carry"), and one of the squire's chief duties was to carry his master's shield and armor to the battlefield. He also helped his knight to put the cumbersome armor on and helped him up on his big warhorse. Once in combat, the squire had to display the pennon of his knight on the end of a lance, dash about the battlefield after the man on horseback to help him back on his horse if he were knocked off, fight by the knight's side if he were outmatched, rescue him if he were wounded or captured, and take charge of all prisoners the knight took. Afterward, he had to keep the knight's sword sharp and his armor clean and shiny. It was a hard six or seven year's apprenticeship, and at the end the squire had definitely earned his promotion to knighthood.

There were two different ceremonies for making a squire into a knight. One involved a great deal of pomp and ceremony. The candidate for knighthood began in the evening with a bath, shave, and haircut. While he was in the bath, two "grave and ancient knights" sat with him to instruct him in the mysteries of chivalry, which he no doubt knew by heart already. Then the grave and ancient knights escorted the candidate, robed in white, to the chapel, where he spent the night in prayer and confession. After this, he was allowed a brief nap until the two guardian knights dressed him in a special costume, and off they rode to the place where the really important part of the ceremony was to take place. The candidate fell on his knees before the king or nobleman who granted his knighthood, and the two top-ranking knights present ritually placed his spurs on his heels. The personage who was to grant the knighthood then buckled on the new knight's sword, embraced him, and gave him a blow on the neck or shoulder, saying "Be thou a good knight." This was called the *accolade* (from an Italian term meaning "embrace"), and it was what made the knighting official. Everyone then went off to the chapel, where the newly-created knight vowed to defend the Church and offered his sword on the altar. When he came out, there was a comic-relief finale as the master cook of the castle claimed the spurs as his fee and threatened to chop them off with his cleaver if the knight—God forbid!—did anything to violate the code of chivalry.

But this lengthy ceremony was such a production that it was seldom used. Most knights were created by a simple accolade in which the conferrer of knighthood struck the kneeling candidate three times with the flat of his sword while pronouncing a brief formula. Scores of knights were created in this way before and after battles, as well as off the battlefield.

The code of chivalry (literally, horsemanship) has been covered with a misleading veneer of sentimentality and wishful thinking. In fact, it was a warrior's code carried to an almost insane extreme. Its underlying principle was bravery in combat, which the knights were always seeking in order to prove themselves and gain honor. It was tempered by rituals of courtesy to those of equal or superior social rank. Women of the gentry or nobility were treated with the most elaborate courtesy, as they were not rivals for honor and status. Toward the common people, knights were free to behave with the utmost contempt and brutality, and usually did.

Knighthood gradually died out as a profession as the development of guns made castles and armor obsolete. True, they could have had bullet-proof armor made, but it would have been so heavy as to be absolutely impractical. By 1500, chivalry itself was defunct except in tournaments and pageants. Knights are still created today, but the knighthood is an honorary rank conferred in recognition of some notable achievement or service to the nation. It entitles the honored person to be called "Sir." Medieval knights would no doubt be disgusted to learn that, in Britain, at least, females are also knighted, with the title of "Dame."

As for squires, that title came to be applied to the largest landowner in a district. Later, it was used as a flattering title for the lesser gentry as well, something like "Colonel" in Kentucky. "Squire" was also used in the United States as a title for such powerful men as big landowners, lawyers, and rural justices of the peace. This usage has gone the way of the passenger pigeon, except for lawyers who pompously append "Esquire" to their names.

Marquis

In the early years of the Dark Ages, when new nations were starting to grow out of the wreckage of the Roman Empire, there were many border areas that neighboring rulers claimed. In the Late Latin that served as a lingua franca, these regions were called *marca* from a Germanic word that meant "border." That word was *becarie* in German and *mearc* in Old English. In medieval English it became *march*, a term that is now obsolete but can still be found in historical novels. But it was in the disputed borderlands between France and Germany that the title of *marquis* had its origin.

Marquis

Rival kings and nobles made frequent bloody raids on the borderlands; to secure them, special counts were placed in charge of their defense. These counts were at first known as *marchio comes*, or "count of the mark." Later, the *comes* was dropped, since everyone knew what a *marchio* was anyway. The Germans took to calling their *marchiones* (the Latin plural) *Markgraf*. The French called theirs *marchis*; the *ch* probably had a deep guttural sound, because the spelling was later changed to *marquis*, the form in which it was brought to England.

Since a *marchio* had special responsibilities, he was compensated by being granted more than one county as a source of income. Other counts were allowed only one. But certain aggressive French counts managed to acquire more than one county despite the prohibition, and they, too, began to call themselves *marchio*. So the title came to mean not the guardian of the frontier but an unusually powerful count, one so powerful that he ranked above other counts and just below a duke. Other Romance-speaking nations followed the lead of France on this point, as they did in so many other matters concerning the nobility.

The title of *marquis* came relatively late to England—the first one was created in 1385. Some great English families took up the fashion of spelling it *marquess* and persist in this affectation to this day. The marquis or marquess best known to Americans—at least to aficionados of boxing—is the eighth Marquess of Queensberry (1844–1900), whose proper name was John Sholto Douglas. Queensberry was an ardent sportsman and patron of sports, especially of boxing. In 1860, when he was still in his teens, he helped to found the Amateur Athletic Club of Britain; seven years later he was one of the authors of a new set of rules for boxing, which made that sport less of a bloody contest of punishment and endurance and more of a contest of skill. The Marquess of Queensberry's rules (they were, of course, named for him to lend the sport respectability) banned wrestling holds, compelled the boxers to wear padded gloves, set a three-minute limit for rounds with a one-minute break between rounds, and established the ten-second knockout count. The Queensberry rules are the basis of those used today.

Mayor
The Mayor is the chief official of a city or town, a powerful man indeed. But his title is derived from the Latin term for an upper-grade servant. In the great Roman households, the chief servant who supervised the others was called the *maior domus*, literally "greater one of the house." This was often abbreviated to simply *maior*. When the Franks marched out of Germany and took over France from the crumbling Roman Empire in the 5th century A.D., they also took over the local variant of Latin. So the royal Merovingian family called the chief of their palace staff *maior palatii*, which is usually translated in history books as "mayor of the palace." (That phrase is always a stumbling block for school children, who know in their hearts that the Mayor is the person who runs the city.)

The Merovingian kings were a pretty sorry lot, more interested in doing each other in than in running their kingdoms; so the mayors of the palace took on more and more administrative functions, and the power that went with them. By the 7th century the mayors of the palace were the real heads of the government, functioning as prime ministers. They took part in the nomination of dukes and counts; they ran the royal tribunals when the king was not there; often they took command of the armies. The office of mayor of the palace became hereditary, passing from father to son while the kings frittered away their time in vice and violence. For one period, the mayor of the palace ruled without any king at all. At last, in 752, the incumbent mayor, Pippin the Short, pushed the figurehead king into a monastery and took the crown himself. Pippin's son was the famous Charlemagne.

Of course, not all mayors were palace mayors or became kings. Most were the chief magistrates of towns or cities. The title of mayor began to be used in England in the 11th century, after the Norman conquest. Before then, English towns were governed by a royal agent called a reeve. The mayors of London and a few other cities, who represented powerful constituencies, were eventually given the title of Lord Mayor.

Americans have never gone in for such wicked foreign fripperies, but we have had some colorful mayors. There was Mayor Curley of Boston, who was imprisoned for corruption but reelected while he was in jail. The equally crooked mayor of Jersey City, Frank Hague, reputedly boasted, "I am the law." Mayor Daley of Chicago, one of the last of the old-time machine bosses, is said to have influenced the Democratic presidential convention of 1952 to pick Adlai Stevenson as the party candidate. On the other side of the coin, we have New York City's beloved Fiorello La Guardia, who ruled autocratically but well. A consummate showman, La Guardia loved to don a fireman's helmet and rush to the scene of a fire, there to be photographed. He also won the hearts of the city's kids by reading the Sunday funnies over the radio during a newspaper delivery strike.

In French, a mayor is called a *maire*. In German, he is a *Bürgermeister* (literally, master of the townspeople). The Latin title of *maior* took a different path and eventually became *mayer* or *meier*, the overseer of an estate. In Spain, even before the end of the Roman period, the Latin *maior* became *maiorinus*. And here the word takes a bizarre twist. Spanish sheep-owners belonged to a large and powerful organization called the Mesta, and the Mesta hired a superintendent of herding operations who was called the *gregum maiorinus*, or "mayor of the flocks." *Maiorinus* was gradually corrupted to *merino*, and the *gregum* fell out of use, so that this important man was called simply "The Merino." The name then came to be used for the sheep themselves and for their wool, so if you see an advertisement for merino wool, you'll know that it has ancient links with Roman overseers and modern mayors.

Monarch In the ancient Mediterranean world, there were many nations that were ruled by a single, absolute potentate. The Greek philosophers, attempting to categorize political systems, devised a term for such a ruler. They called him a *monarch*, from *monos*, "alone," plus *archein*, "to rule." For some two thousand years *monarch* kept this connotation, even though monarchs probably never ruled quite as absolutely as it sounds. Even the most tyrannical of monarchs had counselors to advise him, and, if he would not listen to them, there were always favorites to influence him by playing on his vanity or his sexual frailties. I probably should not refer to the monarch as "he," for there have been some celebrated female monarchs too: Cleopatra, Elizabeth I of England, Catherine the Great of Russia, and Queen Victoria, to name the best known. Today, a monarch is a hereditary sovereign, usually called King or Queen, who reigns but does not rule; that is, the monarch no longer has any power over the government, whereas in the old days he or she always had the last word.

In the 17th century, during the English Revolution, there arose a Puritan sect that called themselves the Fifth Monarchy Men. There had been four great monarchies in the world, they said, all of which had been destroyed because of their sins: Assyria, Persia, Greece, and Rome. But now the time was ripe to establish a fifth monarchy of Jesus and the saints. The Fifth Monarchy Men proposed to do this by overthrowing the exist-

71

ing society and replacing it with a simpler and more virtuous one based on the Old Testament. The sect originally supported Cromwell against King Charles I, but turned against him when he proved not Puritanical enough to meet their standards. Cromwell cracked down on them—he and the gentry who had supported the Parliamentary cause against King Charles I had no intention of overturning the existing order. All they wanted to do was straighten out some of the kinks that the inept and autocratic king had put in it. Off to jail went the leaders and the most eloquent preachers of the Fifth Monarchy movement, and the sect went into a quiescent phase until Cromwell died and royalty was restored to the throne in the form of Charles II. The Fifth Monarchy Men took the coronation of the licentious "Merry Monarch" as their signal to strike. Led by a barrelmaker named Thomas Venner, a band of Fifth Monarch zealots tried to seize London in 1661. God apparently did not favor their attempt, for they were quickly crushed and most were killed. The Merry Monarch, not amused by the attempted coup, had Venner and ten other surviving leaders executed for high treason. After that, the Fifth Monarchy movement faded into an obscure footnote to history.

One can hardly mention monarchy without also thinking of *oligarchy*. That word was coined from the Greek *oligos*, "few," and *archein*, "to rule" and means, logically enough, that power is concentrated in the hands of a few men. At the opposite end of the scale from the powerful few were *hoi polloi*, "the many" or, if you are looking at them from the viewpoint of the ruling class, the masses or the rabble. In English *hoi polloi* has always been used as an expression of contempt. The phrase "the hoi polloi" dates back to the 1660's, when the poet Dryden used it. But Dryden's sneer was bad grammar. "*Hoi* is classical Greek for "the"; so "the hoi polloi" literally means "the the many."

Noble

Noble is among the many French words that crossed the Channel after the Norman Conquest. It comes from the Latin adjective *nobilis*, which literally meant "well-known" or "celebrated." (It was originally spelled *gnobilis* and came from a root, *gno-*, which meant "to know.") By transference it came to mean "of the aristocracy."

In early English usage, *noble* could refer either to a person who had earned distinction by his deeds or his character, or to one of the privileged class. It later took on numerous related meanings such as "admirable," "splendid," and "unusually large"; Shakespeare often used it to mean "of great or lofty character," as in the famous line, "This was the noblest Roman of them all."

Another meaning was "precious." Gemstones were once called "noble stones," and the alchemists termed gold, silver, and sometimes mercury "noble metals" because they did not rust or tarnish, just as a noble's honor was supposed to remain forever bright. In the 18th century, when scientific chemistry developed, platinum was added to the list of noble metals and mercury was dropped. Other non-reactive metals such as palladium were added to the list as they were discovered. Modern chemists call neon, argon, krypton, helium, xenon, and radon the "noble gases" because they are so non-reactive. Like the proudest of nobles, they will not combine with the other herd of elements except under very special laboratory conditions. Even men of science, it would seem, carry this medieval concept embedded in their psyches.

In some languages the concept of nobility of materials went even further. In Swedish, for example, fine woods like mahogany and ebony are called "noble woods." And blue-veined cheeses such as Stilton, Roquefort, and Danish Blue are called "noble cheeses" because the blue streaks of mold that permeate them suggest the blue veins that show through the fair, thin skin of the nobility.

However, the family name of Alfred Nobel, the inventor of dynamite and founder of the Nobel Prizes, has nothing to do with nobility. It is derived from the family's original home, the little town of Nöbbelöv in the south of Sweden.

Parliament The British Parliament, like our Congress, is a great place for talk—and that is what *parliament* originally meant. In Old French, *parlement* meant "speaking." (From the verb *parler*, "to speak." Incidentally, *parlor* comes from the same root and originally meant a special room in a monastery or a convent where the monks or nuns could meet for conversation or talk to visitors.)

At first *parlement* meant a debate, then a formal conference between the king and his advisers, then a meeting of the king and his more important subjects, and finally the national assembly that the king was forced to summon now and then in order to get money to finance his military adventures. We spell the word "parliament" instead of "parlement" because at one early point the French word was Latinized into *parliamentum* for official use.

In Anglo-Saxon times there had been a national assembly called the *witenagemot* (from *witena*, "wise men," and *gemot*, "meeting"). It was made up of the leading churchmen and nobles. The common people were allowed to attend meetings of the *witenagemot* and cheer or boo the arguments, but that was the extent of their influence. William the Conqueror dispensed with the *witenagemot* by simply failing to summon it, and under his immediate heirs there was a kind of three-way jockeying for power between the king, the barons, and the church, with constantly shifting temporary alliances. In 1215 the barons forced King John to sign Magna Carta. Its main importance in parliamentary history lay in the provision that the king could not impose any financial levies without the consent of a council of the leading church officials and the earls and barons. This was the first legal restraint on the king in nearly 200 years.

The common people were still left out, but in 1254 their first representatives—merchants and heads of craft guilds from the towns—were summoned to a national parliament where they sat timidly beside the prelates, nobles, and the knights of the shire who represented the military class. The term *parliament* was first used to refer to the assembly of 1275, in which the commoners were again represented. In 1295 the clergymen refused to attend, wishing to assert their independence. As a result, they lost a great deal of power and influence.

After 1300, the embryo Parliaments became increasingly assertive. In 1327 the Parliament actually deposed the king in favor of his son. Soon thereafter the knights of the shire joined forces with the representatives of the towns (the peasants had no representation and would have none until modern times), and the House of Commons took form.

Parliament has had a checkered history, at times subservient to the Crown and at times boldly independent. In theory, the sovereign or chief of state is part of a parliament, but nowadays the Queen plays only a ceremonial part. She has no vote or veto power, and cannot even lobby for a piece of legislation.

Some Parliaments have earned names such as the Model Parliament, the Addled Parliament, the Drunken Parliament, the Long Parliament, the Merciless Parliament (a.k.a. the Wonderful Parliament), the Rump Parliament, the Good Parliament, and the Useless Parliament. By comparison, the United States Congress, for all the bombast of some of its members, comes off as a pallid bunch of milksops.

Politician
"Coffee, which makes the politician wise, And see through all things with his half-closed eyes," sang the poet Alexander Pope in *The Rape of the Lock*, expressing a skeptical view of politicians that is still widely shared more than two and a half centuries later. Yet the word *politician* had an honorable beginning in the works of Aristotle in the 4th century B.C.

The fundamental unit of Greek society was the *polis*—the city-state, which embraced every facet of Greek life: religious, moral, cultural, and social as well as what we call political. A citizen was a *polites; politike* was politics, the art and science of government. A man who practiced politics was called a *politikos*.

Like many other classical Greek ideas, this was forgotten during the Dark Ages and rediscovered in the Renaissance. French scholars translated *politike* into *politique*, and *politikos* into *politicien*. English writers began to use the term in the late 16th century—the first recorded use was in 1588. From the very beginning, it carried a disreputable image of scheming and intriguing. Of course, it was also used in the complimentary sense of "statesman," but the bad image clung to it. In the 1620s a "politician" was also a term for someone who lived by politics as a trade. Samuel Johnson, in the mid-18th century, defined a politician as "a man of artifice; one of deep contrivance."

Many politicians have worked hard to earn that reputation, engaging in shady schemes and plots to enrich themselves or increase their power. With the rise of democratic ideas and universal male suffrage, politicians found themselves faced with masses of easily controlled, ignorant voters. The notorious political machines grew out of this circumstance. Every now and then, some reform-minded politician would arise to redeem the honor of the breed, but somehow politicians had a tendency to slide back to their old places at the trough. As for campaign promises, hardly anyone believes them any more.

Yet it is a curious paradox that, even though we distrust politicians as a group, we depend on them to get the business of government done. In the days of George Washington and Thomas Jefferson, a man could indeed serve in the Senate or the House of Representatives part of the year and spend the rest of the time at his normal business as a lawyer, merchant, farmer, or what have you. But today running the government is a full-time business, and it is done by people who have made it their profession, the politicians. Perhaps if we gave the profession more respect, we would get better people in it.

Queen In Old English there were two very similar words. One was *cwene*, which meant "woman." The other was *cwen*, without an *e* on the end, which meant a very special woman—the king's wife. These two sister words went on to very different careers. *Cwen* became *queen*, but *cwene* turned into *quean*, a derogatory word that is found in Shakespeare's plays (it became obsolete not long after). Long before Shakespeare's time it had taken on the meaning of "strumpet" or "harlot."

Although a queen's role was seen as providing heirs to the king, there have been many queens who were able rulers in their own right. Hatshepsut of Egypt was one; almost 1,500 years later Cleopatra also ruled Egypt. Hatshepsut wore a false beard to signify that she was as good as a man (at least, her monuments show her that way); Cleopatra conquered men with sexual allure. In the 16th century Queen Elizabeth I of England led her country to greatness and started it on its way to becoming a world power. In the 18th century there was Catherine the Great of Russia. And, of course, there was Queen Victoria of England, who ruled from 1837 to 1901 and gave her name to a whole era, not to mention a rather repressive variety of morality.

In Christian symbolism, the Virgin Mary was honored with the title of the Queen of Heaven from a very early time. On a secular plane, we have beauty queens (but why no beauty kings?). The queen is the most powerful piece in chess, and in playing cards it is the second-highest face card. If the world's dominant cultures were matriarchal instead of patriarchal, the queen might be the highest-ranking card as well.

Party

Party comes from the French word *partie*, which is derived from the Latin *partita*, meaning "parting" or "division." It comes from the same root as *part*, and in fact that is what it originally meant when it first appeared in English in the 12th century. By the end of that century, it had come to mean one side in a contest or dispute or one of the persons involved in a contract. We still use the term "party to a contract," and legal documents drone on about the "party of the first part" and "party of the second part."

At the same time, *party* meant the individuals who made up a side in a controversy, or in a tournament or a real battle. Thus it came to mean any group of people united by a common purpose such as a work party, a hunting party, or a raiding party. In a political sense, *party* seems to have been used as early as the late 14th century, but it only took on its modern meaning toward the end of the 17th century.

There have probably been parties as long as there have been legislative bodies, but for most of history they were the personal followings of aggressive leaders with no programs beyond personal advantage. Otherwise, they were temporary alliances of the enfranchised classes to promote a particular cause or policy. The modern party system, with more or less permanent, organized parties dedicated to definite principles, had its beginning in England, and the first parties were the Tories and Whigs, both names being highly insulting. *Tory*, which came from the Irish *toraighe*, or "pursuer," was an epithet given some years earlier to Irish Catholic outlaws who raided and murdered English Protestant settlers and soldiers in Ireland. It was applied to the supporters of the Duke of York's succession to the throne. The Duke, later crowned as James II, was a Roman Catholic, and many Protestants feared that he would restore the religious persecutions in which Bloody Mary had indulged, just as King Louis XIV of France was doing to French Protestants across the English Channel. Stung to the quick by this comparison to Irish criminals (Protestant or Catholic, the English all looked on the Irish with contempt), the Tories branded their opponents with the epithet of *Whig*, from the Scottish *whiggamore*, a cattle thief or horse thief. It had also been applied to a group of extreme Scottish Presbyterians during the English Civil War.

The names Whig and Tory were first applied to these opposing factions in 1679 and became more or less official in 1689, the year in which James was deposed. Before the American Revolution there were Whigs and Tories in the colonies, although they had no vote in the British Parliament. During the Revolution, the Whigs supported independence, while the Tories supported the King and Parliament. After the war there were no real parties for a time, and George Washington warned his countrymen about the dangers of political parties, which he saw as analogous to the selfish factions that had plagued British politics.

Nevertheless, divisions did arise along party lines. The first appeared in 1787, while Congress was debating whether or not to adopt the Constitution and turn the thirteen quarreling states into one nation. Those in favor called themselves Federalists; their opponents rather unoriginally dubbed themselves

Anti-Federalists. Around 1792, the Anti-Federalists, suspecting the Federalists of plans to restore a monarchical form of government, took the name of Republicans. Soon they changed the name to Democratic Republicans, to indicate that they defended the rights of the common man against the aristocratic Federalists.

After the War of 1812 the Federalists faded away, only to re-emerge after the election of 1824 as the National Republicans. To avoid confusion, the Democratic Republicans dropped the "Republican" a few years later. Certain factions of the Democrats joined forces with the National Republicans to form the Whig Party, whose title was formally adopted in 1834. The Whigs later split on the question of slavery, and the anti-slavery wing founded the Republican Party in 1854. Since then, the Democratic and Republican Parties have been the mainstays of American political life, sometimes widely divergent, sometimes barely distinguishable, sometimes stealing outright from each other's platform.

Many political philosophers have written resentfully about the domination of American politics by two parties not terribly different from each other in outlook and both spanning a wide range of opinion from right to left. However, the alternative would be two large parties of extreme and opposing views, which could lead to civil unrest, or else so many little parties, each representing a special interest, that no one would ever gain a clear majority in Congress and government would depend on shaky coalitions in which very minor—and sometimes fanatical—groups would wield decisive power.

Prince A prince was not always the son of a king—and is not even today. In fact, the title from which *prince* is derived was simply a Latin term for a leader. *Princeps* was the Latin word, formed from *primus*,

"first," and *capere*, "to take." Literally, it meant the first or foremost of a group, thus a leader or a chief. When Augustus took control of Rome, he took the title of *princeps civitatis*, or "first citizen of the state." Historians say that he chose this title as the one least likely to arouse resistance among the supporters of the old republic.

Under the Roman Empire, *princeps* was often used as the title of high officials. After the disintegration of the Roman Empire, the barbarian chieftains who moved into Rome's former territory often proclaimed themselves *principes*; so the word took on the significance of a ruler. It spread into the Romance and Germanic languages: *principe* in Italian and Spanish, *prince* in French, *Prinz* or *Fürst* in German, and so on. (*Fürst* was the native German word that corresponded to *princeps*; it was used for lesser princes. *Prinz* was reserved for the sons of the king.) In the Middle Ages, *prince* or its equivalent was often used to denote the ruler of a small state who was a feudal subordinate of a king or emperor.

Although the word *prince* had been known in England since about 1200, there were no English princes until 1301, when Edward II was created Prince of Wales. Tradition has it that his father, King Edward I, made him Prince of Wales at his birth to satisfy the Welsh demand for a ruler who did not speak English. But in fact he was granted the title by Parliament when he was seventeen years old and presumably spoke a passable English when not speaking Anglo-Norman French. So much for legend.

For several hundred years the Prince of Wales—the first-born son of the King—remained the only prince in England. It was King James I (the same king who commissioned the King James Bible) who broke tradition in the early 17th century and allowed all sons of the reigning king to be called Prince. Queen Victoria, in the 19th century, extended this privilege to her grandchildren, including the girls, who, of course, were called Princess.

81

Princess was not used in Roman times; it dates from about 1400. Originally it meant a female ruler or the wife of a prince. In the early 16th century it began to be used for a king's daughter.

Although the English were very chary of granting the title of Prince, it was quite otherwise on the European mainland. There princes of all grades flourished. Some were members of the immediate royal families; others held the title because the king or the Holy Roman Emperor had granted it to their ancestors. Germany, as mentioned above, used *Prinz* for princes of the blood royal and *Fürst* for all the others. Usually a *Fürst* was outranked by a duke. In France, that prolific monarch Louis XIV went further and established *two* grades of royal princes. One consisted of the King's legitimate sons, the other of the officially recognized royal bastards. In Russia, every descendant of a prince was entitled to call himself a prince too; so the title had very little significance beyond showing that the bearer was an aristocrat.

Today there are only two nations in Europe that are ruled by princes: the tiny countries of Monaco and Liechtenstein. Andorra is called a principality, but its princes are the Bishop of Urgel in Spain and the President of France.

"Put not your trust in princes," urged the composer of Psalm 146 in the Bible. The Psalmist meant that earthly princes had no real power, for only God could save. But a reader of Niccolo Macchiavelli's ill-famed classic *The Prince* would put an entirely different interpretation on it. Macchiavelli described how a ruler could manage to seize power and retain it through a judicious application of fraud, treachery, and violence, and he backed up his theories with many examples from ancient and recent history. Often blamed for teaching rulers to act evilly, Macchiavelli's book was a bitterly cynical treatise on the realities of Italian politics in his day, shortly before and after 1500. It is said that both Hitler and

Mussolini were guided by *The Prince* in establishing their evil empires, but many high-minded men and women have also studied it in order to avoid the conditions it describes.

Senator
In ancient times, people had an inordinate respect for the old, believing them to be endowed with some special wisdom or the favor of the gods. Back then, an individual's chances of surviving to old age were slim. Even in times of peace, if disease did not carry them off, famine often did. So it is no wonder that in those pre-scientific days the few surviving oldsters were regarded with awe and reverence. The Romans shared this view, for they called their highest law-making body the *Senatus*, or Assembly of Old Men (from *senex*, "old man," the same root that we find in *senile* and *senior citizen*). A *senator* was a member of the senate and was by definition a man, if not always old.

The official line of Rome's historians was that the Senate was created by Romulus, the legendary founder of Rome, when he chose one hundred of the best men among his subjects to advise him. The oldest verifiable data, however, tell us only that there was a Senate in 509 B.C.—more than 200 years after the legendary founding of Rome—and that it contained 300 members. All of them were almost certainly patricians, members of the aristocracy.

The Roman Senate was never a democratic body. While Rome was ruled by kings, the kings picked the Senators and could dismiss them from office at their pleasure. After the kings were expelled, around 500 B.C., the Senators were elected by the Patricians, who naturally supported members of their own class. Under the Republic, certain high public officials automatically became Senators when their terms expired. In time, plebeians were allowed to hold these offices, and thus certain select members of the common herd gained entry to that august body. (It is not noted, however, that they spent much time lobbying for the cause of the common man after being appointed.)

As time passed, the Senate of Rome grew larger and larger. By the time Julius Caesar sat in it, the Senate numbered 900. The United States Senate, with 100 members, is streamlined by comparison. Powerful under the Republic, the Senate became a rubber stamp under the Emperors, although membership and its privileges were still coveted. Traditions of its glory lingered on after the Roman Empire crumbled.

In 1787 and 1788, the framers of the United States Constitution had to find a solution for the thorny question of how the states should be represented in the legislature. Should the number of representatives be apportioned according to population? The small states dug in their heels and balked at this idea, since it would enable the larger states to outvote them automatically. Should each state have the same number? The larger states screamed bloody murder at this, for they feared it would put them at the mercy of the envious smaller states. At last a compromise was reached. The new Congress would have *two* houses. The lower house would be apportioned according to population size, while the upper house would be composed of two members from each state. In imitation of ancient Rome, which was held up as a model by people of all political leanings, the upper house was called the Senate. To justify this name, Senators had to be relative elders of at least 30 years of age; mere striplings of 25 could qualify as Congressmen. Political institutions being what they are, it did not take long for the Senate to become a true assembly of elders. Many Senators have served well into their seventies, and a few have held their seats into their nineties.

The framers of the Constitution intended the Senate to function as a brake on the more democratic House of Representatives. To that end, they provided that the Senators should not be elected by the public at large, but by the state legislatures, which they believed would be more responsive to the wishes of the gentry. The man in the street could not vote for his Senators until the 17th Amendment was ratified in 1913. Women had to wait until 1920.

In the 19th century, Senators were often rated by their powers of oratory—in that pre-electronic age public speaking was one of the major forms of entertainment. The public did not care too much about the content of a Senator's speeches as long as the form was flowery, picturesque, and full of big, high-sounding words. Senators also put their oratorical powers to work to block votes on legislation they opposed, a practice that came to be known as *filibustering*, from an old word for "pirate."

The word *senator* entered the English language about 1200 A.D. Impatient reformers, observing the older fogies of the Senate, may think that nothing has changed since that date. But really there has been progress.

Sheriff

Sheriffs have had a bad image problem for centuries. There was Robin Hood's old antagonist the Sheriff of Nottingham, who perpetually oppressed the poor and helpless. In the Old West, there were crooked sheriffs who protected cattle rustlers in return for a pay-off. One notorious sheriff, Henry Plummer, actually headed a gang of robbers in his off hours. In our own day, we have been treated to the spectacle of brutal Southern sheriffs clubbing civil-rights demonstrators and setting dogs on them. And in some increasingly urbanized counties across the nation, maintaining a county sheriff and his department is beginning to look like a wasteful duplication of expenditures for services that city and state police can provide just as well.

Yet the sheriff has a long and honorable history, from his

beginning in Anglo-Saxon England. He was then known as the *scire-gerefa*, or shire reeve. ("Shire" comes from the Old English *scir*, which stems from an older Germanic word, *scira*, which meant "care." A reeve was a sort of overseer and could be anything from a royal district administrator to a farm superintendent.) The *scire-gerefa* governed the shire jointly with an alderman, who was then an official of high rank, not a City Hall hack. The Norman invaders changed many things in English life, but they kept the sheriff because he was so useful in maintaining law and order. As a royal appointee, the sheriff upheld the king and the aristocracy against the common people. Therefore the Sheriff of Nottingham was naturally cast as the opponent of the mythical Robin Hood. On the other hand, historians say that the sheriffs on occasion protected the people against the rapacious barons.

One of the sheriff's duties was to see that sentences of execution were carried out. This gave rise to some grim English gallows humor—literally, because "to dance at the sheriff's ball and loll out one's tongue at the company" meant to be hanged, and "the sheriff's picture-frame" was a hangman's noose. American slang has no comparable expressions. But then we don't have public hangings, either.

Vassal Modern people—if
they know the word at all—often carelessly misuse *vassal* as a fancy substitute for *slave*. But a vassal was not a slave—in fact, he was often a nobleman, and vassalage was the cornerstone of the feudal system under which Europe operated during the Middle Ages.

The feudal system had nothing to do with deadly, hereditary quarrels between families. The term came from the medieval Latin *feudum*, meaning "fee" in the special sense of property held from an overlord in return for allegiance and military or other services. The feudal system was in essence a network of personal contracts and alliances, with the big land-owners parcelling out farms and manors, and sometimes even castles, in return for which they got what amounted to their own private armies. Under feudalism, there was no sense of loyalty or responsibility to the community or the nation—only to one's own liege lord, and, through him, to more powerful overlords all the way up the chain to the king.

A vassal was one who held a fee, or fief, as some liked to call it, from a superior. The fief was usually land but could be the right to some other form of revenue, such as the tolls from a bridge or the exclusive right to operate a mill. To get his fief, the vassal (from the Late Latin *vassallus*, "serving-man") knelt before his lord, placed his hands between the lord's hands, and took a solemn oath of loyalty and service. This was called an act of homage (from the Old French word *ommage* or *homage*, ultimately derived from the Latin *homo*, "man") because the vassal declared that he was the lord's man and bound to serve his interests.

The feudal system was full of variations and inconsistencies, and it often happened that a vassal held a fief from someone whom he outranked socially. A count, for instance, might hold a fief from a viscount. There were even cases of kings holding fiefs from the vassals of their own vassals. Families acquired new fiefs through marriage or by other means, and vassals sometimes found themselves in the awkward position of owing allegiance to two hostile lords.

In fairness to those who confuse vassals and slaves, it should be admitted that around 1500, when the feudal system had pretty well broken down (it was replaced by strong central monarchies), *vassal* was sometimes used as an insult, carrying the meaning of a humble servant or underling. Near the end of the 1500s, it took on the secondary meaning of a slave or a person of the lowest class. But the person at the bottom of the feudal ladder was not the vassal but the serf. The word *serf* comes from the Latin *servus*, "slave," but the serf was not quite a slave, since the lord did not own him personally. But neither was he free. He was bound to the land he farmed and could not leave it without his lord's permission. He also owed the lord innumerable fees and services, including labor and part of his crop. As a result, most serfs lived miserable lives of poverty and humiliation, and there were many bloody rebellions by desperate serfs. Most of the blood was the serfs' own, since they were not allowed to bear arms and had to fight with farm tools as weapons. They were also untrained and undisciplined, while the knights and men-at-arms were well trained and disciplined. But relief of a ghastly sort did come. The Black Death so reduced the number of serfs that landlords had to make concessions to them to get any work done at all. Serfs were allowed to substitute cash payments for many of the hated work details, and in most of western Europe ended up as tenant farmers well before the French Revolution. They were still poor, they still had few rights, but they were no longer tied to the particular fields they tilled.

The French Revolution ended serfdom in France, and Napoleon abolished it in the territories he conquered. In parts of Germany, however, the serfs were not freed until well into the 1800s, and in the vast Russian Empire they were not freed until 1861.

After all this discussion, is it correct to say, "Joe just can't seem to give up smoking. He's a real vassal to the habit."? In the strict sense, no, but inasmuch as with every puff Joe takes he proclaims his loyalty to the tobacco industry and his obedience to their advertising campaigns, perhaps it's not too far off the mark.

Abbot

Most of us know that an abbot is the head of a monastery, but not so many know that this title originated among the early Christians of the Near East, where monasticism had its beginnings. *Abbot* is an English form, via Greek and Latin intermediates, of the Syriac *abba*, "father." (Syriac is a long-dead Semitic language, not spoken since the 13th century, although it is still used in the liturgies of a few Near Eastern sects.)

In the beginning, *abba* was used as a title of respect for all monks. Only later, in the West, was it limited to the head of a monastic community. Originally, most abbots were laymen, as were almost all monks. Monk and abbot alike were obliged to go to the nearest church for their religious needs. But monasteries tended to be built in deserts, mountains, and other places remote from the world and its temptations, and it was often difficult to get to the nearest church for confession and Mass. The Church hierarchy at length realized that a monastery needed a priest on the premises at all times to adminster the sacraments, and so the abbots were ordained. Even so, a number of monasteries in Western Europe were ruled by lay abbots until the 11th century. (In these cases, the abbot had a resident chaplain to assist him.)

From humble beginnings, abbots became quite autocratic and ruled their abbeys like little kings. Absolute obedience was

89

what they expected from the monks, and, if they did not get it, they inflicted harsh punishments on their hapless underlings. During the Middle Ages, many abbeys became wealthy and powerful from donations of land and money made by dying noblemen who had good reason to fear for the welfare of their souls. The abbots became, in effect, powerful lords, differing from their secular counterparts only in having taken vows of celibacy. These abbots enjoyed such wordly pleasures as dining well and hunting with hounds and falcons. When they traveled, they rode on handsome mules with gilded bridles and richly caparisoned saddles, sometimes carrying hawks on their wrists in case they should encounter small game along the way. Church bells rang to salute them as they passed by with their magnificently equipped retinues. But the abbots' days of glory came to an end with the Reformation in Protestant countries, and in Catholic countries in the 18th and 19th centuries. In Russia, however, it took the Bolshevik Revolution to curb them.

Atonement

To *atone* means to make amends for a wrong; in the case of religion, it means to make amends for a sin. Although *atonement* sounds like a Latin word, it is actually of 16th-century English origin and comes from the phrase *at one*, meaning "on good terms" or "in harmony." It was first used in a secular sense of peace or reconciliation between two quarreling parties, such as a king and his refractory noblemen. It was in this sense that *atonement* was first used in print, in a book by Sir Thomas More. The earliest known religious use was in 1526, in William Tyndale's translation of the Bible.

Gradually the sense of "reconciliation" replaced the original sense of "being at one," and eventually *atonement* came to mean the things one had to do to reach a state of reconciliation with God or with one's fellow man. Virtually every religion has some concept of atonement, but the actual means of propitiating the offended deity vary with the ways that people think of their gods. In the most primitive sense, atonement takes the form of enduring punishment, as if the god were a vicious and tyrannical old man who would be satisfied by this demonstration of submission on the sinner's part. Then, as priesthoods developed, one could make sacrifices of animals (which the priests ate in the name of the god), money, or valuable goods. Priests of all religions made a handsome profit out of sin in this way. Lastly, an ethical concept of atonement developed: the sinner could not buy forgiveness by sacrifices or cash payments and then feel free to go out and break his religion's rules again. He had to repent of his wrong action and reform his conduct so as not to repeat it.

The Day of Atonement, *Yom Kippur*, is the holiest day of the year in the Jewish religion. On Yom Kippur, pious Jews fast and pray for forgiveness for all the wrongs they have committed, whether knowingly or unknowingly. But Jewish doctrine teaches that man cannot hope for forgiveness from God until he has made atonement for the wrongs he has done to his fellow man.

Bishop In the early days of

Christianity, the congregations of believers found that they needed leaders to direct their worship and take charge of their affairs. So leaders were chosen by the apostles or their delegates. The people called their new leaders *episkopoi*, which is Greek for "overseers." The term was already used for public officials of the Roman Empire. It comes from *epi-*, "over," plus *skopos*, "watcher." In Latin, *episkopos* (the singular form) became *episcopus* and later *ebiscopus* or *biscopus* as the pronunciation changed. When the Anglo-Saxons were converted to Christianity they further shortened the title to *biscop*, which became *bishop* about the 14th century.

Originally each bishop was in charge of only one congregation, but the rapid growth of Christianity made it necessary to coordinate numbers of congregations and make sure that their doctrines and rituals of worship remained uniform. This job fell on the bishops, who were assigned territories with varying numbers of congregations. These territories were called *dioceses*, from the Latin word *dioecesis*, a term for the jurisdiction of a governor, which itself came from the Greek *dioikeis*, meaning "housekeeping" or "management."

Christianity places great importance on the symbolism of a shepherd and his flock, and the bishop was envisaged as a shepherd in addition to an administrator. It was his task to keep priests as well as laity from wandering off the path laid out by the Church, and he dressed the part. His crozier (from the Old French word *croc*, "hook") is nothing but a symbolic shepherd's crook, the long, hook-ended staff with which a real-life shepherd used to catch a straying sheep by the hind leg and drag it back to the flock. His gaiters, still worn by some Anglican bishops, are copies of ancient Mediterranean shepherd's leggings. His cope, or cloak, is a symbolic shepherd's cloak, highly decorated to befit his high ecclesiastical rank.

Since the bishop was such an important personage, his title was used in popular expressions. For instance, a certain flower was called "bishop's miter" because of its resemblance to the Bishop's ceremonial headgear. Then there was "bishop's weed," also known as "goutweed," which may have alluded to the lavish lifestyle of many bishops, gout being attributed to overindulgence in meat and wine. "Bishop" was the name of a popular drink of the 18th century, which consisted of sweet, mulled wine garnished with a roasted orange (at least, that was one recipe). Of course, the bishop is an important piece in chess: two bishops protectively flank the king and queen, as the church bolstered the secular rulers of bygone days.

In England, when a pot of porridge or some other dish got burned in cooking, people said that the bishop had put his foot in it. A 16th-century Protestant writer said that this was because bishops could burn at the stake anyone whom they pleased. Another explanation is that when a bishop passed through a village, the country folk would rush out of their houses to demand his blessing, forgetting whatever they had on the fire. Then, if the neglected food burned, they blamed it on the bishop.

Cantor

To those who know the cantor as the clerically robed person who chants the prayers in a Jewish congregation it may come as a surprise that *cantor* is not a Hebrew title but a Latin word for "singer." The Hebrew term is *chazen* (sometimes spelled *hazzan*). *Cantor* comes from the Latin verb *cantare*, "to sing," and it was once a Christian title, referring to the choirmaster or leader of singing in a church. It is still used in the Swedish Lutheran Church.

In Old Testament times, there were no cantors in Judaism. All the singing in the Temple was done by Levites, the tribe from which the priests were also drawn. After the Romans destroyed the Temple in the 1st century A.D., the role of singer was open to all Jews. But the *chazen* was originally an all-round functionary of the synagogue. He looked after the building and grounds, kept order during the services, and acted as a general supervisor. It was only in later centuries that he specialized in singing and dropped the other duties.

When 19th-century liberal reforms enabled Jews to move out of the ghetto into the modern world, the cantors became the Jewish equivalents of opera stars. People would flock to certain synagogues to hear a noted cantor sing the service. Twentieth-century technology gave cantors another push toward the big time, and some became recording stars. A few cantors gave up their profession to become secular opera singers. Others have become popular entertainers. However, the famous Eddie Cantor, a stage and film star of the early 20th century, was never a cantor. It was his family name.

Cardinal

A cardinal is a Roman Catholic dignitary second only to the Pope. The title goes back to the 6th century A.D. and comes from the Latin *cardo*, "hinge," the idea implied being of one so important that everything else hinges on him. Originally the title of cardinal was generally used for important churchmen, such as the canons of cathedrals or the heads of important churches. Over the years, usage gradually limited it to the cardinals of Rome, and in 1568 Pope Pius V made it official. Since, then, the only cardinals are the members of the College of Cardinals, the most powerful body in the Roman Catholic Church. The College of Cardinals, or Sacred College, was established in the twelfth century and is limited to seventy members. However, it is seldom filled to the limit; a few seats are almost always left vacant. Although the cardinals have many functions, their most important is the election of the Pope, who is always chosen from among their number.

There are three grades of cardinal: cardinal bishop, cardinal priest, and cardinal deacon. In times gone by, there were also lay cardinals, but there have been none since the 17th century. All cardinals rank as Princes of the Church. In keeping with their rank, they wear large red hats and scarlet robes, traditional colors of royalty. At times, cardinals have played a very large role in secular affairs. The two most outstanding were the French cardinals Richelieu (1585–1642) and Mazarin (1602–61). Richelieu, who was a duke as well as a cardinal, virtually governed France as a dictator from 1630 on. Although he ruthlessly crushed the Protestants of France, he intervened on the Protestant side in the Thirty Years' War to preserve the balance of power. He also kept the great nobles in check and founded the French Academy. Mazarin, who was born in Italy and whose real name was Giulio Mazarini, fought as a soldier in the Papal army and served as the Papal nuncio to France before he entered the French service, under Richelieu's patronage. Although never ordained a priest, he was made a cardinal in 1641 and succeeded Richelieu when that aristocratic prelate died in 1642. Mazarin became the chief minister of Louis XIII and Louis XIV, the famed Sun King who built Versailles. It is suspected that he may have been secretly married to the widowed mother of Louis XIV, Anne of Austria, who ruled France as regent for eighteen years. Mazarin was a renowned diplomat, and one of the classic pieces of French pastry is named for him.

A beautiful American wildflower is called "cardinal flower" because of its bright red color, like that of a cardinal's robes. The colorful cardinal finch is named for the same reason. But the cardinal numbers (one, two, three, and so on) and the cardinal virtues are so called because they are of basic importance —everything hinges on them.

Church
Church comes from the Greek adjective *kyriakon*, meaning "belonging to the Lord," and is a short way of saying "the Lord's house." It is odd that English and the other Teutonic languages adopted this word for a church, because the ordinary Greek word for a church was *ekklesia*, which passed into Latin with only a minor change in spelling. The Greek word, however, stemmed from a term meaning something like "the city council," and so it connoted the body of worshippers more than the building in which they met. Nonetheless, in early Christian usage *ecclesia*

soon came to mean the church building, and this Latin form passed into all the Romance languages. Even today, a language scholar can see the similarity between the French *eglise*, the Spanish *iglesia*, and the Italian *chiesa*. Through Roman missionaries, the Greco-Latin term was spread to the Celtic languages, too. So Irish and Scottish Gaels say *eglais*, Welsh speakers say *eglwys*, and Bretons say *iliz*.

Why the Teutonic languages took up *kyriakon* instead of the much more common *ecclesia* is still a mystery. One theory is that it spread by way of the eastern Goths, who hacked their way into the eastern Roman Empire, became mercenary soldiers, and also became the first Germanic tribe to be converted to Christianity. Another is that mercenaries from a number of German tribes picked up the term from their Greek-speaking Christian clients and spread it to their homelands. Still another theory has it that German raiders learned the word when they pillaged churches in France and Britain. In any case, the original Germanized form was probably *kirika* or something similar. The Anglo-Saxons used the form *cirice* or *chiriche*, and the modern English word *church* is its lineal descendant. In the early Middle Ages, missionaries carried *kirika* north to the Scandinavian lands and east to the Slavs. Thus, in modern German, it is *Kirche*, in Dutch, *kerk*, in Swedish, *kyrka*, in Danish, *kirke*, in Russian, *tserkov*, and so on. In the north of England, people used the form *kirk*, probably due to the influence of the Danes who settled in northeastern England. This form lives on in Scotland.

Not all churches were of equal importance, and the most important in the formative days of Christianity were those in which the bishop had his official throne, or *cathedra*. Each *cathedral church* was the administrative center of its diocese, and by church law was located in a major town or city. Because of their importance, cathedrals were built much larger than ordinary churches, and were usually much more elaborately decorated. Cities and towns vied with each other to build the most magnificent cathedrals. The peak of cathedral building was the Middle Ages, and many fine cathedrals survive from that time. The stained glass windows and stone carvings were functional as well as esthetic. They depicted scenes from the Bible and the lives of the saints for worshippers who could not read—and that was the great majority of the people. They also depicted the deadly sins and the forms of punishment that the Church taught awaited those who broke her rules. Naturally, it cost a great deal of money to construct these huge and magnificent buildings, and most of the money came, directly or indirectly, from the common people, who had little enough to spare after the multifarious dues and taxes they had to pay to their overlords and to the Church. However, the people apparently took pride in the cathedrals that their contributions of money and labor made possible, for there is no record that they ever protested. Even the humblest peasant or laborer could feel that he had a share in creating this house of God, no matter how bitterly he complained about the other exactions of the clergy.

A *chapel* is a place of worship that is not a church in its own right and is usually fairly small. The history of this word is like an ecclesiastical shaggy-dog story, for it comes ultimately from *capella*, Latin for "little cloak," and the story runs as follows. In the 4th century A.D. lived a man named Martinus, who was born in that part of the Roman Empire that is now Hungary. At the age of fifteen, he was forced to become a Roman soldier and was sent to serve in France. One bitterly cold night the young soldier saw a shivering beggar creeping along the street. He took off his cloak, cut it in half, and gave half to the beggar. The next night, according to legend, he had a vision of Jesus telling the angels about Martinus' act of charity, and soon afterwards he was baptized. Leaving the army, he joined the Church and became a highly effective missionary and eventually bishop of Tours. After his death, he was canonized as St. Martin, and his little cloak, or *cappella*, became a sacred relic. The Frankish kings took the *cappella* with them into battle to bring them God's favor, and they also swore oaths on it for greater binding power. Indeed, they took it along on all their travels, in a specially built portable shrine. When not in use, the *cappella* was kept in a special sanctuary of its own—its guardians were called *cappellani*, or chaplains. The sanctuary of the sacred cloak came to be called *cappella* itself, and the name spread to all sanctuaries containing relics, then to all private places of worship, such as the chapel of a castle, and finally to any room or building used for worship that was not itself a church. So today we have college chapels, military chapels, wedding chapels, and specially dedicated chapels inside cathedrals.

Devil

Devil The Devil, Prince of Evil, Satan, Lucifer, Shaitan, arch-enemy of God and man, is a mainstay of Christian and Muslim theology. He represents all the fears and hatreds of man personified, a heritage from our most primitive human ancestors.

Primitive man believed the world was inhabited by a multitude of spirits that caused the wind to blow, the crops to grow, the herds to procreate, the rain to fall, and everything else that affected man. They lived in trees, rocks, rivers, the earth and the air, and often took the form of animals and birds. This belief persisted down into the time of the great civilizations of antiquity (and indeed almost down to our own day) and greatly influenced religion and daily custom.

Since disaster always appears to outweigh good fortune, man early on decided that most of the spirits were evil, unless propitiated with sacrifices and magic rites. Even then, some refused to be propitiated because they took such delight in tormenting mankind. As man's thinking developed, he conceived the idea of evil gods that ruled over the hosts of lesser evil spirits, as an earthly king rules over his subjects. This concept reached its peak in the Zoroastrian religion of ancient Persia, which held that two deities constantly battled for control of the universe: the god of light and goodness, Ahura Mazda, and the god of darkness and evil, Ahriman. These Persian ideas influenced Jewish religious thought in the years after the Babylonian Exile (586–539 B.C.).

In Jewish tradition, there was an archangel of evil whose mission was to test the loyalty of mankind to God, tempt them into sin, and punish the luckless sinners. However, this celestial agent provocateur was not an independent power but an agent of God, whose permission he had to secure for every evil project. The Jews gave this spirit the name of Satan, "adversary," from the verb *sitan*, "to oppose" or "to plot against." In the Old Testament, the word *satan* is usually used for some human villain, but in the Books of Zechariah and Job it becomes The Adversary, the evil angel. When Jewish scholars translated the Old Testament into Greek, they used the Greek term *diabolos* where the Hebrew had Satan. *Diabolos* is not an exact translation of *Satan*, for it means "slanderer." Its roots are *dia-*, "across," and *ballein*, "to throw" (the root of *ballistics* also), thus figuratively one who throws slimy lies across the path of another, a mud-slinger.

Christianity took over the idea of a Prince of Evil from the Jews, but elevated him to much greater importance. At times, Christian theologians held that the entire world belonged to the Devil. But here we are jumping the gun, for we must return to the linguistic part of the story. The Greek *diabolos* became the Latin *diabolus*, and the term was spread by missionaries throughout Europe and the near East. In Old English, it became *diobul* or *deofol*, depending on the dialect of the speaker. (There were many other forms, too). As English developed, it eventually became *divell* or *devil*. In other modern languages, we have the French *diable*, Italian *diavolo*, Spanish *diablo*, German *Teufel*, Dutch *duyvel*, Swedish *djävul*, and so on. Curiously, or perhaps not so curiously, the term was tabooed in virtually every language for fear that pronouncing the dread title would cause the Devil to appear, claiming vengeance. Instead, he was referred to in oblique terms as The Evil One, Old Nick, Old Hairy, Old Harry, the Dickens, the Black One, and the like.

The Devil, feared as he was, performed a useful function. He explained the prevalence of evil in the world God had created. Why an all-powerful and just God would permit an evil spirit to create misery and lure souls into eternal damnation was a question the theologians never did answer satisfactorily. But the Devil was ever present in the medieval world, lurking behind every corner with his insidious temptations. Martin Luther believed firmly in the personal existence of the Devil, who frequently came in physical form to persecute him. This pervasive belief in the Devil was responsible for the horrible witch hunts of medieval Europe, which petered out in the witch trials of Salem, Massachusetts. After Salem, rationality took over.

The Devil also had assistance from multitudes of lesser devils, or demons. *Demon* comes from the Greek *daimon*, which was originally a neutral term for a spirit. A *daimon* could be good or bad, but by the Christian era it was definitely bad. Good spirits were called *angels* (from the Greek *aggelos*—pronounced *angelos*—a messenger). In English, demons were also called *fiends*, from a Teutonic root meaning "enemy," or *imps*, from an old word meaning the young shoot of a tree, thus a young devil.

The Devil so preoccupied the popular imagination that the *Oxford English Dictionary* has five and a half pages devoted to him and derivations of his name. "Devilfish" has been used to express man's abhorrence for large squids, manta rays, and even the gray whale, which had the naughty habit of smashing the boats of whalers who harpooned it. "Devil's dung" was another name for the evil-smelling plant asafetida, once esteemed in medicine. Superstitious folk once called the harmless dragonfly "the devil's darning needle." These, of course, are only a small sampling of the total. Then we have "devilled" food, prepared with burning-hot seasonings that suggest the fires of hell. And there was the printer's devil, the errand boy in an old-time printer's shop. He was so called partly because by the 18th century "devil" was irreverently used to refer to a stand-in or a go-fer, and partly because he was smeared black with printer's ink, the color black being traditionally associated with evil in general and the Devil in particular. And, with reverse psychology, "devil" came to mean a person in a pitiable situation, since evil was deemed to be degraded, contemptible, and doomed to fail. Poor devil!

God

God comes unchanged from the Old English *god*. Language historians have traced it to a hypothetical Indo-European root, *ghutom*, which means either "one to whom sacrifices are made" or "one who is invoked." Curiously, the Old English word was masculine in the singular but could be either masculine or neuter in the plural. This suggests a mystical distinction that was common in the ancient world, between a personalized, individual god (masculine or feminine) and an impersonal force of nature (neuter).

To primitive man, the world was filled with spirits, and nothing happened unless a spirit made it happen. Every animal, every growing thing, had its guardian spirit, as did the wind, the rain, rocks and mountains, lakes, and streams. Certain highly visible entities, like the Sun and the Moon, were worshipped as gods in their own right, and man's lively imagination created many more to keep them company. The beginnings of civilization brought even more gods, as each tiny kingdom and each craft needed its patron deity. Of course, this was good business for the priesthood—the more gods that were worshipped, the more priests were needed. There were sky-gods and earth-gods, gods of childbirth, gods of the herds and flocks, gods of metal-workers and gods of merchants, gods of the sea and the rivers that flow into it, gods of sexual love and of chastity, and for just about any other conceivable quality, activity, or phenomenon of nature.

The belief in many gods was strong, especially since it was backed by tradition and superstition. To pick an example from the mainstream of Western culture, the Romans, in most respects an intensely down-to-earth and rational people, were virtually drowning in deities. At the top of the pantheon were the big, powerful gods like Jupiter, Juno, Mars, Venus, and Neptune (born of a fusion of the native Roman gods with their Greek counterparts). Then there were scores of lesser deities: Vesta ruled the domestic hearth; Cuba watched over the beds of sleeping children, while Levanta helped them get up in the morning; Janus with his two faces guarded doors and city gates; Juno Sororia was responsible for the passage of girls into puberty; and so on, and on, and on. Then there were the innumerable powers that had no names, the impersonal forces that dwelt in animals and plants, in rocks and mountains and springs. The Romans called them *numina* (*numen* in the singular); *deus* (masculine) and *dea* (feminine) were the designations for gods with enough individual characteristics to have names. And every family had its generic household deities, the Lares and Penates. The Lares, which may have originated as the ghosts of family ancestors, watched over the family members and their fields, while the Penates guarded the stores of food. And that was not all. The Roman Emperors, following the Oriental fashion, had themselves declared divine. Their worship was compulsory. Even the City of Rome was deified. Yet even the greatest gods were not all-powerful, for they were subject to the Three Fates. And in daily life it was the humbler gods and spirits of farm and house and workshop that got the greatest attention from the people.

The wild profusion of gods and goddesses led to glaring contradictions between their myths. In addition, the older myths had them behaving absurdly and immorally. So thinkers in various religions began to question the traditional myths, and even to suspect that the world might be ruled by one god instead of many. There was a seed of latent monotheism in many primitive religions: their myths spoke of a supreme god who created the world and then handed it over to lesser gods whom he also created. But then the Creator dropped out of the game, and all the action remained with the other gods.

The first known introduction of monotheism was the work of a Pharaoh of Egypt, Ikhnaton, around 1370 B.C. Ikhnaton, whose name meant "servant of the Sun-Disk," declared that the only god was the sun-god, and he banned the worship of all other gods. The established priesthoods naturally resented this deeply, and when the sickly Ikhnaton died after a rather short reign they declared him an accursed heretic, obliterated his name from the monuments, and restored the traditional polytheism with all its animal-headed divinities.

The first people to practice monotheism were the Jews, and they came to it very slowly. Although the Bible states that God revealed himself to Abraham, he did not reveal himself to the Jewish people until he summoned Moses to Mount Sinai and gave him the Ten Commandments, of which the second declares: "Thou shalt have no gods before me." What this actually did was to establish God as the chief god of the Jewish people, but did not explicitly forbid them from also worshiping other gods in a subordinate capacity. Historically, Moses probably announced the Ten Commandments some time during the 13th century B.C.

Now, God had already revealed his name to Moses before the Exodus: *Yahveh*, meaning "I am that which I am." This is hardly a name in the ordinary sense, but men of the ancient worlds still held fast to the primitive belief that to know someone's true name was to have power over them. God was apparently using a cunning subterfuge to cloak his true identity. Even the name Yahveh was so powerful that it was not to be spoken aloud, except once a year by the High-Priest on the Day of Atonement. When written down in prayers, it was never pronounced. Instead, worshippers said *Adonai*, "My Lord." Piety took this process a step further, so that today Orthodox Jews ordinarily refer to God as *Ha-Shem*, "The Name," or *Ha-Kodosh*, "The Holy One."

In written form, the four consonants of God's name came to be known as the Sacred Tetragrammaton (Greek for "the four-letter thing"). When vowel markings were added to the Hebrew alphabet, the Tetragrammaton was written with the vowels for *Adonai* so that no one would inadvertently pronounce the sacred name aloud. Christian scholars, not versed in the Jewish tradition, misread the word and interpreted it as *Jehovah*.

In the Old Testament, God is often referred to as *Elohim*, a plural noun which can be roughly translated as "Powers." Some Biblical scholars believe that the fact that it is plural indicates that Yahveh had absorbed the powers of rival gods. *El* was also the name of a powerful god worshipped by many Semitic peoples, and it was as El that God first revealed himself to Abraham. For some time after the giving of the Law on Mount Sinai, the Jews apparently continued to worship local *Baalim*, or "masters," as well as Yahveh. But in the 9th century B.C. the prophets Elijah and Elisha spread the message that Jews should worship Yahveh alone. This still acknowledged the existence of other gods, whom other peoples worshipped. It was not until the Babylonian Exile in the 6th century B.C. that the Second Isaiah proclaimed that there was no God but Yah-veh, and no others existed—the first true monotheism.

When Christianity split off from Judaism, the Christians took the Jewish idea of monotheism and combined it with pagan concepts to produce a single God with three separate aspects: Father, Son, and Holy Spirit. These three aspects were termed *personae*, from the masks worn by actors in Greek and Roman dramas. Uneducated converts, unable to comprehend the subtle concept of the Trinity, came to believe that the three *personae* were actually three separate individuals fused mystically into one. The illogic only made it seem more holy. In the 4th century A.D. there was a grave theological dispute over whether the Son and the Father were in fact one or two deities. The Nicene Council decreed that the Son and the Father were of the same substance, which did not really answer the question. In the meantime, the ordinary believers battled in the streets over it, and many died to defend their contesting dogmas. There were later disputes over the status of Jesus when in human form, and over the status of the Holy Spirit. Church councils produced semantically ingenious explanations, but in the end relied on the sword to enforce their decisions.

The third great monotheistic religion is Islam, whose founder, Mohammed, drew heavily on Jewish and Christian concepts. To Muslims, the true name of God is *Allah*, literally "The God." In practice, Allah is usually referred to by one of his ninety-nine titles, such as "The Merciful" or "The Mighty."

The people of ancient civilizations thought of their gods as generally malignant. They had all the bad qualities of human beings, and few of the good ones. To keep them from venting their malice on man, they had to be constantly propitiated with rituals and sacrifices. Even the God of Israel was originally cast in this mold, as a vindictive patriarch constantly on

105

the lookout for disobedience that he could punish. But the Jewish Prophets of the Old Testament came to regard God as just and merciful.

The history of religion is filled with intolerance, cruelty, and superstition. Men and women have committed the most damnable cruelties and injustices in the name of God, upon whom they have projected their own most destructive emotions and secret wishes. But man's concept of God (or the gods) has gradually evolved from a vindictive, malicious entity to a God of justice and compassion. And therein lies hope. And who among us is so presumptuous as to claim that he truly knows God?

Heaven

Heaven comes from the Old English *heofon*. (Other forms are *hefene* and *heben*.) Originally it referred to the sky and the upper air, where the stars hang in their places and the birds fly. In the plural form it still does, for astronomers still scan the heavens, and we refer to stars and planets as heavenly bodies. But about A.D. 1000 *heaven* took on another meaning that is now its primary one: the place where God resides, and the souls of the virtuous go after death. English may be unique, at least among Indo-European languages, in having different words for the physical sky and the supernatural abode of God. In French, Spanish, German, and Dutch, to name a few, the same word does duty for both "sky" and "heaven." Only the context lets you tell which one is meant.

The idea that the gods dwell on high is probably universal among humanity. In some cultures, the gods are believed to live in the sky, in others, atop lofty mountains, like the Greek gods who dwelt on Mount Olympus. Primitive man probably came to this conclusion because he could see that the Sun and Moon were up in the sky. Wind and rain, and thunder and lightning also came from the sky. (However, the very important Eskimo goddess Sedna lived at the bottom of the sea, where she controlled the sea mammals and fish on which the Eskimos depended for their existence.)

In the ancient Middle East, it was believed that heaven was a kind of solid dome or firmament that covered the earth as a lid covers a pot. The Hebrew word for it, *raqia* (the thing that is hammered out), implies that the firmament is made of metal. Other ancient cultures, depending on their degree of technological advancement, conceived of the heavenly lid as made of iron, brass, cloth, or animal hide. The Assyrians believed it to be embroidered with the stars. Cultures ranging from American Indians to Finns and Africans, as well as Middle Easterners, believed that the chief function of the firmament was to keep a celestial ocean off the face of the earth. Many are the creation myths in which the Creator separates the Upper Waters from the Lower Waters to create the land. In the heavenly dome are windows that God (or another deity) opens to let the rain pour down to the thirsty land, or closes tightly to punish sinning mankind with drought and famine.

Heaven is also where the souls of the righteous go after death. However, various cultures have envisioned this in very different ways. The Greeks thought that most of the dead went to the underworld, where they spent eternity in a shadowy, discontented state. Wicked people went to a place of torment that the Greeks called *Tartarus*. A privileged few were sent to the Elysian Fields, where they enjoyed eternal youth and friendship, and perpetually good weather. The Elysian Fields were located either in a special part of the underworld or in some distant part of the earth that no mortal could reach.

For many peoples, the afterlife was just like that on earth, except better. Among the ancient Egyptians, dead people not only had their possessions buried with them but also a stock of food for the next life. Effigies of slaves and domestic animals also went into the tomb to serve the dead person, if he or she had been rich enough to own them in life. Death was not a way for Egyptians to enhance their social standing. The hunting tribes of North American Indians believed in a Happy Hunting Ground, where life, again, was like that on earth, but much easier, with game always plentiful and easy to kill. The Norsemen fantasized that their brave warriors were conducted at death to Valhalla ("Hall of the Fallen") by female spirits called Valkyries ("Choosers of the Fallen," a word that may have been borrowed from an Old English term meaning "battle witch"). In Valhalla, the dead warriors hacked away happily at each other all day long, giving and receiving glorious wounds. In the evening, restored to life and health, they feasted on the flesh of a miraculous boar named Hrymnir, who was also restored to life each morning. Mead was the bountiful beverage, served by beauteous maidens.

The Aztec and Maya civilizations believed in a graded series of heavens, to which the dead were assigned according to their social rank on earth. The Aztecs had thirteen heavens, the Mayas fewer. Whether you had been virtuous or sinful had very little to do with how you spent your afterlife. The Mayas, however, were more humane than the Aztecs, for they had a special heaven for suicides. The Eskimos postulated two heavens, one in the sky and one deep within the earth. Only brave hunters and women with large and beautiful tattoos were admitted there.

The Old Testament makes no statements about the afterlife. In ancient times, Jews believed that the dead went to an undergound realm called Sheol, where they spent a very boring time waiting for the resurrection and final judgment at the end of the world. Later Jewish theologians preached that the good would be rewarded by going directly to Paradise (usually identified with the Garden of Eden), but there has never been any official dogma about immortality. There is no agreement, either, about how the dead spend their time in heaven, except that they are filled with happiness at being close to God.

Early Christians were also vague on the activities in heaven. Some liked the idea that the souls of the dead sat about in spotless white robes with nothing to do but play sacred melodies on their harps—the early Christians were drawn chiefly from the poorer classes, and this was their idea of virtuous luxury. Some allowed themselves the extra pleasure of being waited upon by their former masters. It sounds like a tedious way to spend eternity, but Roman Catholic doctrine holds that the Beatific Vision—the direct contact of the soul with God—is so structured that it never cloys. Modern Christian theologians tend to think of heaven as a state of being rather than a place.

Perhaps the kind of heaven where the good are rewarded is better referred to as Paradise, whose name is derived from an Old Persian word for a walled garden or park—the ultimate delight for dwellers of the barren Near East. In the Muslim concept, the souls of the male faithful go to just such a paradise, where they feast and drink in beautiful gardens with lush, green grass and disport themselves with supernaturally beautiful maidens called *houris*, whose virginity is miraculously renewed every morning. There is no provision for the souls of women, however. Many Muslims believe they have no souls.

Hindus believe the dead go through a cycle of heavens and hells and reincarnations until by virtuous living they lose their identities and merge with the World Soul. For Buddhists, the highest heaven consists of non-existence and liberation from the painful cycle of existence and reincarnation.

Since ancient times, seven has been a sacred and magical number with great power, and in Jewish and Muslim tradition there are seven heavens, ranked according to virtue. The seventh and highest is where God has his throne. So to be in seventh heaven is to achieve the highest possible happiness.

Hell

Just as there had to be a place for the souls of the good, so mankind's developing sense of justice called for a place of torment for the wicked. This is the place we call *Hell*, a name that comes from a Germanic root, *hel-* or *hal-*, that means "to conceal." This ties in well with the psychological background, for with striking uniformity mankind agrees that Hell is located underground, which is certainly a place of concealment. Man probably arrived at this idea from his practice of burying the dead, which in turn was done to prevent their spirits from returning to harm the living.

Originally, Hell was not a place of punishment, but the kingdom of the dead, where everyone went without regard for his conduct during life. Most religions agreed that life for the dead was pretty dreary. The Greeks, for instance, imagined that the deceased existed as insubstantial shadows, flitting listlessly about. Their only treat came when a family descendant —or someone who wanted to consult them—sacrificed an animal to them. Then they would eagerly lap up the blood, squeaking and chittering like bats. The ancient Jews believed that the dead went to an underworld called Sheol, where they wandered in deep darkness, tormented by constant thirst. The Norse underworld was called *Niflheimr* ("fog-home") or *Hel*, after the goddess who ruled it. As its name suggests, it was a place of perpetual mist and cold. The stench of rotting corpses added to its unpleasantness. For the Eskimos, Hell was a place just beneath the ground where the souls of cowardly or lazy hunters and women who could not stand the pain of tattooing languished with nothing to do. Their only food was an occasional butterfly.

When man began to think that evildoers deserved punishment after death, he devised the most elaborate tortures that his imagination was capable of. Fire was the usual accompaniment to the stabbings, beatings, flayings, and other ministrations of the demons. But some people rebelled against the idea of eternal punishment for one's sins. Hindus and Buddhists decided that the soul is reincarnated after a term in Hell and can work off demerits by living virtuously in its next life. Jewish theologians developed the theory that the soul can work off its demerits during its term of punishment. Eternal punishment was limited to particularly wicked transgressors, such as adulterers and those who shamed their fellow man. During the Middle Ages it was popularly believed that God shut down Hell every Sabbath to give the tormented souls a rest. Roman Catholics believe in a subsidiary Hell called Purgatory, where all but the worst sinners can win release to Heaven; the obdurate remainder end up in Hell itself.

In Biblical times, the place of punishment was given the name of *Gehenna*, from *Ge-Hinnom*, the Vale of Hinnom. This was a deep valley on the outskirts of Jerusalem where the pagan Ammonites used to burn children in sacrifice to their god Moloch. So the Vale of Hinnom was an abomination to God-fearing Jews, even though some backsliders revived the practice during the reigns of King Solomon (10th century B.C.) and the idolatrous King Manasseh (7th century B.C.). After the Babylonian Exile, the people of Jerusalem turned the infamous valley into a garbage dump, and its name into an abomination of another sort.

The Romans called their hell *infer* or *infernus*, meaning "the place below." It comes from the same root as *inferior*. This passed into Christian parlance as the "inferno," which by extension later came to mean any horrifying fire.

The idea of grades of Hell is widespread. Buddhism postulates seven hells, in which sinners are variously cut to pieces, crushed between colliding mountains, and burned. Lamaism —the Tibetan variety of Buddhism—adds to these eight hells of cold. The Aztecs had nine hells of varying degrees of severity; to reach them, the soul had to undergo a terrifying, four-year journey that was a punishment in itself. Clashing mountains, deserts, serpents, and freezing gales filled with obsidian knives menaced the soul until it reached the Lord of the Dead. Islam recognizes seven hells, all fiery and increasing in heat to fit the sin.

The idea of Hell is usually coupled with the idea that the soul faces judgment right after death. In Greco-Roman mythology, the soul is tried by a panel of three dead kings: Minos, Rhadamanthos, and Aeacus. The Egyptians believed that the soul, questioned by a small army of gods, was weighed in a balance against an ostrich feather. If its sins outweighed the feather, it went to the place of torment. Muslim doctrine holds that the soul must cross a narrow and perilous bridge that leads to Paradise over the pit of Gehenna. The wicked lose their balance and fall in.

Belief in Hell has probably never been so strong as in Christian Europe during the Middle Ages. A whole category of lore and legend sprang up about it, and how to evade being sent there. The Protestant Reformation clung to the theory of Hell to frighten believers into obedience. Fortunately, scientific discoveries have discredited the idea of a physical Hell (except for people who want *very* much for such a place to exist for the reception of their enemies), and modern theologians tend to envision Hell as a state of being rather than an underground torture chamber.

Idol

Idol comes from the Greek word *eidolon*, which means "image" or "likeness." *Doll* comes from the same original, but a doll is a child's plaything, and an idol is an object of worship. Apparently the original Greek significance was that of a phantom, then of a reflected image, as in a mirror, and finally a statue or painting. To Jews and early Christians, an *eidolon* meant an image of a pagan god, and was false by definition.

Idol

The practice of making images to worship originated in pre-historic times. In the secret recesses of caves, Ice Age hunters painted images of the animals they hoped to catch. No one knows just what their rituals were, but probably they hoped that creating the images would give them magical power over the animals themselves. Then came fertility-images, such as the so-called Venus of Willendorf, a faceless female figure with grossly exaggerated breasts and hips. But by the dawn of civilization, man could make admirably realistic statues of his gods, when he chose to. Sometimes he chose not to, for his gods were blends of animal and human. Thus the Egyptians had falcon-headed statues of the god Horus, cow-headed ones of the goddess Hathor, and cat-headed statues of the goddess Bast, to name but a few. The Philistine god Dagon was represented as a man below the waist, a fish above. In India, the god of wisdom and literature, Ganesh, is always depicted with an elephant's head. The most grotesque idols of all are those of Tibet, where gods are depicted in raging, blood-thirsty form, with extra eyes and arms and heads, bedecked with human skulls, corpses, and other deliberately frightful regalia. The idea is that by portraying them in terrifying form they will scare away the millions of demons that infest the Lamaist cosmos.

"Thou shalt not make unto thee any graven image, or any likeness of any thing that is in heaven above, or . . . in the earth beneath, or . . . in the water under the earth," God ordered the Twelve Tribes of Israel in the Ten Commandments, thereby setting the Jews apart from almost every other people of the ancient world. Although this prohibition was not always observed strictly in the early days of the Jewish people, after the Babylonian exile the Jews followed it zealously, even accepting martyrdom rather than do obeisance to the idols of heathen conquerors such as the Romans.

The first Christians followed the Jewish pattern and consid-

113

ered idols an abomination. But as Christianity grew apart from the faith which Jesus had practiced, the ever-growing numbers of pagan converts insisted on having images of the saints. Many Church leaders deplored this practice, but the craving of the laity for their images was not to be halted. In the West, Pope Gregory the Great (590–604) more or less settled the question by declaring that images and statues were necessary to guide the prayers of the ignorant, but should not be worshipped in themselves. In practice, they were treated as objects of worship.

In Byzantium, iconoclasts ("image-smashers") and iconodules ("image-venerators") fought a long struggle, with one side or the other in ascendancy depending on the sympathies of the Emperor or Empress. At one point, an angry crowd of iconoclasts stoned an image of Christ, claiming that idolatrous practices had led God to punish the Eastern Empire with invading hordes of barbarians. In the end, though, the image-lovers won, as the legacy of Byzantine and Russian religious art testifies.

In the ancient world, men believed that the god actually lived inside the idol. Through this visual representation, he could eat and drink the essences of the sacrifices that people made. Then, pleased, he would reward the worshippers. At the same time, the people had—or thought they had—a certain advantage over the god. If he failed to respond to the proper sacrifices and supplication, they could punish him by cutting off his rations. If this did not cow him into cooperation, the next step was to insult and threaten the image. In extreme cases, images were thrown into the fire or broken up into little bits.

Monk
The word *monk* is derived from the Greek *monachos*, which means "solitary" and

probably dates from the 3rd century B.C. At least the practice
of monasticism can be traced that far back, to St. Anthony's
decision to flee the world and its temptations. According to
Church history, about A.D. 285 Anthony left the Egyptian village where he had been leading an ascetic life and secluded
himself in a ruined fort on the banks of the Nile. There he remained for twenty years, never coming out and never seeing a
human face (one wonders what he lived on!). But other devout
and ascetic persons, inspired by Anthony's example, made
their way to his hiding-place and lived as hermits in caves in
the desert nearby. The word *hermit*, in fact, is derived from
the Greek *heremia*, "desert," and literally means a desert-
dweller. In response to their pleas, Anthony emerged from his
retreat and gave them spiritual guidance. However, the hermits had no group life and no organization.

Monasticism as we understand it now, that is, men or
women living apart from the world in organized religious
communities, was the creation of another Egyptian saint
named Pachomius (292?–346). Pachomius became a Christian
while serving in the Roman army; supposedly directed by an
angel, he founded a community of religious men near Den-
dera in Upper Egypt. Strictly organized, this community had a
head to give orders, and the members lived, ate, prayed, and
worked together according to detailed rules. By the time of his
death, Pachomius had founded nine monasteries and one nun-
nery, and the coenobitical system, as it is called, was on its way
to success. *Coenobitic*, although it suggests strange perversions
or fossils, is nothing more than Greek for "living in common"
(from *koinos*, "common," and *bios*, "life").

Monastic communities like those of Pachomius multiplied as
devout and socially maladjusted Christians sought refuge from
the world with like-minded souls. Typically, they were located
in remote and inaccessible regions such as deserts or mountains. But, even though the monks sought to flee the world,

they ended by exerting a great influence on it. For one thing, in western Europe the monks preserved what was left of the learning of Greece and Rome. They contributed to medicine by studying the uses of herbs, and their gardens of medicinal herbs became an important resource. Their paintings of sacred subjects and their beautifully illuminated manuscripts helped keep the arts alive during the Dark Ages. Certain orders, like the Cistercians, were active in farming and helped to spread settlements through the forests of Europe. Perhaps most important, the monks believed that work was worthwhile for its own sake and thus planted the seed of the belief in the dignity of labor. They also developed disciplined work habits that some historians claim set the pattern for the industrial age.

Everyone who has read the tales of Robin Hood will remember the jolly Friar Tuck. A friar is not, strictly speaking, a monk, but belongs to a different class of religious order. A monk, to be precise, lived in a self-supporting community that raised its own food and often had enough of a surplus to sell to the public. A friar, on the other hand (the title comes from the Latin *frater*, "brother"), belonged to an order that lived by begging. The great mendicant orders—the Franciscans, the Dominicans, the Carmelites, the Augustinian Hermits, and the Servites, were all founded in the 13th century. The rationale was that the friars should go where they were needed, among the poor laboring classes of the burgeoning towns, and that they should live in poverty like that of the people they ministered to. Although St. Francis originally intended his disciples to support themselves by the work of their hands, the increasing demand for their spiritual services left them little time for work, and they came to rely on begging from the public.

Another difference between monks and friars is that a monk is attached to a particular monastery; it is his family home. A friar, however, is attached to his order rather than to a particular community, and he can feel at home wherever his superior sends him.

Monk

During the Middle Ages, the monasteries became very wealthy by means of gifts from laymen (and women too) who were worried about the fate of their souls. Bequests of money and land came in from the nobility and the richer bourgeoisie. Often a monastery was the greatest landowner of its district, and the abbots, if not always the rank-and-file monks, lived in luxury. The monastic orders thus became tempting targets for greedy sovereigns. Henry VIII was quick to seize the monasteries' wealth for himself when he broke with Rome, and much of their land he parcelled out among his supporters. The same thing occurred in other countries where the Protestant Reformation succeeded. Even in Roman Catholic countries, some orders were suppressed and their lands taken by the state. However, the late 19th century saw a comeback of monasticism.

So far we have been looking at Western Christian monasticism. Actually, monasticism is far older than Christianity. It probably originated in India, the idea spreading west along the ancient trade routes. The Jewish sect of the Essenes, which strongly influenced Jesus, practiced a kind of precursor of monasticism in which devout men and women lived ascetically in strictly disciplined communities. However, they did not practice celibacy.

The tradition of monasticism is strong in Hinduism, and in principle every man when he reaches a certain age—the signs are gray hair, wrinkled skin, and the existence of a grandson—is supposed to abandon his family and possessions and live a hermit's life in the forest.

Buddhism is famous for its monasteries. Monasticism reached its peak in Tibet, where the whole country was ruled by the chief monk, the Dalai Lama, from 1270 to 1959, when the current Dalai Lama fled the Chinese Communists. Before the Communist takeover, one Tibetan male in every four was a monk, and the lamaseries dominated the landscape. The most famous of them, the Potala in Lhasa, is said to contain over 1,000 rooms, 10,000 altars, and 200,000 statues. Even larger than the Potala was the nearby monastery of Drepung —the largest in the world—which contained 10,000 monks and owned 25,000 serfs to work its vast landholdings. Like the Potala and the other monasteries of Tibet, it is now a museum.

Nirvana

Nirvana is a Buddhist term that is generally misunderstood by Westerners. It is a Sanskrit word that literally means "blowing out" or "disappearance," from the verb *nirva*, "to blow." In the original Buddhist scriptures, it means the dying out in the heart of the flames of the three cardinal sins of sensuality, ill-will, and stupidity, as a man might blow out a lamp. In the West it is taken to mean the extinction of the soul, which gives relief from all the pains and frustrations of individual existence.

Actually *nirvana* is only one of a number of names that the Buddhist scriptures use for the state of ultimate enlightenment, and it happened to be the one that the first Westerners who wrote about Buddhism fixed upon. Since their versions of Christianity taught them to despise this world and hope for salvation in the next, they concluded that the Buddhists shared this view and that *nirvana* could only be attained after death. Actually, *nirvana* describes a state of mystical union with the supreme spirit, with a corresponding dying out of all desires and passions, and, according to Buddhist doctrine, it can be attained in this life. There is a similar doctrine in Hinduism.

A companion doctrine that was much noised about in the 1960s is *karma*, which is the Sanskrit word for "action" or "fate" and has come to mean the way in which one's actions in this life affect one's fate in the next reincarnation. *Karma*, often defined as a Buddhist concept, is also one of the bases of Hindu theology. The sum of one's evil acts can be outweighed

118

by the sum of one's good actions so that one is not punished by being reborn in a lower form, but each sin must nevertheless be atoned for. In the trendy cant of the 1960s, when young people made a shallow search for the wisdom of the Orient, *karma* also meant an aura, an atmosphere, or "vibes," as in "This place has a bad karma."

Nun

A nun is a Roman Catholic woman who has taken religious vows of obedience and abstinence and wears a strange and forbidding costume—or is she? In Roman Catholic law, the term *nun* is, strictly speaking, restricted to those women who have taken particular vows and live in a monastery for females. The life of such a nun consists primarily of contemplation and self-mortification. But in popular use it also covers the sisters who do nursing, teaching, and missionary work.

The word *nun* actually means "old woman." In the early days of monastic life, the young members of a monastic community would call their elders *nonnus* (if they were male) or *nonna* (if they were female) as a title of respect. Eventually *nonnus* dropped out of use, and male monastics were called *monachus*, which became our *monk*. Today, Italians call their grandparents *nonno* and *nonna*, but they do not give them quite the reverence that is due a nun.

Pope

The Pope is the head of the Roman Catholic Church and one of the most powerful individuals in the world. But his title is simply a version of *pappas*, the Greek word for "papa." Early Christians used this as a title of affection and respect for their priests, and in the Eastern Orthodox Church some form of it is still the title of a parish priest. In the West, it came to be applied to bishops at least as early as A.D. 250. By the reign of Leo the Great, in the mid-

5th century, it was used for the Bishop of Rome in particular, and after 1073 only he had the right to use the title of *Papa*. The claim of the Bishop of Rome to supremacy rests on several factors. The most important is the doctrine of apostolic succession from St. Peter, who carried his missionary message to the city of Rome and was martyred there. Then, too, Rome was the center of power and influence in the early days of the Christian Church. Another factor was the Donation of Constantine, a document purporting to be a grant by the emperor Constantine (*c.*274–337) to Pope Silvester of spiritual and temporal dominion over Rome, Italy, and the "western regions." Curiously, this document did not appear until the 9th century, and both the prelates of the Eastern Church and the Holy Roman Emperors of the West denounced it as a forgery. Modern scholars agree with them, but it convinced a majority of the Catholic faithful in the Dark Ages.

One of the Pope's many titles is that of Supreme Pontiff. This title harks back to the state religion of ancient Rome, whose highest religious body was a college of priests called *pontifex*, literally "bridge-maker." The head of the college was the *Pontifex Maximus*, or greatest bridge-maker. Once Christianity was established as the state religion of the Roman Empire, the title was sometimes applied to important Christian clerics. In the Middle Ages, bishops were sometimes called pontiffs. Now the title is used only to refer to the Pope.

Almost from the beginning, the Papacy has been involved in international politics. Ambitious secular rulers saw the Pope as a powerful instrument and tried to dominate him; equally ambitious Popes tried to bring kings and nobles to heel in the service of the Church. In the 10th century, the Papacy fell into the hands of a noble Italian family, the Counts of Tusculum, who tried to convert the office into a hereditary family fief, and nearly succeeded. In 1075 the King of Germany called a national assembly of bishops who declared the current Pope unfit for his office and refused to obey him. The Pope struck back by excommunicating the King and releasing his vassals from their oaths of allegiance. Faced by outright insurrections, the king had to knuckle under. At this time, too, the Pope received a grant of the lands of the pious Countess of Canossa, so that the Church became the owner of a broad belt of territory stretching from coast to coast across central Italy. Here the Pope ruled as a temporal sovereign.

The lowest point of the Papacy was reached in the 14th century, when the Popes were virtually owned by the King of France. This episode began in 1305, when the newly elected Pope, a Frenchman, refused to leave France and set up new headquarters in Avignon. Subsequent Popes, most of them French, continued this arrangement and built a splendid new papal palace there. In 1367 a Pope returned to Rome but was forced to flee back to France by civil strife. His successor in turn went to Rome but died after only a year. The ensuing papal election resulted in two rival Popes, one supported by the French, the other by the German interests. The French Pope, naturally, returned to Avignon, and the two men spent their time hurling denunciations at each other and excommunicating each other's followers. Their deaths did nothing to solve the problem, and the Great Schism continued to the dismay of the faithful. At one point there were actually three popes simultaneously claiming jurisdiction. Things went back more or less to normal in 1417; the new Pope refused to yield to pressure to reside in Germany and returned to Italy, but prudently settled in Florence. Not until 1449 did the Popes decide it was safe to return to turbulent Rome.

The Popes retained the Papal States until 1870, when the newly reconstituted nation of Italy took them over by military force—the Pope had declared that he would never hand them over otherwise. Since then, the Popes' temporal rule is limited to the tiny but independent territory of the Vatican, but spiritually they are more powerful than they have been for several centuries.

Priest
Priest comes from the Greek word *presbyteros*, meaning "elder," and it dates from the early days of Christianity. The first Christian congregations considered all believers equal before the Lord, and they had no exalted specialists to mediate between them and God. Instead, the senior members of the congregation led the prayers and performed the rituals. This changed as the Christians gained power and developed an organization in which specialists established themselves in charge of all communications between man and God, following the pattern of other religions.

The institution of priesthood dates back to prehistoric times, when certain persons convinced their fellow-tribesmen that they were particularly skilled at dealing with the supernatural beings that controlled their world. These primitive priests sometimes "controlled" the supernaturals with magic formulae, sometimes manipulated them with flattering prayers. Songs and dances, formulas and incantations were all part of their arsenal. Modern anthropologists call these proto-priests *shamans*, from a Siberian tribal word.

The development of agriculture and civilization brought organized priesthoods to serve the various deities and conduct the sacrifices that kept them in a favorable mood. The priests of the ancient world also doubled as soothsayers, interpreting the intentions of the gods by magical lots, clouds, the stars, the entrails of sacrificial animals, and other ingenious if superstitious means. In many societies the kings served as the chief priests of the land, as did the Pharaohs of Egypt.

Among the ancient Jews, the term for a priest was *kohen*. The priests were drawn from the tribe of the Levites, though not all Levites were priests. For a parallel example, in the

United States most policemen were once Irish, but not all Irishmen were on the police force. In the early days, it is probable that all male Levites were eligible to become priests, but after the Exodus from Egypt, only descendants of Aaron could become priests and conduct sacrifices and prayers. The other Levites served as Temple singers, as janitors, and in other subordinate capacities. In the time of King Solomon, the clan of Zadok gained the sole right to the temple priesthood. In the time of Jesus, the Zadokites were also a political faction, and they and their supporters were the Sadducees of New Testament notoriety. The Jewish priesthood was entirely connected with the rituals of the Temple in Jerusalem, and after the Romans destroyed the Second Temple in A.D. 70, they had no more function and disappeared. Their place was taken by the rabbis, who were teachers and interpreters of the religious laws.

The Greek term for a priest was *hiereus*, from *hieros*, "holy." From the same root we get *hieroglyphics*, literally "priestwritings," and *hierarchy*, which comes from *hierarches*, or "chief priest" and only in the 16th century came to mean a formal structure of ranks.

The Romans called their priests *sacerdos* (plural, *sacerdotes*), from *sacer*, "sacred" or "holy." *Sacer* has given us all kinds of ecclesiastical terms, such as *sacrament* ("something consecrated"), *sacrifice* ("sacred-making"), and *sacrilege*, which originally meant the stealing of sacred objects. Among Romans, as among Greeks, the priesthood was concerned only with ritual, not with morality, and it did not claim exclusive control of the God–man relationship. Worship was centered in the home, and the father of the family conducted the prayers and sacrifices.

As the priesthood developed in Christianity, the priest had two roles. He administered the ritual sacraments, as the Jewish and pagan priests of old had offered sacrifices, and he was a pastor (Latin for "shepherd") giving his flock spiritual guidance and tending to their morals. In the Roman Catholic and Eastern Orthodox Churches he retains this dual role; most Protestant sects have done away with the ritual part and regard their clergymen as pastors only. In fact, in English and some other languages, they are not called priests but ministers or pastors. *Parson* was originally a 13th-century term for a parish priest, since he represented the *person* of the Church. In Roman Catholic and Eastern Orthodox dogma, only a priest can grant forgiveness for sins; in Protestantism, this is a private matter between the individual and God.

Purgatory

In Roman Catholic doctrine, purgatory is a place or a state of being where souls must spend a period of punishment and torment in order to purify them for admission to heaven. As the rules are written, almost all souls that do not go directly to hell end up in purgatory. The word comes from the Latin *purgatorium*, "place of purification," from *purgare*, "to purify."

There is no mention of purgatory in the preachings of Jesus; in fact, it was not originally a Christian doctrine. The early Christians had no place for it in their eschatology, since they expected the momentary return of Jesus, followed by the Day of Judgment when all souls would receive the reward or punishment they deserved. When it became evident that the Second Coming was not imminent, the Christians had to make some interim provision for the fate of souls. In late Biblical times, there was a Jewish doctrine that souls spent a brief period of penance in Sheol before going to heaven, and that the prayers of the living on their behalf could shorten their stay there. The Christians apparently adapted this belief to their own evolving faith. However, the early Christian theologians were rather vague about the nature and scope of this purgative process, and it did not become official Church doctrine until the reign of Pope Gregory the Great in the 6th century A.D.

Catholic doctrine holds that a soul's term in purgatory can be reduced by several means: prayers, special Masses, and indulgences purchased for them by the living. In the Middle Ages this developed into a kind of celestial trafficking in pardons, which was very profitable for the priesthood. Popular preachers vied in terrifying the public with lurid descriptions of the tortures that souls in purgatory suffered, although serious theologians tried, in vain, to damp down this sensational sin-mongering. The Protestant reformers regarded the whole idea of purgatory as nothing more than a corrupt scheme to enrich the priesthood, and Protestantism does not recognize it.

The Eastern Orthodox Church believes in a state of purgatory, but does not define it precisely. Hinduism and Buddhism, which hold that souls pass through many hells and heavens on their way to eternal peace, have an equivalent concept.

Rabbi

Rabbi, the title of Jewish clergymen, literally means "my master" (from the Hebrew *rav*, "master"). It dates back to the period of the Jewish sage Hillel, who taught from about 30 B.C. to A.D. 10. At that time it was used mainly for outstanding religious scholars and teachers. In the New Testament, Jesus is represented as criticizing the scribes and Pharisees for their insistence on being called "rabbi," as a pompous Ph.D. today might insist on being called "Doctor" (Matthew, 23:7). However, he was willing to accept it himself from enthusiastic disciples (John, 1:49 and 3:2).

The role of the rabbi actually took form during the Babylonian Captivity several centuries earlier. With no temple—the only authorized one was in Jerusalem—the priests could not function. Religious leadership passed instead to scholars of the divine Law, who served as judges, arbiters, community leaders, and teachers and interpreters of the religious laws. Under these men, who were not yet known as rabbis, Judaism became less and less concerned with ritual and more and more concerned with ethics.

Time passed; Cyrus the Great of Persia conquered Babylonia and let the captive Jews return to their homeland. The Temple was rebuilt, and the priesthood regained its influence. But the role of the teacher was now firmly established. After the Romans destroyed the Second Temple in A.D. 70, it was these men who kept the Jewish religion alive. They had not yet, however, become clergymen. Anyone could—and did—lead the daily prayers at the synagogue. The rabbis spent their time studying and discussing the Law.

It was in the Middle Ages that the rabbis really came into their own, and the title of Rabbi came to be commonly used. More and more the rabbis became leaders of their flocks as the people relied increasingly on their judgment. In Christian and Muslim lands alike, Jews were denied citizenship and forced to live in segregated communities. In compensation, they were allowed to live by Jewish law, and it was the rabbis who administered it. However, for centuries rabbis were not paid, as the teaching of the Law was felt to be too sacred to be debased by fees. The rabbi was expected to support himself at some honorable trade. On the other hand, Jews believed it was meritorious to support a scholar so that he could devote his full time to sacred studies, so that some rabbis were supported by private grants.

The 19th century brought changes. Enlightened attitudes on the part of the Christians allowed the Jews to emerge from the ghetto into the modern world. Congregations began to hire rabbis on a full-time basis; at the same time, the rabbis lost their official position as judges because the Jews were now subject to civil law. Instead, they took on pastoral functions like the Christian clergymen. It is the rabbi who conducts the services, preaches, officiates at weddings and bar-mitzvahs, and does social counseling. He is often called upon to act as a spokesman for the Jewish community to the Gentile majority. For all this, a rabbi claims no special relationship with God, as do Christian priests and ministers. He may hear the confessions of guilt-stricken sinners, but it is God, not the rabbi, who grants absolution. In Judaism, no one stands between man and God.

Saint

Saint was originally the Latin word *sanctus*, meaning "holy." From an adjective describing certain men and women of outstanding holy qualities, it became with use a title. It is easy to see how *Sanctus Petrus*, "the holy Peter," could change to "Saint Peter." The idea of sainthood is not confined to Christianity, but it is particularly important in that faith; so let us go back to the years that followed the death of Jesus.

In the beginning, the Christians used "saint" to describe all members of their sect, for they believed that they were a holy army of believers battling the evil of the rest of the world. In much the same way did the Pilgrims on the *Mayflower* call themselves "saints" to distinguish themselves from the other, less religious passengers, and the Mormons call themselves the "Latter-Day Saints." Then the term was used to refer to the blessed souls in Paradise; when someone died, his friends would say that he was among the saints—unless he was a notorious reprobate. But Christians grew more discriminating, and by the 2nd century limited "saint" to those who had died as martyrs for the Christian faith. Later, the famous ascetics who tortured themselves in the name of Christ were added to the list. Later yet, persons who had led lives of exceptional holiness were qualified for canonization.

The idea of venerating the saints began in the late 2nd or early 3rd century A.D. with the martyrs. Each church had its own list of martyrs who had once been members of its congregation, and on the anniversaries of their deaths the priests and laity would assemble at their tombs to honor them. In time, the churches began to pay honor to each other's saints, and a uniform list was established.

By the 4th century, the custom of venerating the saints had added a dimension: people now prayed to the saints to intercede on their behalf with God. Some Christian theologians objected that this was paganistic and exalted the saints to the status of gods—albeit minor ones—in their own right. They were outvoted by their colleagues at various church councils. Besides, the people, the mass of whom were still imbued with pagan ideas and pagan longings, demanded it. Soon pious biographers created legends of the lives of the saints and of the miracles they worked, even after death. Pilgrimages to their tombs became popular. The pilgrims hoped to acquire divine favor to cure illnesses, to bring success in their enterprises, or to ease their passage into Heaven. The clerics who kept the tombs profited handsomely. A lively traffic sprang up in relics of the saints, which in themselves were held to be wonder-working. Originally the relics were cloths that had been laid over the tomb to absorb some of its magic, but later, actual parts of the dead saint's body were removed and, encased in rich containers, prayed to. In the age of credulity, bogus relics were common, which caused some Christians to question the whole concept of the efficacy of relics. These questioners were silenced by the Church, by force if necessary.

Roman Catholic and Eastern Orthodox dogma insists that saints are not actually worshipped, merely venerated. To an outsider watching the faithful pray and make offerings to saints' images, it is a very slender distinction.

During the Dark Ages and the Middle Ages, legends and

myths that originally belonged to pagan gods and heroes were grafted onto the existing body of saint-lore. Among the peoples of the Baltic shorelands, for example, St. George became the Christian substitute for the pagan god Kalvis, the divine dragon-slayer. The Virgin Mary took on many of the attributes of the ancient Mother Goddess of the Near East. Centuries later, this tendency reached an extreme in the Voodoo and Candomblé cults of the Negro slaves in the Caribbean and Brazil. Thus, Legba, the god of crossroads and entrances, was metamorphosed into St. Peter, the doorkeeper of Heaven. Damballa Wedo, a serpent god, became St. Patrick, who drove the snakes out of Ireland. The Virgin Mary was the new form of the love goddess Ezilie Freda. The slaves found that images of the Catholic saints made perfectly acceptable icons of their African deities whose worship the Church forbade.

The cult of patron saints also goes back to the first triumphal spread of Christianity among the pagans. It was well established by the 6th century A.D. Again, this was in effect a transfer of pagan belief to a Christian framework. Just to give an idea of the scope of this cult, St. Barbara is the patron saint of miners and artillerymen; St. Christopher and St. Anthony of Padua are among the patrons of travelers; St. Vitus, of the neurological disease called St. Vitus' dance—and of comedians as well; St. Luke, of physicians, painters, and butchers; St. George, of farmers; St. Cecilia, of musicians and poets. There are many, many more. Although the patron-saint cults grew up with the approval of the Church, they crept in from below via the laity. The hierarchy did not designate them except in a few instances.

Eventually the number of saints grew so large that the Catholic Church undertook a review. In 1969, 200 saints were dropped from the rolls as not being of proven sanctity or not having existed at all. Such popular saints as Christopher, George, Vitus, Patrick, and Nicholas were among them. This still left an estimated 2,500, and the Church is constantly scrutinizing new candidates, particularly from Asia, Africa, and the New World. Nowadays, the candidate for sainthood must have led a life of exemplary Christian virtue and must, after death, have produced a miracle attested to by experts. In the old days, it was enough that popular word-of-mouth claimed that the miracles had happened.

The Protestant Reformation largely did away with the cult of the saints, although churches are still named after them, and a number of Protestant countries still have their traditional patron saints: St. George for England, St. Andrew for Scotland, St. Olav for Norway, and so on.

In every religion that has anything analogous to saints, a saint must practice rigorous self-denial as well as performing good deeds. In Judaism, the saints are called *tzaddikim* ("righteous men"). They were originally conceived of as inspiring others to holiness by the example they set, and the title is still used by Hasidim (an ultra-pious sect) for their leaders. But folklore soon magnified the powers of the *tzaddikim*, and they were credited with miracles just like Christian saints. However, they were not prayed to. In the Middle Ages, Jewish mystics in Eastern Europe developed the legend of the Thirty-Six Saints who exist in the world at any one time. In Yiddish, they are called *Lamed-Vovniks*, from the Hebrew numerals for 36. The Lamed-Vovniks lead a secret existence, for they lose their powers if their identities become known, and it is only their sanctity that keeps God from destroying the world for its uncountable iniquities. Only in time of grave peril to the Jews may a Lamed-Vovnik appear for a brief moment to effect a rescue. However, none appeared to stop any anti-Jewish atrocities from the Crusades to the Holocaust.

In Buddhist thought, a saint is one who has attained Buddhahood but delays his entry into the state of Nirvana to help all mankind. He helps animals as well, for Buddhism holds that every soul goes through a series of incarnations in animal as well as in human form.

Orthodox Islam does not have saints, but the mystical Sufi sect has hundreds, both male and female. In Sufi doctrine, a saint can work miracles during his or her lifetime as well as posthumously. Believers, who are mostly uneducated, make pilgrimages to their tombs and ask them to intercede with God, as in Christianity. A Sufi saint is called a *wali*, literally a "friend (of God)." In India and Pakistan there are networks of holy men called *pirs* who have not quite attained sainthood but are understood to be very close to it. Through their followers, the *pirs* exert considerable political power. A skeptic might comment that renouncing the world appears to confer a great amount of worldly power.

Sin

Sin   *Sin* comes from the Anglo-Saxon word *synn*, of obscure origin; it may possibly come from a Germanic root meaning "debt." The dictionaries define *sin* as a transgression of divine law, or, in simpler terms, breaking God's rules. The simplest working definition of a sin is something that makes God angry, angry enough to punish the sinner, his family, his nation, or even all mankind. All the major religions have a concept of sin, although they disagree on just what constitutes a sin. To a devout Jew or Muslim it is a sin to eat pork; to a devout Christian it is no sin at all (indeed, until recently, eating pork was considered a virtue by many Christians, as a show of contempt for the rival faiths). To Roman Catholics, it is a sin to remarry after divorce; for Protestants, Jews, and Muslims it is perfectly permissible. A devout Buddhist considers it a sin to kill an animal, including fish; yet he will happily eat an animal that someone else has killed, for the sin is then on the slaughterer's head, not his own.

The concept of sin is very ancient. It probably originated in man's fear of breaking the taboos that his shamans said the spirits had laid down. Breaking a taboo led to disastrous consequences: the game would disappear; the coconut tree would wither; enemies would raid the tribe and kill everyone; or the sinner himself would die in agony. As the religions of the early civilizations developed, sin continued to be mainly a matter of failure to observe the religious rituals correctly. But ethical concepts were added along the way. Almost all religions agreed that murder was a sin; they banned adultery and incest; they condemned any tendency by man to set himself up against what the priests declared to be the will of the gods.

The Old Testament, in its original Hebrew, has about twenty words to express different types of sin. In modern Judaism, the generic word for sin means "error," and God is believed to prefer that the sinner turn from his evil ways and be forgiven rather than to punish him. Christianity introduced the doctrine of Original Sin, which is that all mankind have been infected forever by the transgression of Adam and Eve in the Garden of Eden. According to this doctrine, every child is born sinful, and only by strenuous effort can he save himself. Judaism does not have a doctrine of original sin, although the rabbinical sages hold that all men and women have a built-in "evil inclination," which comes to almost the same thing. Islam does not preach original sin, either.

All higher religions recognize a difference between major and minor sins, between sins of commission and sins of omission, and sins committed intentionally and unintentionally. But they tend to classify almost every kind of human act or thought as either sinful or potentially sinful. This enables them to terrify their believers into submission. It is also productive of fees with which the sinners hope to buy forgiveness. In medieval Christianity there was almost a fixed scale of penalties for the various sins, and certain monastic orders sold indulgences —a kind of spiritual credit balance that could be used against future sins.

The early Christians classed seven sins as particularly serious. They called them the Seven Deadly Sins, for they brought the penalty of eternal hell unless they were atoned for. They were pride, anger, envy, lust, gluttony, avarice, and sloth. For some reason, dishonesty was not listed among them, nor was cruelty. Perhaps this tells us something about the value system of the world in which the early Christians operated.

Synagogue

A synagogue is a Jewish house of worship, but the word itself is Greek. It is derived from the Greek *synagoge*, meaning "assembly." (The *-ue* ending is a French variation on the Greek spelling.) This was the word chosen by the translators of the Septuagint to render the Hebrew *keneset*, "assembly" or "congregation," for originally *synagogue* referred to the people of the congregation. Only later did it come to mean the building where the congregation met for worship. Jewish tradition speaks of a Great Synagogue or Great Assembly of 120 scholars, founded by Ezra the Scribe around the middle of the 5th century B.C., who compiled and edited the Old Testament.

No one is quite certain when the synagogue originated, but the experts believe that it began during the Babylonian Exile, when the transplanted Jews in Babylonia organized prayer meetings to take the place of the sacrificial services in the Temple at Jerusalem. However, the synagogue first became the center of Jewish life, social as well as religious, in the 1st century A.D.

One of the Hebrew names for a synagogue is *Bet ha–Tefillah*, or "House of Prayer." Another is *Bet ha–Midrash*, or "House of Study." Aristotle is said to have exclaimed that the Jews must be a race of philosophers because they discussed religion in their houses of worship (pagan temples were for sacrifices only). One of the chief roles of the synagogue was, in fact, as a place to study the laws and commentaries. Jewish men traditionally spent most of their free time at the synagogue listening to the experts debate the fine points and occasionally adding a comment themselves. Today the synagogue is a social as well as a religious center, but the tradition of discussion continues.

Temple
Temple comes from the Latin term *templum*, a staked-off enclosure where the augurs could interpret omens from the flight of birds. In later Roman times it meant the building where a god dwelt in his statue. Temples were the most impressive buildings of the ancient world, from the Greco-Roman area to Egypt, India, and China. They were built with the intention of overawing the visitor with their size and magnificent decorations, and thus impressing him with the power of the resident god or goddess and his/her priests.

Egyptian temples were dark and gloomy, their interiors largely filled with the massive columns needed to support their lofty roofs. However, they must have given the worshippers a pleasant change from the blazing desert sun. Greek and Roman temples were light and airy, and brightly decorated with paint and gold leaf. The chaste whiteness we so much admire today is simply a result of weathering.

The temples of Hindu and Buddhist divinities were also magnificent. The idols were often covered with gold leaf and decorated with precious gems. The Shwe Dagon Pagoda in Rangoon, Burma, has a 326-foot dome covered with gold leaf and topped with a huge cluster of diamonds and other precious stones.

The temples of the Aztecs and Mayas were built atop towering stone pyramids that rose step by narrow step. The actual temple was small, a stone representation of the aboriginal

134

thatched hut. The sacrificial altars stood outside, so that all the people could watch the ceremonies and vicariously take part. The reason for placing the temples on top of lofty pyramids was probably to bring them closer to the gods' abode in the sky. This was also probably the case with the famed ziggurats of Babylon, which scholars believe were an attempt to duplicate the sacred mountains where the gods were thought to dwell.

Probably the most discussed temple in Western thought is the famous Temple of Solomon in Jerusalem. Completed about 950 B.C., it was probably built along the lines of one of the great Phoenician temples, with an outer courtyard where worshipers could meet and chat and sacrificial animals were sold, and an inner building where the services were conducted. At the rear of the building was the Holy of Holies, a dark chamber where the Ark of the Covenant rested. Only the High Priest was permitted to enter there, on certain special occasions.

The Bible dwells in loving detail on the splendors of Solomon's Temple: richly carved panels of aromatic cedar wood lined the interior of its massive stone walls; carved cherubim—fearsome angelic spirits—touched wings across the top of the interior, which was lit by narrow windows. The dim and mysterious light was relieved by the brilliant gold leaf with which the altar, the cherubim, and all the other decorations were covered. The roof, too, and even the floor (if the Biblical scribes are not indulging in pious exaggeration) were covered with gold. Outside on the porch were huge bronze caldrons, costly just in terms of their metal, and infinitely more so because of their elaborate decorations. The largest of the caldrons was over fourteen feet across and seven and a half feet deep, bigger than many a modern backyard swimming pool. The temple, built by hired Phoenician craftsmen, took seven years to complete. Its stones were pre-cut to size so that they could be fitted together on the site with no impious din of iron hammer and chisel (iron also had an evil symbolism because it was the metal of weapons). The size of the Temple was not remarkable by modern standards—one estimate is 150 feet long by 70 feet wide by 45 feet high—but it was very impressive for the former hilltop fortress that was Jerusalem. And it certainly added to Solomon's glory as well as to the Lord's.

This temple was destroyed by the Babylonians in 587 B.C. It was rebuilt in 515 B.C., probably on the old foundations, which were too massive to be easily destroyed. The Second Temple, less magnificent than the first, still served as a spiritual focus for the Jews, who by now were scattered all over the Mediterranean world. Even Gentiles made pilgrimages to the Jewish Temple to gain the favor of the mysterious Jewish God who had no bodily form and whose name might not be spoken.

Around 20 B.C., King Herod undertook to remodel the Temple. Its size was to be doubled, and the decorations were to surpass the original splendor of Solomon's Temple. His plan was to attract visitors from all the lands of the known world, thereby benefiting Jerusalem and ingratiating himself with his Jewish subjects, who regarded him as a half-foreign interloper and a collaborator with the detested Roman colonialists. But Herod's temple was destroyed by the Roman legions of the Emperor Vespasian ("Waspish"), in A.D. 70, following a desperate revolt by the Jews against Roman tyranny. In the 7th century A.D. the conquering Muslims built the famed Mosque of Omar on the site of the Temple. The Jews were permitted only to approach the western wall of the ancient foundations, the so-called Wailing Wall, to pray and to insert slips of paper bearing petitions to God into the crevices of the massive masonry. Since then, Jews have believed that it is God's will that no new temple be built. Even though Israel regained the Temple Mount in 1967, no attempt has been made to recreate the vanished Temple. It lives on only in literature and legend.

Astrology   In the mud-brick
cities of ancient Sumeria, nearly 5,000 years ago, scholars
watched the stars make their slow, seasonal progressions
around the sky. They mapped out constellations (somewhat
different from ours, since they were drawn from a different
mythology) and laid out the first zodiac. They plotted the
paths of the stars and planets and worked out elaborate calculations to predict when each one would appear at a given point
in the sky. They were the first astrologers.

Astrology is a study based on the belief that the stars and
planets control human destiny. It has been described as the
application of scientific methods to unscientific ideas. Scientists consider it pretentious balderdash; yet, even today, millions of people believe in it fervently, including a good many
who should know better. But astrology is also the parent of astronomy; so even the most skeptical owe it a debt.

The belief that the heavenly bodies control our fates probably originated back in prehistoric times, when men noticed
that certain bright stars (they would not have paid attention to
the dim ones) appeared at certain positions in the sky at different times of the year. Year after year the stars went through
the same performance, so that the hunters and gatherers were
able to correlate the stars' positions with the changing seasons.
Having made this basic observation, they made the mistake of

137

thinking that the stars controlled the seasons. From there the next step was to assume that these godlike bright sparks in the heavens controlled the fates of men and women.

The Sumerians' empire perished under the assaults of warlike neighbors, but their astrological lore lived on. It was taken up by their successors, the Babylonians, who improved upon the Sumerians' calculations so that their priests could make more accurate predictions of the changing relationships of the stars and planets. Excellent mathematicians, the Babylonians were infatuated with the numbers twelve and sixty. It was probably they who gave us the division of the Zodiac into twelve houses, just as they divided the day into twelve hours.

The Babylonians' ideas about astrology spread throughout the Middle East, and reached Greece around the middle of the 4th century B.C. The Greeks, who loved to speculate, added greatly to the store of astrological lore. It was they who gave us the term *astrology*, which comes from *astron*, "star," plus *logos*, "word," and can be translated as "commentaries about the stars." An *astrologos*, "one who tells about the stars," was the equivalent of an astronomer. *Astronomy* is a later word that Greek scholars used while the people talked about "astrology." It comes from *astron* and *nomos*, meaning "arranging." Thus, an astronomer was someone who "arranged" the stars on sky maps.

Greek speculations about the stars' and planets' power over the lives of men and nations traveled to India and from there to China, where they formed the bases of the native "sciences." They were also taken up by the Romans, who admired everything Greek except the Greeks themselves. Astrology was tremendously popular in Rome, for the Romans were intensely superstitious and looked for omens in everything, even the entrails of birds. Astrologers in Rome called themselves Babylonians or Chaldeans, trading on the reputations of these civilizations just as in our century chefs used to call themselves

French. (The Chaldeans were a later culture that flourished in the Babylonian area.) The Romans took astrology so seriously that a man in public life would keep the day and hour of his birth secret until he found an astrologer willing to give him a favorable interpretation.

It was the Greeks, however, who loaded astrology with the details that delight its believers to this day. It was they who invented the horoscope (from *hora*, "hour," and *skopos*, "watcher"), which purported to analyze a person's character and fate based on the positions of the heavenly bodies at the exact moment of his birth. Of course, without accurate timepieces, the ancient astrologers could not determine the precise moment of anything, but that didn't bother them nor the credulous faithful. The Greeks also perfected the ancient concept of the Zodiac, a term that comes from *zodiakos kyklos*, or "circle of the animal signs." Each of the twelve houses of the Zodiac was identified with a mystical sign, and nine of them were animals. Two were human, and one was a set of scales. Each sign of the Zodiac conferred certain arbitrarily assigned qualities upon people born under it. For example, persons born under Aquarius are supposed to be kind-hearted, helpful, and gentle. Aries people are supposed to be aggressive, headstrong, and liable to go overboard in their enthusiasms. Scorpios—I am one —are supposed to be intelligent (so true), strong-willed, and passionately devoted to causes. They are also supposed to be oversexed, egotistical, and very critical of others (Lies! Lies! All lies!). Of course, we all know people who fit the descriptions assigned to them under the Zodiac, but we also know a lot of others who don't fit them at all. Astrology fans say these folks are just exceptions.

There was more to the Zodiac. The planets, as they wandered through the Zodiac, also exerted a strong influence. Indeed, each planet ruled one or more signs of the Zodiac, and also its appropriate day of the week. Mars, for instance, ruled

Tuesday; Sunday was the Sun's day, and so on. Each Zodiac sign and each planet was assigned its appropriate colors, flowers, gemstones, metals, parts of the body, and even diseases. These last two were based on the doctrine of the Grand Man, a figure drawn bent backward around the circle of the Zodiac so that his head was pressed against the soles of his feet. Since Aries is the first sign of the Zodiac, the head was placed there. The feet went under Pisces, the last sign. The parts of the body in between were governed by the signs under which they fell. Some doctors took this falsely founded theory so seriously that they refused to treat a patient if the signs that ruled the ailing part were not in the right position.

Few people distinguished between astrology and astronomy until Copernicus' discoveries were firmly accepted, in the 16th century. Until then, the two words were used interchangeably. Chaucer, for instance, in his 14th-century *Treatise on the Astrolabe*, a practical manual, wrote of "astrology" when it was astronomy he meant. In the Middle Ages, astrology was divided into "natural astrology," the study of the stars themselves, and "judicial astrology," which was the study of the stars' effects on human affairs. By the 17th century science had advanced far enough that educated people used "astrology" only to refer to this fortune-telling aspect.

Astrology still retained a powerful hold, however. For example, Queen Elizabeth I of England had a court astrologer, Dr. John Dee, whom she consulted before making important decisions. So did many of her contemporary rulers. In our own day, Adolph Hitler was a fervent believer in astrology. In 1975, Isabel Peron, the widow of the Argentinian dictator Juan Peron, had an astrologer as her chief cabinet minister. This man was able to make his predictions about violent ends for many Argentinians come true, as he was also the head of the secret police.

In the United States, tabloid newspapers and trashy magazines regularly carry horoscope columns. Books and magazines on astrology are sold on newsstands. For several years in the 1960s, golden years for anti-rational quackery, a large computerized astrologer's booth stood in Grand Central Station. For $5.00 you could get a detailed character reading. For $7.50 you could get your horoscope for the next twelve months. People stood in line to make their offerings at this shrine of pseudo-science.

Once, when I was working on the staff of a well-regarded encyclopedia, I asked a fellow worker how an educated, intelligent person like her could believe in that nonsense.

"Well, I don't really," she grudgingly conceded, "but you gotta admit it's fun to talk about!" And so astrology does serve some purposes even if it is not grounded in fact. It is a good opener for conversations and a handy gimmick for starting flirtations. It is also a facile excuse for bad behavior: "I can't help it if I lose my temper a lot. I'm an Aries, you know!" As long as people do not take it seriously, astrology is probably harmless. In any case, it will have a devoted following as long as people like to believe in mysterious powers beyond our control.

Augur An augur is not, as some poor spellers might think, a tool for boring holes in wood. (That's spelled with an *er*.) The augur was an important official of ancient Rome, and his job was to predict events by such omens as the entrails of sacrificed animals, lightning in the sky, and, above all, the behavior of birds. *Augur* may come from the Latin *avis*, "bird," and *garrire*, "to chatter," as in *garrulous*. Thus, the augur was one who talked incessantly about what the birds were doing.

Before taking an augury, the Roman augur would go out at midnight on a clear, windless night, accompanied by a magistrate. The two men would ascend a hill from which they had a wide view. After praying and making a sacrifice, the augur marked off a consecrated space, or *templum*, and pitched a tent. With his head covered, he sat in the tent, facing south, and prayed to the gods for a sign.

Since the augur was facing south, the east, which was the direction of good luck, was on his left. Anything taking place on the left hand, therefore, was a portent of good fortune, while anything on the right boded ill. (The Greek augurs sat facing north; so the right side was the lucky one for them, and the Romans eventually followed suit. In fact, in most matters the Romans, like most people of the pre-scientific age, considered the left side evil and the right side good. The Latin word for "left" was *sinister*, from which the current word is derived.)

The augur looked to the sky for guidance because the sky was the domain of the chief god, Jupiter. Lightning was one of Jupiter's attributes. It was, of course, a very powerful omen, as one would expect of a god-hurled bolt from the heavens that could rend huge trees in half, set houses on fire, and kill people. Lightning going from left to right was lucky. Lightning going from right to left was unlucky. But lightning was such a dread force that the sight of a lightning flash was cause to cancel all public business for the day. However, lightning did not occur very often in the skies over Rome; so public business went on for the most part uninterrupted. The augur was forced to look for other aerial signs of the gods' will, and here the birds played their part. Birds flying from east to west were lucky; a flight the other way made many a Roman defer his plans. Whether north and south had any significance in the augur's vaticinations I do not know.

Another method of taking auguries from birds was to watch the feeding behavior of the sacred chickens. The augur flung a scoopful of grain to the consecrated fowls. If they ate it greed-

ily, it was a good sign; it was especially good if they ate slop-
pily and dropped bits of grain from their beaks. But if they ate
slowly or not at all, it was a bad omen. Roman generals took
cages full of sacred chickens with them on their campaigns,
and made no move without consulting them. They may not
have been above influencing the chickens' predictions by
starving them beforehand. One Roman leader, wanting a good
pep talk from his chickens before a sea battle, flew into a rage
when they dawdled over their prophetic meal. Remarking bitterly, "If they won't eat, then let them drink!" he threw them
into the sea to drown. That very day he was killed in the battle;
pious Romans said that this was punishment for his irrever-
ence.

Originally the augur was called an *auspex*, or "bird-
watcher," from *avis* and *spex*, "observer." The plural of *auspex* was *auspices*, a word we still use to signify the outlook for
a project. Since the 17th century, *auspices* has also meant "patronage" or "protection," since it was the all-powerful gods
who supposedly controlled the auspices. So, we might say:
"This study is being carried out under the auspices of NASA."
We could also say: "The weather looks auspicious for launch-
ing the new space probe," or "Today is inauspicious to see the
boss about that raise."

Charm "Charmed, I'm sure,"

is a classic English formula for greeting strangers to whom one
would much rather not be introduced. Actually, *charm* has
been used in English since the late 13th century, when it was
taken over from the French word *charme*. Its real origin, however, goes back to the Latin *carmen*, which ordinarily meant
"song" but could also mean "incantation," literally a "singing-
in" of a magic spell, or "enchantment." (Both come from *in-
cantare*, "to enchant," from *in-*, "in," plus *cantare*, "to sing.")

Originally a charm was a magical verse to be sung or recited. By extension, it came to mean an amulet or other small object that people wore to ward off evil or bring good luck, such as a rabbit's foot or a four-leaf clover. As a verb, "to charm" meant to influence people by means of magic. Animals could be charmed, too. A "charmed life" was one that was magically protected.

A few centuries later, *charm* took on a figurative sense. A *charming* person was one who had such powers of personal attraction that they seemed magical. A *charmer* now (I mean the late 17th century) was a fascinating woman rather than a sorceress. *Enchanting* took on this same figurative meaning even earlier; Shakespeare used it in 1606. Today "charming" has lost all its original meaning of magic and simply means "attractive" or "quaintly appealing." But charm is not entirely out of date. It is also a quality that nuclear physicists attribute to certain sub-atomic particles. And what could be more up-to-date—or mysterious—than that?

Coven
A *coven* is a congregation of witches who have gathered to worship Satan. The word seems to be a Scottish form of *covent*, which in turn is an old form of *convent*, and *convent* comes from the Latin *convenire*, "to come together." Nuns and witches make a strange pair, but there you have it. The word *coven* first appears in a 17th-century Scottish pamphlet on witchcraft. Why Scottish? I cannot say, except that the Scots in the 16th and 17th centuries were as obsessed with witchcraft as any nation has ever been. King James VI of Scotland (who became James I of England) himself wrote a treatise upholding the reality of witchcraft, and some terrible witch hunts took place in both Scotland and England with the king's blessing.

The ideal number for a coven was thirteen, a number that

for some reason has always been associated with ill luck and unholiness. Covens would meet at midnight, the traditional "witching hour," when the powers of light and good were at their weakest and the powers of darkness and evil at their strongest. The witches would go through the usual rituals of devil-worship, with the Devil impersonated by a male witch. It is believed that the witches' sabbaths usually ended in a sex orgy, which may have been a factor in attracting new recruits to the witch cults.

Demon

Demon comes from the Greek word *daimon*, a term for a supernatural being who was not powerful enough to rank as a god. The *daimon* was not necessarily evil; it could just as easily be benevolent. Greeks at the time of Plato and Socrates believed that everyone had a guardian *daimon* to watch over them. The identification of the word "demon" with evil probably originated with Hellenized Jewish scribes of the pre-Christian era, who identified the Greek term *daimon* with all the evil spirits that stalked, flew, and crawled through Middle Eastern folklore. Such, for instance, were the hairy, satyr-like *seirim*, which hung about ruins to prey on travelers, and the insubstantial but terribly dangerous *shedim*, which Jews of the Hellenistic era identified with pagan gods. Then there was Lilith, Adam's disobedient first wife, whom God turned into a demoness as punishment; Lilith, whose name is Hebrew for "screech-owl," became the mother of hordes of demons that plagued mankind. She visited men in their sleep and gave them erotic dreams. Sometimes she copulated with them and later gave birth to a new generation of horrifyingly deformed demons. Lilith also sucked the blood of children and killed women in childbirth.

Despite the prevalence of evil spirits in the Middle Eastern melange of religions and folklore from which the ancient Jews drew these beliefs, demons receive very little mention in the Old Testament. The priestly scholars who wrote and edited the Bible regarded any attribution of powers to these malign godlets as detracting from the supreme power of God. In fact, they were sometimes forced by their logic into claiming that evil spirits were sent by God, a singularly unpleasant accusation to make against the Creator.

Demons were of many kinds, and every culture from the most primitive Australian hunter-gatherers to the highly sophisticated Chinese, not to mention Europeans and Africans, has believed in them at one time or another. In many primitive societies, all sickness and death was blamed on demons who acted either on their own or on the orders of witches, since nobody could conceive that these were natural occurrences. Insanity and epilepsy were considered *ipso facto* evidence that the victim was possessed by a demon, and this belief persisted down to quite recent times in the more backward parts of the Western world. (On occasion epileptics were thought to be possessed by God. Mohammed was an epileptic, and there is a theory that the Hebrew prophets were similarly afflicted.)

In many pre-scientific societies, people believed that demons were everywhere. In Korea at the turn of the century, for example, the common people believed that demons infested the chimneys and the rooms of their houses, sat on cooking pots, lurked in vegetation. When a person went outside, a cloud of invisible demons swarmed around him like gnats. In Egypt, at the same period, the peasants dared not pour water on the ground without asking permission of the *jinn*, who hated getting wet and were liable to do something nasty in return.

In Muslim lore, demons tended to be stupid and could sometimes be outwitted by a clever man. In Hindu and Buddhist lore they were sly and crafty. To medieval Christians, they were diabolically clever, and man stood no chance in matching wits with them. His only chance was to menace them with a crucifix, an amulet, or a holy relic, or to recite a charm quickly before the demon could act.

It was not only the ignorant who believed in demons. Philosophers and churchmen shared the belief. In our own country, we have the example of Cotton Mather, who lived well into the 18th century. Mather was a leading clergyman in Massachusetts and a sufficiently distinguished scholar to be made a member of England's prestigious Royal Society. He pioneered inoculation to prevent smallpox. Yet Mather was one of the driving forces behind the notorious Salem witch trials of 1692, and to the end of his life he believed that New England was infested by demons. It was a great step forward when rationality began to prevail and man began not to take demons seriously.

Vampires and werewolves are special classes of demons, and we will cover them separately. But vampire lore is filled with unwholesome sexual fantasies, and the belief in sexual relations between humans and demons was widespread. Medieval Europeans took over the pagan Roman beliefs in the *incubus* and the *succubus*. The incubus—his name comes from the Latin verb *incubare*, "to lie upon"—was a male demon that seduced women as they slept. The succubus ("the one who lies underneath") was his female counterpart. Both civil and church law recognized the existence of these beings. It was a convenient excuse for erotic dreams, which religion classified as sinful. Chinese and Japanese lore is filled with stories of fox-demons who take the shape of beautiful women and seduce men. Each time they make love, some of the man's life force goes into the fox-demon, until eventually the demon has it all and the man dies. But what a way to go!

Ghost

Have you ever wondered why *ghost* is spelled with a *gh*? It turns out that we owe this odd spelling to the first printer in England, William Caxton (1421–91). Caxton for some reason fell under the spell of the Flemish word *gheest* (Flemish for *ghost*), and due to his influence we are still stuck with it. Even so, it did not become standard until a century after Caxton gave up the ghost. In Anglo-Saxon times the word was *gast* or *gaest*; it came from a West Germanic root carrying the meaning of "anger" and may possibly go back to a very old Indo-European root with the meaning of rending or tearing to pieces.

Ghost is a word of many meanings. Its original meaning seems to have been the soul or spirit in the sense of the life force, what you lose when you "give up the ghost." It could also mean "breath," one of the signs of life. Then it could mean the soul, as distinct from the body; a person (as nowadays we would metaphorically say a "soul"); an angel or an evil spirit; God himself (surviving nowadays only in the phrase "the Holy Ghost"); the soul of a dead person living among the other shades of the dead; and lastly and currently, a dead soul making an appearance to living persons.

Some of the old spellings of *ghost* include *goost*, *goist*, *goast*, *ghoast*, and *ghaist*. *Ghastly*, from a root meaning "frightening," is distantly related to *ghost*.

High-toned synonyms for *ghost* are *apparition*, *wraith*, and *spectre*. *Apparition* comes from the Latin verb *apparere*, meaning "to make an appearance." *Wraith* is of Scottish origin, and no one knows what it originally meant, although *wraith* is also a Scottish pronunciation of "wrath," which would tie in neatly with the original Germanic root of "ghost." *Spectre* is a loan-word from 16th-century France and comes ultimately from the Latin *spectrum*, "appearance" or "apparition," from the verb *specere*, "to look at." *Spectrum* originally had the meaning of "ghost"; when Isaac Newton and other 17th-century scientists discussed the spectrum of light, they were speaking metaphorically of the ghost of the light.

Folksy equivalents are *spook* and *hant*. *Spook* is of North German or Dutch origin and made its apparition in North America before it reached England. It was undoubtedly introduced by the 17th-century Dutch colonists. *Hant* is an uneducated pronunciation of "haunt," the activity for which ghosts are famous. *Haunt* comes from a 12th-century French verb, *hanter*, which had twin meanings. One was to do something habitually; the other was to hang about a certain place or person. Originally, *haunt* had no supernatural meaning. Its mundane meanings linger on in usages like: "For months Harry haunted the dockside bars, searching for his lost love," or "The Sunnyside Coffee Shop was one of this tragic poet's favorite haunts."

The belief in ghosts, that is, the souls of the dead returning to haunt the living, dates back to prehistoric times. Some of mankind's oldest funeral rituals were designed to prevent the dead person's soul from coming back. People thought of the souls of the dead as malevolent—consumed with rage because they could no longer enjoy the good things of life—and eager to vent their envy and wrath on the living, especially on their own families. As a result, the families had to make regular sacrifices to propitiate the souls of their ancestors.

With this sort of background, it is no wonder that living men and women fear ghosts, and that encountering a ghost strikes terror into the luckless mortal who meets the wraith. Ghosts are not only malevolent, for the most part, but credited with magical powers. They can materialize and dematerialize in the twinkling of an eye, pass through walls, fly through the air, pass through earth and water, and do all kinds of other nifty things that living people cannot.

It is no wonder, either, that traditional ghosts of all cultures may be sad or may be evil, but are never happy. Many is the European castle through which a Lady in White or a Lady in Gray floats eerily, possibly uttering piteous moans, or a male ghost, often grandly dressed, clanks about in chains lamenting his fate. Humbler ghosts, at least in Western tradition, appear in sheets. These were actually the winding sheets in which corpses were wrapped for burial. Sometimes the ghost was depicted as having eyes of flame, in consonance with the hellish character that mankind attributed to the dear departed. This traditional sheet is deeply enshrined in popular culture, which is why today's comic strips and television cartoons have conventionalized the ghost as a sheet with the powers of speech and locomotion. (But, in order not to frighten the little children who are the prime consumers of this trivialized occult lore, cartoon ghosts have been processed into comical, friendly beings.)

Ghosts also haunt some of our most famous works of literature. In Shakespeare, we have Banquo's ghost, which spoiled the triumphal celebration of Macbeth by appearing at the banquet and usurping Macbeth's chair, dripping blood from its many wounds. Only Macbeth could see the ghost, and he was frightened silly. His henchmen thought he had gone mad and began to lose confidence in him. But Banquo's ghost had a valid excuse for its bad manners, for Macbeth had murdered Banquo. Then there was the kingly ghost of Hamlet's father, which walked the battlements of the Castle of Elsinore dressed in armor, until it was able to talk to Hamlet and set him on his course of vengeance against the old king's brother. Again, there was a good reason for the ghost's appearance, for the treacherous brother had poisoned him in his sleep in order to steal both wife and throne from him.

From the works of Charles Dickens we have the ghost of Jacob Marley, deceased partner of the callous miser Scrooge. No royal armor for the petit-bourgeois moneylender Marley, but sheets and chains of which each link was forged from a cruel deed. Henry James' *The Turn of the Screw* features the ghosts of an evil governess and steward who continue to exercise a malign influence on the children they once looked after.

Ghosts have also given us less spooky metaphors. In photography we have "ghost images," faint secondary images that result from double exposures. Ghost images sometimes appear on television screens to send the owners of the sets screaming to the repair shop. Ghost crabs and ghost shrimps are light-colored species that fade into the sand like ghosts. There are the ghost towns of the western states, one-time flourishing communities that were abandoned when the mines or whatever else sustained them gave out. And there is the ancient and honorable institution of the ghost writer, an anonymous person who creates the text to which another person sets his name. Ghost writing has kept many a professional writer from real ghosthood. But I swear on the bones of my ancestors that a ghost did not write this essay.

Glamour *Glamour*, like *enchanting* and *charming*, is a word that once had a magical meaning. Would you believe that it is related to the study of nouns and verbs, the parsing of sentences, and all the other dreary business of grade-school grammar? In fact, it is a Scottish corruption *gramarye*, a medieval variant of *grammar*. *Gramarye* originally meant simply grammar or learning in general, but in an age when the common people could not read or write, it was assumed that any kind of learning was magical, and so *gramarye* came to mean occult knowledge or black magic. A further perversion of *grammar* (this time by the French) gave us the *grimoire*, a handbook of spells.

Glamour and *gramarye* existed happily as peasant words until Sir Walter Scott introduced them to literary language in his novels in the early 19th century. Then they took on a hideous life of their own and have infested supernatural fiction ever since. (I mean the kind of supernatural story whose author tries to compensate by exotic and arcane language for his lack of a plot.)

So, *glamour* originally meant "magic" or "enchantment." But writers, ever on the lookout for the picturesque, converted it into "magical attraction." When we say that such-and-such a person is glamorous, or that advertising is a glamorous profession, we are really saying that the allure is not real, but due to unsanctified sorcery.

Goblin

A goblin is a minor demon, of limited powers but still dangerous if crossed. The name apparently comes from *gobelin*, the name for a local malevolent spirit of a town in Normandy. It was probably brought to England in the 14th century by Norman travelers. (The famous French Gobelin tapestries are named for the original manufacturers. Why they were called "goblins" I do not know.)

A hobgoblin (vintage early 16th century) is a mischievous, half-friendly household spirit. The name comes from *Hob*, a rustic diminutive for Robert. (In the same guttural way, English peasants turned Roger into "Hodge" and Richard into "Hick." You can make a reasonable facsimile of the sound by making a purring noise between the middle of your tongue and the roof of your mouth.) A modern equivalent would be "Bobby Goblin." *Hobgoblin* was also a nickname for Robin Goodfellow, also known as Puck. Country folk used to believe that hobgoblins would do useful chores under cover of night if bribed with a little gift of food. Later, *hobgoblin* became a synonym for a bogeyman or other imaginary terror. Ralph Waldo Emerson, the 19th-century Massachusetts sage, once opined that "A foolish consistency is the hobgoblin of little minds."

Imp, more or less synonymous with *goblin*, originally meant a young shoot or bud of a plant, used in grafting, an art practiced in ancient times and known to the Anglo-Saxons as *impian*. By extension, *imp* came to mean a child, and as late as the 17th century it was used occasionally to mean the scion of a noble family. The witch-hunting mania of the late 16th and 17th centuries led to the popular use of the expression "imp of Hell" or "imp of the Devil." In the early 17th century the expression was practically a household word, and the "of Hell" and "of the Devil" were dropped because everyone knew what *imp* implied. Imps, which were understood to be little devils, were believed to be the familiars of witches, taking the form of a common animal such as a cat or dog. Toads, flies, bees, and spiders were also common forms for familiars, the witch-hunters proclaimed. Yet even at the height of the witch mania, in the mid-17th century, people playfully called a mischievous child an imp. Even a professional witch-hunter could hardly believe that a naughty child was actually a devil in disguise.

Magic

Magic comes from the Latin *ars magica*, "the art of the Magi." The Magi (*magus* in the singular) were the priestly caste of ancient Persia, and were credited with awesome powers of sorcery. The Greeks, eager believers in the supernatural, adopted *Magus* as a title for a super-magician, and the Romans picked the term up from the Greeks.

Of course, magic itself existed long before the name did. It was one of the ways in which man tried to control the natural world. The other was religion, which took the path of propitiating the gods and the lesser spirits.

Long ago, magic divided, like an amoeba, between black magic, whose aim was to injure others or to gain wealth, power, or beautiful women illegitimately, and white magic, whose goal was to cure illness or counter black magic. Black magic always involved trafficking with evil spirits, whereas white magic did not. White magic was formerly called "natural magic," and it was one of the forerunners of science.

According to the *Oxford English Dictionary*, black magic and white magic are terms invented by modern writers—that is, writers of the 18th and 19th centuries. Yet as far back as the 14th century we encounter the term *nigromancy*, whose first half is the Latin for "black." Actually that word, now obsolete, is a blend of the Latin *niger* with *necromancy*, from the Greek *nekros*, "dead," plus *manteia*, "prophecy." Necromancy was originally the art of calling up the spirits of the dead and making them foretell the future. There were many other kinds of "mancy" practiced in the ancient world, such as *tyromancy*, predicting the future by the curdling of cheese, *chiromancy*, better known today as palmistry, *pyromancy*, or telling the future by the behavior of a flame, and *catoptromancy*, which made use of mirrors. All were equally unreliable, but the people came on just the same.

Ogre

In 1697 a French author named Charles Perrault published a collection of fairy tales that he called *Contes de ma mère l'oie* (Tales of Mother Goose). The book was quickly and greedily mined by other writers, and gave us such staple images as Bluebeard. It also gave us the word *ogre*, which appeared there for the first time. An ogre is generally agreed to be a man-eating giant, and hideous to boot. But the origin of the word is very dubious. One theory, generally pooh-poohed by experts, is that it is a distorted form of *Ugri*, an old name for the Hungarians, who ravaged central Europe in the 5th century A.D. The ill-famed Attila the Hun was one of them. But then the Goths and Vandals and plenty of other tribes behaved just as badly, and no one named a monster after them.

A somewhat more plausible explanation is that ogre is a mangled form of *orco*, an Italian word for "demon," derived from *Orcus*, a Latin name for Hell and also for the Lord of the Underworld. In post-Roman folklore, Orcus/Orco became a man-eating demon who lurked in the woods. From there the transition to a simple giant who gourmandized on human flesh would have been easy.

Pirated from Perrault, *ogre* found its way into English in the early 1700s. It soon took on a metaphorical meaning of someone who was particularly cruel, brutish, or ugly. As a four-letter word that is neither obscene nor scatological, I think it deserves a revival.

Omen

An omen is usually defined as a portent, and vice versa, a classic example of a circular definition. Both are prophetic signs of something that is fated to happen—unless you take the proper ritual measures to fend it off. *Omen* is a Latin word that the experts believe is derived from *audire*, "to hear." The underlying idea is that the god who is being consulted on the upcoming events "speaks," usually symbolically, and is "heard" by the anxious mortals. *Ominous* (*ominosus* to the Romans) originally meant "portentous" (here we've come round the circle again). It could be either good or bad. But by the 18th century the favorable aspects of this word had been forgotten, and only the menacing ones were retained.

Portent comes from the Latin *portendere*, "to stretch forth" —in symbolic terms, a stretching forth to see the future.

One of the oldest and most widespread sources of omens is

the liver of an animal. Pigs, cattle, sheep, and chickens were major contributors—albeit involuntarily—to man's search for knowledge of the future. The liver was thought to be the seat of the life principle and of the soul. When an animal was sacrificed to a god, its liver was supposed to reflect the soul of the god. Since the ancients believed the mind was part of the soul, it also reflected the mind of the god. A trained priest could thus "read" the mind of the god by interpreting the appearance of the liver. And since the gods controlled everything that happened, knowing what the god had in mind was the same as knowing what events were going to befall one.

The god's thoughts revealed themselves in such phenomena as the shape and color of the lobes of the liver and its subsidiary parts, and in the patterns made on its surface by the veins and ducts. These signs were the clues on which the priests based their predictions. They were usually careful to make their prophecies ambiguous and to phrase them as loosely as possible. But the ancients took this mumbo-jumbo with utmost seriousness. The Etruscans, who taught the art of liver-gazing to the Romans, used bronze models of livers to train omen-takers, and the liver was the professional symbol of the omen priest. Numerous statuettes have been found of robed men carrying a liver in one hand.

Bones were often used to furnish omens. The ancient Chinese were particularly fond of scapulomancy, the interpretation of the cracks made in a fresh shoulder-blade when it is thrown onto a fire. Ancient Greeks and Romans cast lots with knucklebones—the patterns they formed when they came to rest were the clues to the future. Later, they used dice. They would surely have used cards, too, had cards been invented then.

The ancient Hebrew priesthood also cast lots to ascertain God's will at any particular moment. The High Priest at Jerusalem wore on his jeweled breastplate two mystical objects called *urim* and *tummim*, which seem to have been some sort of oracular devices. It has been suggested that they were pouches that contained mystically marked dice or knuckle-bones; when the High Priest leaped about in an oracular dance, the lots would eventually drop out and reveal the intentions of God.

Dreams, too, have always been regarded as omens—think of Joseph's famous dreams in the Bible, and of the dream books still bought by credulous people today. And man has also used natural phenomena as prophetic signs. The Roman augurs, for example, based their prophecies on such phenomena as lightning and the flight of birds. Nowadays we are more scientific: we use such portentous indicators as supply-demand curves and stock-market quotations.

Soothsayer

Sooth comes from the Old English *soth*, "truth"; so a soothsayer is one who speaks the truth. It is an odd choice of name for people who make prophecies based on guesswork, and which most of the time don't come true. Perhaps there was wishful thinking at work in the 14th century, when the word first appears. But by the 16th century, some people had become skeptical about soothsayers, for certain writers identified them with conjurers, witchcraft, and Satan.

A related practitioner was the *seer*, literally a see-er. *Seer* is a word from the late Middle Ages, and it means someone to whom God grants prophetic visions. A seer may also use a crystal ball, which was a rare and very valuable commodity all through antiquity and the Middle Ages, in fact, until modern technology made glass plentiful and cheap.

An oracle is another member of the prophetic fraternity. The word *oracle* comes from the Latin *oraculus*, which is derived from *orare*, "to speak" or "to pray," plus the suffix *culus*, which carried the meaning of an instrument. The oracle was the instrument through which a god spoke, like a celestial public-address system. *Oracle* could also mean the place where the god liked to transmit messages, or the message itself. A very well-known oracle of the ancient Greeks was the priestess of the Pythian Apollo at Delphi. The temple in which the priestess performed her visionary role was located on the flank of legend-haunted Mount Parnassus. The very setting was overpoweringly impressive, a steep-cliffed valley with mountains looming above it. The priestess, whose title was the Pythoness, was a married woman over 50 years of age. To prepare herself for prophesying, she chewed laurel leaves and drank from a sacred spring. She then sat on a sacred bronze tripod above a cleft in the earth through which volcanic gasses issued. The ancients believed that the mephitic vapors put her into a prophetic trance, but much more likely it was substances in the laurel leaves that had a hallucinogenic effect. In her trance, she probably muttered unintelligibly, and interpreters called "The Holy Ones" translated her noises into rational Greek. They were helped by the fact that all questions had to be submitted beforehand; so they could figure out a plausible answer to give.

The most renowned of all the Greco-Roman oracles were the Sibyls, *Sibyllai* in Greek. (The name is believed to be a dialect variation of the Greek *Theou Boule*, "the will of God.") The Sibyls prophesied in what must have been an epileptic fit, foaming at the mouth, with distorted features and frantic, uncontrollable gestures.

The Greeks and Romans recognized ten sibyls, scattered over Greece, Italy, North Africa, and the Near East. The oldest and most famous was the Cumean Sibyl, whose shrine was at Cumae, near Naples. This prophetess operated in a huge and gloomy cavern sacred to Apollo. It was regarded as one of the entrances to the dreaded Underworld. The Cumean Sibyl was unusually methodical. According to tradition, she wrote down enough prophecies to fill nine books. All of them concerned pre-Roman and Roman affairs, since that was what the Romans who made up the traditions were interested in. Not only did these books contain predictions of what was to befall the rulers and their subjects; they supplied instructions for rituals to avert the bad omens.

The Sibyl, growing old, offered the prophetic books to Tarquin the Proud, the last Etruscan king of Rome. Tarquin thought her price too high and refused the deal. The Sibyl haughtily burned three of the precious books and offered him the remaining six at the same price. Again Tarquin refused. She burned three more. Tarquin, now thoroughly cowed, bought the last three for the price that would have fetched him all nine had he not been minded to haggle. The books were brought to Rome and placed under the custody of a select body of guardians. At the command of the Senate, these grave and solemn men would consult the Sibylline Books, not to learn the exact details of coming events, but for the religious rituals that must be followed to avert earthquakes, plagues, and other calamities. Only the interpretation that the guardians considered suitable was released to the public, not the original revelations. Someone must have slipped up in the rituals, for the Sibylline Books were destroyed by fire in 83 B.C. New prophecies were collected, but these replacements were eventually destroyed around A.D. 400 by Stilicho, a Vandal general in the service of Rome. It's things like that which make history buffs wish the ancients had had Xerox machines.

Superstition
It has been said that one man's sacred beliefs are the next man's superstitions. If we define superstition as beliefs or practices based on ignorance of scientific facts (often in defiance of plain common

159

sense), this is certainly true. Many of the tenets of the world's major religions are in fact superstitions, or developed out of superstitions of earlier times. And older dictionaries usually define superstition in religious terms.

The word *superstition* comes from the Latin *superstitio*, a compound of *super*, "above," and *stare*, "to stand." It has no logical connection with its meaning, though hard-pressed etymologists have suggested that the Romans who created the word pictured a person standing over something in amazement or awe. An old definition of superstition is, in fact, an unreasoning fear or awe of the unknown or the imaginary. Over time, it acquired additional meanings such as a belief in magic or in things that just plain were not so.

Superstitions range from faith in good-luck charms such as a rabbit's foot or a plastic hunchback (carried by superstitious Italians to avert the Evil Eye) to a belief that God has scheduled the end of the world on a particular day, usually not far off. Witchcraft and magic, being based on irrationality, fall into this category too. Faith in the accuracy of a fortune-teller's cards or a palm-reader's interpretation of the lines on your hand is superstition. Astrology is a prime example.

In bygone days, superstition was a part of daily life, a kind of sub-religion. Many of the old beliefs hang on stubbornly, although few people take them very seriously any more. We still knock on wood to avert bad luck, and some people still say "Gesundheit!" (German for "health") when another person sneezes. Black cats are still symbols of bad luck; in Sweden, you are supposed to spit three times if you see a black cat. A surprising number of high-rise buildings do not have a thirteenth floor because so many people will not rent an apartment or an office with that unlucky number. People change their names in order to engineer a more favorable occult influence from the magical values of the letters that make them up. And so on *ad nauseam*.

In some cultures, if a friend asks how you are, you are expected to respond with a string of complaints. If you admit that things are going well, you might stir up the envy of evil spirits, who would punish you, or else of your neighbors, who would put you in your place via the evil eye. A modern variant of the evil eye is the whammy, a short-lived curse. Baseball fans used to try (and for all I know still do) to put the whammy on the opposing team's players when they came up to bat. Or your opponent in a game of pool would put the whammy on you as you were trying to make a tricky shot.

Superstitions often take bizarre expression. North African Arabs used to believe that touching the head of a Jew would bring good luck. In Italy, you could rub the hump of a hunchback for the same effect. One could write many books and still not cover all the superstitions that man's fertile imagination has spawned. As the chorus of an oldtime Yiddish comedy song tells us, "If you wanna believe it, it's true."

Vampire

Vampire–Dracula must be one of the quickest association pairs we have. But the vampire myth is far older than the 1897 English novel that gave us the suave, sinister—but wholly fictional— count. And it is by no means limited to Transylvania; some form of the vampire myth is found in almost every part of the world.

The word *vampire*, however, does come from Central Europe. Some experts derive it from a Magyar word, *vampir*, while others claim the same word is really Serbo-Croatian. Another version, used by some 19th-century authors with a taste for the high-flown, was *oupire*, a French spelling of the Russian word for a vampire, *upir*. Some authorities trace all the European forms back to a Turkish word for "witch," *uber*. That is not as far-fetched as it might seem, since the Turks at one time controlled almost all of the Balkans, a hefty chunk of

Hungary, and a large part of southern Russia. Our current vampire lore, at any rate, was definitely born in eastern Europe, particularly in Hungary. In the early 1730s that country had a real vampire craze, and horrifying reports of attacks by vampires on innocent people flooded all Europe.

The idea of the vampire, a sort of bloodsucking monster that returns from the dead to prey upon the living, is very old. The ancient Sumerian myth of Gilgamesh, some 5,000 years old, mentions vampire-like ghosts. In Hebrew lore, Lilith, the first wife of Adam, was transformed into a bloodsucking night creature. Greeks and Romans shuddered at stories of the *lamia*, a female spirit who preyed on children. (The first Lamia was one of Zeus' many mortal loves, but her children by Zeus were destroyed by his jealous consort, Hera. Lamia died of grief and spent her afterlife in destroying other people's children in a misplaced revenge.)

The Chinese believed in vampire-demons that inhabited corpses, moving from one to another at will. These vampires, or *ch'iang-shih*, did not even need a complete corpse: they could reconstitute a cadaver from a skull or a few half-decayed bones. Their eyes were red; their hands and feet were armed with razor-sharp talons. Their bodies were covered with long, pale-green or white hair, that resembled a hideous mold. When no living victims were at hand to be drained of blood, the Chinese vampires dug up corpses and ate their flesh.

Unpleasant as were the vampires of China, those of Malaya were even more horrifying. They were nothing but a head with dangling entrails. These vampires, always female, usually lived in treetops, concealed by the foliage, for they could float through the air. They favored the blood of newborn infants, although they would drink anyone's blood in a pinch. To protect the newborn, Malays would string thorns around all the doors and windows of the house so that the vampire's dangling intestines would catch on them. The Malays also had another kind of vampire, a beautiful woman in a long, green robe. She sucks the blood of children through a hole in the back of her neck.

In European lore, vampires are usually created by being bitten by another vampire. A sort of spiritual virus is transmitted by the bite, and when the victim dies, he or she becomes a vampire, recognizable by the body's perfect state of preservation and fine, ruddy complexion. (Logic tells us that if vampirism really did spread by contagion the world would long ago have been populated exclusively by vampires, but logic seldom troubles superstitious people.) But suicides and sorcerers could also become vampires under certain circumstances. Even the most innocent of persons could become vampires if a cat jumped over their corpse before it was buried.

A proper Christian vampire was not only practically immortal; it could materialize and dematerialize, entering a room as a mass of vapor. It could turn itself into a large variety of animals that European peasants regarded as devilish, such as cats, bats, wolves, and rats. It had superhuman strength, inhuman cunning, and much, much more. Vampires dreaded only daylight, which made them crumble to dust, a crucifix, and garlic. They could be killed by driving a stake through their hearts or by shooting them with a silver bullet. Stabbing them with a silver knife would probably have the same effect, if the vampire, with its supernatural strength, didn't wrest the weapon from your fear-paralyzed hand and use it on you.

Was there a real Dracula? Yes, and, though not a vampire, he was more bloodthirsty than his fictional namesake. The real Dracula was a Transylvanian prince named Vlad Tepes (Vlad the Impaler), who lived from 1431 to 1476. He was also called Draculya, which can mean either "little dragon" or "little devil." His father, a renowned warrior, was called Dracul, "the Dragon," after the banner under which he fought. The name was passed on from father to son. Vlad got his nickname

"The Impaler" from his sadistic practice of impaling Turks, rebellious noblemen, and anyone else who annoyed him. This was done by forcing a stout pole up the anus of the victim, planting its butt end in the ground, and leaving the poor wretch to writhe away his life in agony propped up in the air. On one occasion Vlad taught a lesson of court etiquette to a deputation of Turkish diplomats who declined to remove their turbans in his presence because it was against their religion. Crying, "I shall strengthen you in your faith," he had the turbans nailed to their skulls. It is not known whether any of the Turks survived the experiment.

Much of what we know about the real Dracula comes from complaints written by some of his subjects, Germans who had settled in his domains. They painted him as a combination of Hitler, Torquemada, Pol Pot, and Stalin, if we may use an anachronistic analogy. Some of these 15th-century pamphlets came to the attention of an imaginative English author named Bram (short for Abraham) Stoker, who studied them in the British Museum while gathering material for a vampire novel. Stoker, impressed by the atrocities of the man, decided that Dracula was the ideal model for his villain. Drawing freely on other authors' vampire novels and on Eastern European folklore, he constructed his masterpiece, which was published in 1897 and has inspired many film versions.

Transylvania is in northwestern Rumania. In Rumania, the evil Vlad is a folk hero because he fought the Turkish occupiers and persecuted the native nobles, thus acquiring an undeserved reputation as a Transylvanian Robin Hood. Although the Rumanian government does not recognize the existence of any vampire legends, it is nevertheless restoring Dracula's ruined castle for the benefit of tourists.

Voodoo   Drums throbbing in the tropic night . . . bloody rites of sacrifice to the African devil-gods . . . wild, savage dances . . . indescribable sexual orgies . . . mysterious witchcraft and magic whose workings are known only to the natives—and, of course, *they* won't tell . . . these are the images of voodoo. Often this heady brew is given further spice by allegations of inter-racial sex (shocking only a generation ago) and the titillating sacrifices of young, blonde virgins, preferably beautiful. And, of course, there is the famous voodoo doll, a little wax mannikin made with hair, fingernail clippings, or blood (best of all) from a person, crooned over with spells, and then mutilated to make the person sicken or die.

What is the reality? As far as objective reporters can find out, the real voodoo is a blend of the native religions of slaves drawn from a number of West African tribes with the Roman Catholicism of their Spanish and French masters. The word *voodoo* may be a corruption of the Yoruba word *vodun*, meaning "god," or it may come from *Vodu*, the proper name of a snake-god of the Ewe people. It is impossible to say which is correct, for voodoo is a loose and elastic faith, with dozens of major gods and hundreds of minor ones. Practices vary from island to island in the Caribbean, where voodoo originated, and also in those places on the mainland where it is practiced. In addition, the *houngans* (priests) and *mambos* (priestesses) develop their own variations on the rituals, as a skilled violinist creates a myriad variations on what a composer has written. And new ideas, as from European and Oriental occultism, are always creeping in.

Voodoo gods are called *loas*, an African word, and a typical voodoo service takes place on a Saturday night. Voodoo was a slave religion, and the slaves certainly would not have been allowed to take time off for worship—and *heathen* worship at that!—during the working day. Also, they had to keep it hidden from their masters and the representatives of the Church. This meant that any voodoo worship had to be held under the protection of darkness. And, since even slaves were given some time off on Sunday, Saturday was the logical night.

A voodoo service is joyous when a good god is being worshipped, gloomy and even frightening when one of the many gods of death is the focus. But even a service for a death god has its moments of levity to relieve the tension. The service begins with prayers, both Catholic and voodoo. Then the priest or priestess makes sacred, symbolic drawings on the ground with cornmeal or sand. The drawings are emblems of the gods who are to be honored, and they are fed symbolically. The drummers strike up an intricate beat—traditional African music excelled in rhythm, though weak on melody and harmony —and the worshipers dance and sing voodoo hymns to the old gods. The gods are not content with this; they demand sacrifices. Usually the sacrifice is a chicken, since most voodoo worshipers are very poor and cannot afford a larger animal. For an important festival, a goat or even a bull may be sacrificed. Then the drawings are "fed" again, and the most important part of the service begins: the loa takes possession of one or more of the worshipers, or so they believe. In Haiti, the possessed person is called the "horse," and the loa is said to mount him (or her). The horse behaves like an evangelical Christian who believes himself entered by the Spirit of God. He cries out, trembles, jerks about spasmodically, and "talks" in unintelligible sounds. Then, as the loa takes more complete control, the worshiper speaks for the god in perfectly clear Creole (or other local dialect). He may issue prophecies, scold the sinners among the congregation, praise the virtuous, deliver a sermon, and so on. No objective observers have ever reported sex orgies at a voodoo service, much less human sacrifice.

In Haiti, gods of death are particularly popular because life is so grim. One of the chief death gods is Baron Samedi ("Baron Saturday"), also called Baron Cimeterre ("Baron Cemetery"). His symbols are a cross and a skull, and he is traditionally depicted dressed like an undertaker. Perhaps the most revered of the voodoo gods is Damballa, a snake god, who is often represented by pictures of St. Patrick because of that saint's snake legend. Ogun is the god of iron and of blacksmiths; Legba, or Baron Carrefours (Baron Crossroads) is the god of crossroads and cemeteries; Agué is the sea god; Erzulie Freda, usually identified with the Virgin Mary, is the goddess of love.

In Brazil, the counterpart to voodoo is called *candomblé*, and the gods have different names. The rituals, however, are much the same. Usually the worshipers, as in Haiti and elsewhere, drink a good deal of cheap rum, which has the effect of relaxing their inhibitions and leaving them open to the god's taking possession of them.

Magic is an important component of voodoo, and the most respected *houngans* and *mambos* are also recognized as powerful magicians. The power of your magic is a visible sign of the influence you have with the deities. There are spells for almost anything: attracting a spouse or a lover, winning a lawsuit, keeping the neighbors' animals out of your garden, and that old staple of sorcery, harming an enemy. The notorious voodoo dolls do exist, though they may not be of African origin. The slaves may have learned about them from Europeans. There is also an element of terror in voodoo. Some authorities speculate that the slaves spread horrifying hints to put fear into their cruel masters; others believe the voodoo priesthood themselves cultivated it to keep their congregations properly awed.

Perhaps this sinister element is a carry-over from the African past. In certain West African nations, before European colonialists took them over, there was a secret cult called Porro which specialized in frightfulness. It was used by the black elite to keep the common people in line through fear. Certainly the late dictator of Haiti, Dr. François Duvalier, recognized this grim element of voodoo and used it with masterful skill to keep his subjects terrorized. Not only did "Papa Doc" maintain a large and dreaded force of secret police, called *Tonton Macoutes* after an evil voodoo spirit, but he spread rumors that the very dogs and tarantulas of the island brought him reports on the people.

Werewolf
Werewolf comes from the Anglo-Saxon *werewulf*. The *wulf* is, of course, a wolf. The *were* is probably an old Anglo-Saxon synonym for "man." this would seem logical, because the names for a werewolf in many other languages also mean "man-wolf" or "wolf-man." The best known is the Greek *lykanthropos*, which we recognize in the high-sounding term *lycanthropy*. Intellectuals in ancient Greece considered lycanthropy a kind of insanity in which the victim imagined that he had been turned into a wolf, but the peasants believed that there really were men who became wolves, and could revert to human shape at will.

The first werewolf recorded in Greek mythology was Lycaon, a legendary king of Arcadia. Lycaon made the mistake of offering Zeus a feast of human flesh and was punished by being turned into a wolf. He lacked the power to resume human form, however, and so was not a true werewolf.

The idea that humans can voluntarily (and sometimes involuntarily) shift from human to beast shape and back again is very old and widespread. There is more of a factual basis for the werewolf myth than for that of the vampire, since there have always been deranged people who imagine they have been turned into ferocious beasts; at some periods in history such unfortunates have been common. While the wolf is the most usual were-animal in European lore, in the Scandinavian countries and northern Russia shape-shifters frequently became bears. In Africa, people believed in were-hyenas and were-leopards. In South America there were myths of were-jaguars, and in the Pacific islands, which generally lacked any animals larger than men and pigs, there were were-sharks.

Indonesia was the home of the most versatile shape-changers, at least in its mythology. Depending on the ethnic group, a man—it is notable that very few werewolves are women—can send out his soul to take the shape of a cat, a tiger, a wild pig, a deer, or any other creature. Indonesians believe (or used to believe) that a person has three souls, so that one can be off doing its evil business of werewolfery while another is guiding the body through its daily routine and social contacts.

The were-man seeks out a victim who is by himself, since he dare not risk observation. He magically puts the victim into a deep sleep and chops the body up into little bits, which he tosses carelessly about on the ground. The only part of the body he eats is the liver. Having enjoyed this delicacy, the were-man carefully reassembles the victim's body from the scattered parts and reanimates it by licking it with his long tongue. The victim awakens thinking that he has merely enjoyed a nice nap, and goes home as if nothing happened. But in a few hours he sickens, and in a day or two he dies. Sometimes he is able to name the were-person who harmed him, but it is hard to catch the evil-doer. He can disguise himself not only as an animal but even as an ordinary object such as a leaf, a stick of wood, or an ant's nest.

An Indonesian werewolf can be recognized while in human form by his long tongue and his shifty, greenish eyes with deep shadows beneath them. Indonesian lore says that some persons receive were-powers as a divine gift, while others get them by contagion. You can contract the condition by touching blood, by eating a werewolf's left-overs (from ordinary meals, that is), or even by leaning your head against a pillar where the werewolf has recently leaned his.

The classic European werewolf, in contrast, is brutally direct in his attacks on victims, leaping at them and tearing their throats out. He can be recognized in human form by the hair on the palms of his hands and by the ring finger on each hand, which is longer than the middle finger. In European folklore, a person usually becomes a werewolf by being bitten by one. In some cases, the werewolf has made a pact with the Devil; in others, he is bewitched or the unhappy victim of a curse. There are even legends of Catholic saints punishing sinners by turning them into wolves. European werewolves seldom have the power of voluntary transformation. At the full moon they change shape willy-nilly.

Werewolves were not always evil; in some cases they behaved like exemplary Christians. In the year 617, for instance, a pack of werewolves invaded a monastery and tore several heretical monks to pieces. In England, a werewolf guarded the head of the saintly king Edmund the Martyr—a relic of great power—from wild beasts. In Renaissance Italy, pious werewolves killed a band of sacrilegious mercenaries who attempted to sack a rich convent. These were comforting exceptions, however. For the most part, werewolves were regarded with fear and loathing as demonic monsters.

In 16th-century France, werewolves were regarded as heretics rather than supernatural monsters. At that same time the country suffered a veritable plague of lycanthropy. Dozens of alleged werewolves were arrested and tried. Surprisingly, almost all confessed freely. But in 1603 a court put an end to this nonsense by declaring that lycanthropy was nothing but an "insane delusion." The peasants, however, continued to believe.

About that time, too, King James I of England struck a blow for rationality by decreeing that "warwoolfes" were mere victims of delusion. Wolves had been wiped out in England a century earlier, and it was very difficult to believe that men could be so transformed when no wolves at all had been seen for a hundred years. The ignorant still believed that witches could turn themselves into small animals such as weasels, cats, and hares, but somehow these never inspired the same degree of terror as a full-sized werewolf.

Witch

Witch comes from the Old English *wicce*, which in turn comes from a verb that may be connected with an old word for "to know" or with a similar word that meant "to turn aside." (The connection with magic would have been in turning aside evil forces.) The verb in question was *wiccian*, and our word *wicked* is probably derived from it too.

In Anglo-Saxon times a witch was anyone who practiced illicit magic, either male or female. Today a witch is by definition a woman; a male witch is usually termed a *wizard*, which comes from the medieval English word *wysard*, "wise man." It is amazing to discover these evidences of the mistrust in which wisdom and learning were held in bygone days.

Another old term for a male witch is *warlock*. It comes from the Old English word *waerloga*, meaning "enemy," "traitor," or especially "devil." While today it is a synonym for *wizard*, some of its older meanings included an oath-breaker, a wicked person, a damned soul in Hell, a conjurer, and the Devil himself. Quite a bundle of pejoratives!

Sorcerer and *sorceress* come ultimately from the Latin *sortiarius*, one who foretold the future by interpreting lots. (The Latin word for a lot was *sors*.) Sorcery was considered sinful by Christian theologians because it was an infringement on God's prerogatives. Only the Almighty had the privilege of knowing what was to come—man's duty was to wait humbly until it happened. Eventually *sorcery* lost its original meaning and became a synonym for black magic.

Witchcraft, like religion, concerns the spiritual world, and in man's primitive past they were often indistinguishable. As human cultures developed the two split apart. The priest was the official representative of the gods; the witch often worked against them. Put another way, the priest was a company man, while the witch was a free-lancer.

In many cultures, a witch practices both black (harmful) magic and white (helpful) magic according to the client's wishes. In European culture, black and white witches are distinct. The black witch invokes evil spirits or the Devil himself for aid; the white witch invokes God and the saints.

The Old Testament states "Thou shalt not suffer a witch to live," but in this case a witch is someone who calls up spirits to prophesy the future, as the Witch of Endor did for King Saul. All Saul got for his trouble was a prophecy of defeat and death. Christianity absorbed the Jewish and pagan conceptions of witchcraft. Nevertheless, Church doctrine insisted that witchcraft was merely a superstition and that witches had no real powers. Penances were imposed on those who proclaimed their belief in witchcraft, and those who professed to practice it were punished under civil law, but few witches were executed.

This changed in the 13th century, when the Roman Catholic Church decided to identify witchcraft with heresy. It was a useful weapon against dissident sects such as the Cathars and the Waldensians to identify their unorthodox varieties of Christianity with devil-worship. In the eyes of the Church it was devil-worship that was the real crime. The magic was a minor offense. The most abominable tortures were inflicted on men and women accused of witchcraft in order to extort a confession, whose details were usually suggested by the interrogators. Naturally, confessions were sooner or later forthcoming from the accused, provided that they didn't die first under the torture. It is almost certain that the stories of organized witch cults and witches' sabbaths—a kind of recognized anti-religion—got their start from this tactical invention of the Church.

Ignorance and malice gathered strength, and charges of witchcraft were frequent. Often they were political ploys against powerful noblemen. Frequently they were brought by envious acquaintances. Even the clergy were not exempt. One of the most telling charges against the Order of Knights Templars, a military-monastic order, was that of witchcraft. The real reason for the attacks on the Templars, however, was their wealth and power.

The Inquisition waged a fearful war on suspected witches—in one year in Germany alone over 100,000 perished at the hands of the sanctified. The witch hysteria was at its worst from the 15th through the 17th centuries. The Protestant Reformation did nothing to lessen it. Indeed, religious fervor stimulated the hunt for witches, the secret allies of Satan. But Catholic countries did not lag far behind Protestant lands in fanaticism. It was a dreadful period of history.

King James I of England—the same King James who commissioned the famous version of the Bible—was a firm believer in witchcraft and the author of a learned manual titled *Daemonologie*. On coming to the throne of England in 1603, he decreed that all types of witchcraft should be punished by death. Yet the king began to suspect that perhaps he was mistaken, and toward the end of his reign declared that witchcraft was mere illusion. James' example did encourage a reaction against the excesses of the witch-hunters.

The last notable flare-up of witch hysteria were the notorious Salem witch trials of 1692. Apparently politics lay in the background. Cotton Mather, a renowned clergyman, was disgruntled because he felt the people of Massachusetts were not sufficiently devout. (Some historians think this was Mather's way of saying that they paid more respect to rival clergymen than to him.) So Mather, who believed that New England was a nest of pagan devils that the Indians had worshipped, issued a fusillade of sermons to prove the reality of witches, and also published an inflammatory book. Governor Phips of Massachusetts, himself in political trouble, encouraged Mather's campaign as a diversionary tactic. So when some bored and mischievous adolescent girls in Salem accused an old black slave woman named Tituba of afflicting them with fits, they had an audience ready and eager to believe them. Fifty-two innocent people were accused of witchcraft, nineteen were hanged, including an unpopular Congregational minister, and one pressed to death beneath heavy stones before the hysteria had run its course. After that there were no more trials for witchcraft in New England, though they occurred sporadically in Europe until late in the 18th century.

One of the more lurid aspects of witch lore is the witches' sabbath, also known to the cognoscenti as *sabbat* and *esbat*. These blasphemous rites featured the presence of the Devil, who was worshipped in a parody of the Catholic Mass, and ended in a sexual orgy. Actually, the witches' sabbath was invented by overstimulated members of the Inquisition. When real witch cults were organized in the 16th and 17th centuries, they patterned their rituals after what they had learned from the forced confessions of accused witches and from inquisitors' manuals. Based on such unwholesome fantasies, the rituals were grotesque. A male member of the coven stood in for the Devil; an artificial phallus enabled him to fulfill the ritual sex acts with his female colleagues. Another well-known peculiarity of witches was their ability to ride through the air on a broomstick, a talent in which accused witches apparently believed firmly. In reality, before attending a sabbat, witches would rub themselves with herbal salves containing such powerful drugs as hyoscyamine and scopolamine, which produced hallucinations including those of flying.

While all kinds of evils, from crop failures and deadly epidemics to the family cow going dry, were blamed on witchcraft, most of the actual business of witches was done in the fields of sex and revenge. Witches sold love potions and charms to attract a mate or lover; to wives with straying husbands they supplied impotency spells. They created charms to bring the plans of one's rivals to disaster. They made wax dolls that could be tortured to inflict pain or illness on an enemy. With harsher treatment of the doll, the enemy was supposed to die. Witches also dealt in poisons that were much more certain than their spells. On the benign side, they attempted to cure ailments of man and beast, usually with better success than the officially recognized physicians. The witches had a good working knowledge of medicinal herbs and were not burdened with an immense legacy of nonsense from long-dead pseudo-authorities.

Some scholars believe that one strand in the witchcraft complex is an ancient pagan cult that worshipped a horned god (hence the popular conception of the Devil as goatlike). Members of this fertility cult also worshipped brother-and-sister deities named Dia and Diana, and scattered bodies of believers in the "Old Religion" may have survived until the 18th century. Modern witch cults are based on this hypothesis of a benevolent nature worship. They do not profess to practice magic, except of the most benign and harmless kind, and they have nothing in common with Satanist cults. A few self-proclaimed witches have even appeared on television talk shows, a sure sign that people no longer take witchcraft seriously.

Zombie
Zombie, the living dead, staple of inferior horror films and cheaply thrilling nov-

els. Reanimated corpses, swaying to eerie moans as the devilish voodoo drums throb in the background, carrying out the wishes of evil magicians. Such stuff is familiar fare to addicts of fantasy, like myself. There may be a grain of fact behind the fantasy.

The word *zombie*, sometimes spelled *zombi*, came from Africa with the slaves. It may be derived from a word in the Kongo language, *zumbi*, meaning "fetish." But for centuries it has had a special meaning in voodoo parlance. It can be either a body deprived of its soul or a soul deprived of its body. The former meaning is the familiar one.

Supposedly, an unscrupulous *houngan*, or voodoo priest, would dig up a recently buried corpse and reanimate it to use as a slave. The soulless, mindless body would react to commands and carry them out like an automaton. (I would say like a robot, but robots are getting pretty smart nowadays.) It never talked back to its master, never asked for pay, didn't even have to be fed. Haitians whispered tales of zombie laborers and servants, and even now there are tales of zombies turning up in cities and villages. All the reputed zombies that have been investigated have turned out to be frauds or mentally retarded persons. But the possibility remains that zombies may actually be drugged men and women exploited as slaves. It is also speculated that evil *houngans* know of drugs that produce a temporary semblance of death. A few hours after the "corpse" is buried, the *houngan* secretly digs it up and gives it an antidote to revive it. However, the poor zombie's mind has been wiped out, and it can only respond rather clumsily and sullenly to orders. Haitian folklore holds that the master of a zombie must speak harshly to it and beat it often to make it fear him; otherwise it will rebel against him and do him harm. Is this the wish-fulfillment fantasy of generations of maltreated slaves?

EATING
and
DRINKING

Bar A bar, as anyone knows, is an establishment that serves beer, wine, and strong drink. It also exists in sissified form as a milk bar and a coffee bar. Everyone also knows that a bar is a long, thin piece of metal, wood, or other rigid stuff. There is a connection between the two, believe it or not.

Bar is a word of Latin descent, stemming ultimately from the Late Latin *barra* by way of French. In the sense of a bar of wood or metal, it was first used in English some time after the middle of the 14th century (it was then spelled *barre*). In the late 1500s it was used to denote a place where drink and food were sold to the public over a barrier or counter. To safeguard the liquor from the customers, it was usually served from a little cubbyhole with a barred window. This early kind of bar can be seen in taverns at historical restorations such as Old Williamsburg in Virginia and Old Sturbridge in Massachusetts, and it lasted into the early 19th century.

The earliest English word for a drinking establishment was *tavern*, which dates from the late 13th century and comes from the Latin *taberna*, meaning "hut" or "booth." (The same word gave us *tabernacle*, literally a little booth or tent, which now has purely religious connotations.) Drinks were also sold at inns, but these catered to travelers and provided lodging as well as food and drink—the ancient equivalent of today's mo-

177

tels. *Inn* originally meant a dwelling, the idea being that of a place with people *inside*.

Another term for a drinking establishment is *saloon*. This euphonious word came from the French *salon*, which originally meant a large, grand room for receptions. In the 19th century, the British middle and lower classes appropriated this aristocratic word and used it to mean any special-purpose establishment open to the public, such as a billiard saloon or tonsorial saloon. In the United States, however, *saloon* came to mean just one thing: a bar. Barbershops and billiard halls might call themselves "parlors" for a spurious touch of class, but "saloon" was just not respectable. As the prohibition movement gathered strength after the Civil War, the corner saloon became one of the most potent symbols in their anti-liquor propaganda.

When Prohibition cast its dread mantle over the land in 1919, people could only obtain alcoholic beverages illegally. They might buy the stuff directly from a bootlegger (so named from an early 19th-century smugglers' practice of concealing small valuables in the tall legs of their boots) or go to a clandestine bar called a speakeasy. *Speakeasy* dates from the 1880s and presumably refers to the need for speaking softly to avoid attracting the attention of the authorities, for even then many states and counties had already gone dry by local option, and illegal drinking flourished mightily in those areas.

Gaining access to a speakeasy sometimes involved a furtive ceremonial. You looked around to see that no one was watching, slunk up to the door, and knocked discreetly. A peephole would open, and an eye would examine you suspiciously. You would then deliver a secret password such as "Louie sent me," and be admitted to the temple of vice. But when the police were well taken care of by the owner, you could just walk in.

A particularly low-grade, sordid speakeasy was called a "blind pig," perhaps suggesting that only a blind pig would enter such a place. "Blind tiger" was another name for a blind pig; the idea in this case may have been that the liquor served there was poisonous enough to make you blind and so raw that drinking it felt like swallowing an angry tiger.

Beer   "Old Bill the Kaiser/Is a friend of Budweiser/And Budweiser's a friend of mine!" ran the end of a popular turn-of-the century drinking song, showing the connection between beer and Germany in the American imagination. Yet beer was invented not in Germany, but in the Near East, at least 5,000 years ago and possibly earlier. It was there, in the region known as the Fertile Crescent, that man first learned to raise grain, and beer is made from fermented grain of one kind or another. The secret of beermaking grew out of baking. Historians believe that early housewives discovered that soaking the grain and letting it sprout (a process known as malting) before grinding it up produced a bread that tasted better. The reason was that the malting process changed the starch of the grain into sugar. "Beerbread" was baked into hard biscuits that kept for a long time, and needed to be soaked in water to make them easy to chew. Soaking the beer-bread enabled wild yeasts and bacteria, always floating around in the air, to feed on the sugar and change it into alcohol. Clever brewers added herbs and spices and dates for flavoring. By 3000 B.C. the Sumerians were brewing at least nineteen types of beer of different colors and flavors. The Egyptians made only five types, but it seems to be they who developed the first true brewer's yeast, giving the beer a more uniform quality, about 1500 B.C.

Brewing, like baking, was for a long time done at home, and the first brewers were women. Women also operated small beer shops in their houses. In ancient Babylonia, these beer shops got such a bad reputation that King Hammurabi (about

1750 B.C.) issued an edict that set minimum strengths and maximum prices for the beer and also threatened the owners of the shops with death if they let political conspirators plot on their premises.

Toward the beginning of the Christian Era, grains were used mostly for food, and beer was made from dates. One Greek critic praised the Egyptian date-beer as being so sweet and aromatic that it was almost as good as wine. Otherwise, the Greeks disliked beer, which they considered fit only for barbarians. The Romans followed the Greek taste in this, as they did in so many things.

However, beer was very popular among the Celtic and Germanic tribes of northern and central Europe, where the climate was too damp and chilly to grow decent wine grapes. Grains flourished, however, particularly the hardy barley. In fact, the word *beer* itself may be related to an Old English word for barley, *bere*. The actual Old English name for beer was *beor*, pronounced *bay-or*.

From Anglo-Saxon times down to the 19th century, beer was thick and soupy, as much food as drink. In Shakespeare's day, farm workers were given a daily beer ration of two quarts as part of their wages. The Pilgrims took a supply of beer with them on the *Mayflower* in 1620, and one of the reasons they settled at Plymouth was that their beer was running out. This was no frivolous excuse: in the Europe of their day beer was safer to drink than water. Wells and streams were usually contaminated by barnyard wastes or the nearby household privy; the beer-brewing process began by boiling the malted grain and water, which killed disease organisms.

During the Middle Ages, brewers added a variety of bitter, aromatic plants to the brew to preserve it (its keg life was short at best). One of the additives was heather. Another, popular in Germany, was a mixture called *Gruit*, which consisted of bog-myrtle, wild rosemary, and yarrow. The first recorded use of hops in brewing was in 822, at a French abbey. It was not until about 1500 that hops became the standard additive. King Henry VIII of England must have disliked hops, for he banned their use in English brewing, and the ban was not lifted until several years after his death.

Although the Anglo-Saxons had a perfectly good word for beer, they preferred to call their brew *alu* or *ealu*, from which we get our word *ale*. To this day, Englishmen insist that "beer" means only the stuff that has been made with hops, while ale is not. American brewers, in contrast, define ale as being stronger and having more hops than beer. No other language that I know of makes a distinction between beer and ale.

Ale was such an important part of medieval English life that all kinds of parish festivals were called "ales," after the predominant beverage drunk at them. Lamb-ales celebrated the conclusion of the lamb-shearing season; leet-ales were held at the sessions of the local court; church-ales were held at major religious holidays such as Christmas and Easter to raise money for the church. Wedding parties were called bride-ales; our word *bridal* comes from this custom.

Lager beer originated in Germany. The name *Lager* means "storehouse"; lager beer was aged in storage for six weeks to six months before being drunk, while other kinds were drunk as soon as fermentation was completed, before they could go bad (this was before the age of pasteurization). Lagers are light in color and body; almost all beers made in America today are lager-type. Pilsner is a type of lager originally brewed at Pilsen (now Plzen) in Czechoslovakia.

Guinness is a proprietary name for a brand of *stout*, a heavy, dark, bitter beer named for its body and strength. *Porter* is a type of stout that was favored by English market porters in the 18th century.

We began this essay with a song; we shall end it with a celebrated quotation from the English poet A.E. Housman:

"Oh many a peer of England brews
Livelier liquor than the Muse,
And malt does more than Milton can
To justify God's ways to man."

Booze There is a tradition that *booze* comes from a popular brand of Pennsylvanian rye whisky of the early 19th century, sold in bottles stamped with the name of the distiller, E. M. Booz. The truth is even more prosaic than the tradition: *booze* is a modern spelling of a 13th-century English verb, *bousen*, which meant about the same as *to booze* does today. The earliest written reference is to monks who "bousen wel" but care for nothing else. However, *bouse* was not used commonly until it became thieves' cant in the 16th century. There were all sorts of derivations from the mother word, such as *bousing-ken*, which was an ale-house or a gin-shop. The current spelling dates from the 18th century.

A truly American synonym is *hooch*, which is short for *hoochinoo*. The *Oxford English Dictionary* claims it is an Alaskan Indian word for a kind of crude spirit made by the Indians from a mixture of rum and molasses or distilled from a mash of such ingredients as sugar and graham flour. In the first case the molasses was probably needed to disguise the taste of the rum, for the lowest grade of liquor was always used for trading with the Indians. On the other hand, the Indians took great pride in their ability to endure discomfort, and fur traders often adulterated their rum and brandy with pepper and vitriol to give it the bite that the Indians esteemed. The worse it tasted, the more prestige you earned for being able to swallow it.

Hoochinoo, according to the *OED*, was the name of a small tribe of Alaskan Indians who produced this local specialty. The name apparently did not attract the white man's attention un-

182

til after the great Klondike gold rush of 1896, for the *OED*'s first reference to it is 1899. Probably popularized by returning miners, and through the colorful verse of Robert Service, it became a synonym for any kind of bad (and probably illegally distilled) liquor, and during Prohibition it came to mean hard liquor in general.

Moonshine definitely takes us into the world of the illegal. It began as a late 18th-century English name for smuggled liquor. "Moonshine" had an elegant double meaning: the smugglers worked by night, with the moon to light their way, and the goods in question were light-colored spirits such as gin and white brandy. In the United States it came to refer to liquor distilled illegally in secret hideouts, often in remote mountain coves. Again, the distillers were said to work by night to escape the attention of the detested revenue agents. Since moonshiners were usually ignorant backwoods folk with no training in the finer points of distillation, their product was almost always harsh and raw, with enough of a load of impurities to produce a truly horrifying hangover the day after. Some of its many nicknames give an idea of its quality: popskull, forty-rod (admirers said it would drop a man at that distance), redeye, white mule (because of its kick), and white lightning (self-explanatory). Moonshining probably reached its height in the dry states of the South and declined when those states relaxed their puritanical restrictions in the years after World War II. The trade was not helped, either, when large numbers of poor people in Southern cities were blinded, paralyzed, or even killed outright by drinking moonshine that had been adulterated with gasoline and wood alcohol. A popular 1920s song gave excellent advice when it counseled: "Keep away from bootleg hooch/When you're on a spree"—and that goes double for moonshine.

Brandy The story of *brandy* takes us on a pleasant excursion back to about 1100 A.D., when alchemists first learned how to distill the "spirit" of wine. Evidence points to the medical school of the University of Salerno, in southern Italy, as the place where this momentous discovery was made. Alchemists had already been distilling "essences" and "spirits" of various substances for centuries, such as perfumes and flavorings, but the discovery of concentrated alcohol had profound social consequences.

Delighted with their discovery, the alchemists investigated its properties. They found that if they made it strong enough it would actually burn, so they named it *aqua ardens*, Latin for "burning water." (American Indians half a world away and half a millenium later would call it "firewater," but that was because of its taste.) Another early name for the spirit of wine was *aqua vitae*, or "water of life," which still exists in the Scandinavian *aquavit* and the French *eau de vie*.

Druggists and monks, both involved in the preparation of medicines, found that alcohol made an excellent solvent for the essential oils of medicinal herbs and spices, and that adding sugar made the aromatic beverage taste very pleasant. Medicinal liqueurs were probably being made as early as 1300, and they were common by 1400. The use of distilled beverages was given a big boost by the epidemic of the Black Death in the mid-1300s (1348–52)—people drank them to ward off the usually fatal infection, and at least the alcohol relieved their tensions temporarily.

The Dutch called wine spirits *brandewijn*, or "burnt wine," from the fact that the wine was heated over a fire to distill the alcohol. They probably adopted this name around 1400. A century or so later, the English adopted the name and turned it into "brandy-wine." The short form *brandy* did not take hold until the 1650s. The Germans call brandy *Weinbrand* or

Branntwein, which mean the same thing as the Dutch *bran-dewijn*. The Spanish call it *aguardiente*, a direct descendant of the old *aqua ardens*. Although brandy is often defined as being made from wine, it can also be made from other kinds of fermented fruit juice. Brandies made from apples (applejack and calvados), pears (perry), and plums (*Quetsch*, *Mirabelle*, and *Slivovitz*) are popular in some regions. Locally made peach brandy used to be a standard tipple in the Old South. The best-known brandy of all is *cognac*, named for the region in France where it is produced. Cognac has become an international word. *Napoleon brandy* is an especially fine and expensive cognac that was allegedly put into casks to age and mellow during the reign of Napoleon I. If any real Napoleon brandy is left now, it is almost certainly undrinkable, for distilled liquor deteriorates with time. It is said, however, that French law permits a bottler to call his cognac Napoleon brandy if it contains a tiny proportion of the original stuff. Thanks to this miraculous method of propagation, you can find Napoleon brandy on the shelves of better liquor stores anywhere. *Vive l'ingéniosité française!*

Chocolate
When Cortez and his conquistadors marched into the Mexican heartland in 1520, they found the Aztec nobles and rich men drinking a strange beverage they called *chocolatl*. It was dark, thick, and bitter in itself, but it was flavored with wild honey and vanilla pods to make a delicious drink. For some reason, the Aztecs also liked to spike it with hot peppers, which they used freely in their cookery. *Chocolatl* was whipped to a froth before it was drunk from costly mugs. The mighty Moctezuma, the Aztec emperor, drank his from goblets of gold that were thrown away after one use, thus demonstrating his wealth and power. The Mayans, too, drank *chocolatl*, mixing it with corn-

meal to stretch the expensive brew. Indeed, *chocolatl* was so highly valued that the cacao beans from which it was made served as currency. One hundred beans was the price of a slave among the Aztecs.

Cacao (pronounced *kah-kow*, to rhyme with *now*) is the Spanish version of the native Aztec name for the beans, *cacahuatl*. Why did the Aztecs have one name for the bean and another for the drink they made of it? Why do we call grapes "grapes" and their fermented juice "wine"? *Cocoa* is an English mispronunciation of *cacao*, possibly caused by confusion with another tropical product, the coconut.

Spain was always on the lookout for valuable crops, and Cortez took back samples of cacao beans with him when he returned to the motherland in 1528. The Spaniards took enthusiastically to *chocolatl*, which they simplified to *chocolate* (pronounced *cho-co-lah-tay*, not *chah-klit* or *chaw-klit*). The Spanish recipe used sugar instead of honey for sweetening, but kept the hot peppers. For a century, chocolate was a monopoly of Spain, supplied not only from Mexico but from plantations the Spaniards had established in the Caribbean islands and the island of Fernando Po, off the coast of West Africa.

In the 17th century, other European powers began to set up their own cacao plantations in their recently acquired tropical colonies. The chocolate fad spread to England, France, Italy, and beyond. By 1657 a London chocolate house was advertising itself, and in 1664 Samuel Pepys noted in his diary that he had been to a coffee-house to drink "jocolatte." "Very good," was his comment.

It was the English who began the custom of adding milk to the chocolate drink (by this time the hot pepper must have been dropped). In the early 18th century chocolate houses were fashionable gathering places for writers, politicians, merchants, and anyone who wanted to pick up interesting gossip.

Chocolate was so highly esteemed that the great botanist Linnaeus chose the name *Theobroma*, neo-Greek for "food of the gods," as the scientific name for the cacao tree.

Chocolate was originally considered a medicine—it was exotic and costly; so it *had* to have curative powers. It was also, for the same reasons, considered an aphrodisiac (although if you look at the list of foods considered aphrodisiac by various civilizations you might conclude that all most people needed was a few square meals). Chocolate is actually a powerful stimulant, as it contains an alkaloid that is chemically similar to caffeine.

A chocolate revolution took place in 1828, when a Dutch chemist named C. J. Van Houten invented a way to press the fat out of cacao beans. The remaining "chocolate cake" could then be ground into powder which could be made into cocoa just by adding hot water. In the old method, the dried beans first had to be mixed with water to a paste, which then had to be thinned down with more water, like a can of condensed soup. Twenty years later someone hit on the idea of adding some of the squeezed-out cocoa fat back to the powder and molding it into bricks to make eating chocolate. Even though sweetened with sugar, this dark chocolate was still too coarse and bitter for many people, but in 1875 an enterprising Swiss named M. D. Peter added milk to the chocolate bar to create the bland, sweet confection that most people find irresistible. Today, chocolate is one of the world's favorite flavors, in everything from cakes and cookies to ice cream. Whole cookbooks have been devoted to it, and there is even a "chocoholics' " association for chocolate addicts who want to kick the luscious but fattening habit.

Cocktail Eighteenth-century

Americans were fond of mixed drinks; during the American

Revolution, tradition says, one popular mixed drink was decorated with the tail-feather of a cock. It was, logically enough, called a *cocktail*. This particular bit of folklore sounds quite believable, even though the first written reference to a cocktail was in 1806. At that time, "cocktail" was not a general term for mixed drinks but a specific drink made from "spirits of any kind, sugar, water, and bitters." The bitters were apparently the essential ingredient, as a cocktail was also called a "bittered sling." Even as late as the early 1860s, a cocktail by definition contained bitters. The recipe for the original Martini cocktail in 1887—it was then called *Martinez*—also called for bitters along with the gin and dry vermouth. (Nowadays, sophisticates demand a Martini that is virtually pure gin.) Not until near the end of the century did drinkers relax their terminology enough to let "cocktail" mean mixed drinks in general.

Some of the favorite early cocktails, even though not yet known by that name, were cherry bounce (rum and cherry juice), bumbo (rum, molasses, and water, sometimes flavored with nutmeg), and sherry cobbler, a kind of lemonade spiked with sherry. The famous mint julep originated in an attempt to ward off malaria, which was very common in the early days of the United States, by taking a pre-breakfast tonic composed of home-made bitters (made by infusing rum, whiskey, or brandy with herbs) plus sugar to make it more palatable. Someone thought of adding a sprig of mint to freshen up the mixture, and a Southern tradition was born.

Some cocktails have been named for people, such as the Tom Collins, the Martini (was it named for a bartender called Martinez?), and the Tom and Jerry, named for two characters in a popular and raffish British novel of 1821. And we must not forget the Gibson, supposedly named for a Mr. Gibson who had to take long, liquid business lunches. In order to stay awake and sober, Gibson hit on the stratagem of having the bartender fill his "Martini" glass with plain water and to mark the substitute by garnishing it with an onion instead of the traditional olive. The onion garnish became a fad, and Gibson's sober subterfuge is now just another variant of the standard Martini. The Bloody Mary was reputedly created by a bartender on the liner *Queen Mary* as a hangover cure sometime in the 1930s.

A number of cocktails have been named for places. The Manhattan, an old standard; the Bronx (popular during Prohibition but rarely encountered now); and the Daiquiri, which was named for a town in Cuba where there was an American military base during the Spanish-American War. There are probably dozens of others, briefly popular but now languishing in utter neglect. One that was popular during World War II and immediately thereafter was the Moscow Mule, which actually honored two of our allies by combining Russian vodka and British ginger beer. It was served in a copper mug and for a brief time seemed like the acme of wickedly un-American sophistication. It tasted pretty good, too.

A great deal of sheer fantasy has gone into cocktail names. Silver Fizz, Pink Lady, Stinger, Grasshopper, French 75 (after a big artillery piece of World War I), Black Russian, Harvey Wallbanger, Foxtrot, Jamaica Ginger . . . the list could go on endlessly. At the risk of seeming Old Fashioned (whiskey, bitters, sugar, and ice, much like the original Cocktail except for the slice of orange that decorates it), I'll close the bar here.

Coffee According to Arab

tradition, around 850 A.D. a goatherd in the mountains of Yemen noticed his goats eating the bright-red berries of a certain shrub. He also noticed that the goats seemed unusually lively and frisky after this snack. The herdsman tried some of the cherry-like fruits himself and found that he, too, was stimulated. Whatever the truth of this story, local Arabs soon found out that the effective part of the fruit was its beanlike seed, and they learned how to roast the seeds, crush them, and boil them in water to make a stimulating beverage. They called their thick brew *qahwah*, which Arab lexicographers say was once the name of a kind of wine. (Another theory is that the name came from the Ethiopian highland province of Kaffa, where the coffee plant was also native.)

Qahwah quickly became popular with the Arabs as a substitute for wine, which their Muslim religion forbade. Devout Muslims also found it useful in keeping them awake during long religious services. At this, the moralists pounced and denounced *qahwah* as an intoxicant, every bit as bad as the wine the Prophet had banned. Despite the fanatics and their threats of death and God's displeasure, soberer heads prevailed, and coffee-drinking became a regular ritual of Arab and Islamic society. In Turkish, *qahwah* became *kahveh*, and Italian traders in Constantinople probably picked up this name along with the drink itself. It is believed, at any rate, that the Italian word *caffè* is the ancestor of the French and Spanish *café*, German *Kaffee*, Scandinavian *kaffe*, and English *coffee*.

Coffee houses were popular in Constantinople, and by the early 1600s they had spread to Europe. European moralists, like their early Arab confrères, were ever ready to denounce anything that appeared to give people pleasure, no matter how innocent it seemed, and they fought against the introduction of this heathen beverage from the land of the detested Turk. In Germany, for instance, one had to obtain a license to roast coffee. In England, King Charles II attempted to ban coffee houses on the grounds that they were centers of political plotting against him. However, it was no more effective than Prohibition in the United States. During the 17th and 18th centuries, coffee houses were gathering-places for intellectuals, politicians, and journalists. There, rather than in the wine-bibbing, beer-swilling taverns, was where the action was.

Coffee came early to the American colonies, and the first coffee house was licensed in Boston in 1670. But it yielded in the 18th century to tea because the price of tea was so much less. Americans began to turn to coffee again only in the War of 1812, which cut off the supply of tea from England. Coffee, however, was now being exported from South America, and this filled the gap. Coffee-drinkers were encouraged by the early temperance propagandists, who were promoting anything that could substitute for alcohol. By mid-century all but the poorest were drinking coffee.

Two popular contemporary institutions owe their names to coffee and the coffee house. The Spanish name for a coffee house was—you guessed it—*cafetería*. In the early 20th century Americans decided that this was a good name for a self-service restaurant. The usage may have begun in California, where from the days of the Gold Rush there was a romantic infatuation with all things Spanish.

In France, coffee houses came to be known as *cafés* for short. In the 19th century, cafés invaded English as a kind of restaurant where one could buy meals along with the coffee. But the French also had another kind of café, the "singing café," where the patrons were beguiled by singers and musicians as they ate and drank. People began going to the singing cafés for the entertainment rather than the food, and today a café is almost always is a nightclub, not a restaurant.

Corn

One of the baffling experiences of my youth was having to learn about the English "corn laws" in European History and finding out that they governed the importation of wheat. For *corn* in 19th-century England meant first of all grain in general and secondly wheat, the principal grain that English farmers grew.

Corn comes from the Old English *corn*, which has closely

related words in all the Germanic languages. Scholars trace them all to an ancient Indo-European root, *grnom*, which carries the meaning of a worn-down particle. The Latin word *granum*, a grain or seed, from which the English word "grain" is descended, comes from the same root. In Anglo-Saxon times, *corn* could mean either a small particle of something, such as sand or salt (today we would call it a "grain"), or else the kind of grain we use for food. *Kernel* is a diminutive form of *corn*. Although *corn* meant grain in general, it also meant the chief kind of grain in a given region. Thus, in England it meant wheat, in Scotland and Ireland oats, in Germany rye, in the Scandinavian countries barley.

So it was that when the starving Pilgrims unearthed a cache of the Indians' grain in the grim November of 1620, they called it "Indean corne." It remained "Indian corn" for a long time, and it became the mainstay of the early American colonists. A standard kind of bread was "rye-and-Injun," a mixture of corn and rye flour. (Wheat grew poorly in eastern New England, but rye, which could stand cold and damp much better, did all right.)

The first Europeans to encounter corn, however, were not Englishmen but the Spanish sailors of Columbus, in the West Indies. The Arawak Indians called this big-seeded, yellow grain with gigantic ears *mahiz*. Columbus reported this fact to his royal Spanish backers, and it has remained *maíz* in Spanish ever since. In almost all European languages, it is known by one variation or another of the Arawak-Spanish name. (Columbus is also responsible for the fact that we call the natives of the Americas Indians, for the goal of his first voyage was India, and he refused to admit that he had not reached it. He felt so strongly about this that he threatened to court-martial any member of his expedition who questioned his assertion.)

Although corn was the main food for many Indian civilizations, it was not popular in Europe. The climate was not right for it, and if it grew at all, it tasted bad. So it was fed to animals instead of people. The exceptions were in the north of Italy, where it was made into a mush called *polenta*, Rumania, where it was made into a similar dish called *mamaliga*, and Hungary, where it was eaten on the cob.

Corn, like wheat, rice, oats, rye, and barley, belongs to the grass family. Its ancestor is believed to be a now-extinct wild grass with fat, spike-like seed heads that grew in southeastern Mexico. It is thought to have been a type of pod corn, that is, each kernel had a little, separate husk around it instead of one husk enclosing the whole ear. This allowed the seeds to be dispersed when they ripened. Modern corn cannot do this. If a ripe ear falls to the ground, the seeds—assuming they are not eaten up by animals or insects—will all sprout together in a dense clump and choke each other out. For this reason, corn is the only grain that cannot reproduce without the help of man. Some researchers believe that the original wild corn crossed with another wild grass to form a cornlike hybrid called *teosinte*. Later, it crossed again with teosinte to give something more like modern corn. The oldest known corn—found in an ancient, disused cave in Mexico—may be as much as 7,000 years old. The tiny cobs are the diameter of a dime and an inch or less in length.

From this beginning, American Indians bred many kinds of corn, yellow, white, red, brown, purple, blue, and many-colored. Indian farmers of the parched Southwest grew dwarf corn only three feet tall; in Central America there is a variety that reaches twenty feet, and its stalks are strong enough to make houses and fencing. The Indians ate mostly starchy corn, the kind we call field corn. They also had sweet corn, but most tribes either disliked it or had bad luck growing it. The Iroquois were among the few tribes that raised sweet corn. However, almost every corn-raising tribe liked and grew popcorn.

All the American Indian cultures that raised corn gave it an important place in their religion, and they had elaborate ceremonials to honor the corn gods. One of the most famous was the Busk, or Green Corn Festival, of the Southeastern Indians, which celebrated the ripening of the corn crop in the fall. To begin it, the men and women of the village separated. The women cleaned out the houses, and the men swept out the council house and repaired it. All fires in the village were put out. The next day, the people purged themselves and fasted. A day of feasting on the new corn followed. On the final day, the men bathed in a river, washing away the sins of the past year, and the shaman, or priest, lit a new sacred fire in the council house. Coals from this were distributed to all the women, to relight their own fires with. And so the new year began with more feasts and a final bath of purification for everyone.

The Indians ate corn boiled, roasted, and in stews. They dried the shelled kernels and pounded or ground them to a powder which they baked into bread or the thin pancakes that the Spaniards dubbed *tortillas*. Cornmeal mush, known by a variety of names such as *suppawn*, was another common dish. Indians of the eastern United States mixed shelled corn with beans and sometimes meat to make succotash (from the Narragansett *msiquatash*). Hominy, prepared from the starchy part of the kernel, with the germ removed, is another food for which to thank (or blame) the Indians.

Gin During the Middle Ages and the Renaissance, the juniper tree and its misty-blue berries enjoyed an almost miraculous reputation as medicines. The smoke of juniper wood was supposed to prevent infection with plague and leprosy; oil of juniper rubbed into aching joints gave relief from arthritis and gout; the berries were believed to cure a long list of ills. So it was no wonder that at some point, probably in the late 1500s, druggists made an alcoholic extract

194

of juniper berries, combined with other herbal ingredients for greater effect. They called the alcoholic elixir *genèvre*, the French name for *juniper* (in modern French it is *genièvre*.) One theory is that this medicinal compound was devised by a French count who was a son of Henry IV. In the 1600s the Dutch began to make this juniper extract. They called it *jenever* (pronounced *ye-nay-fer*) because they had no sound for *zh* in their language. In the early 1700s the English took to jenever, which they often spelled Geneva, like the Swiss city, because it was difficult to keep all those confusing foreign names straight—especially when you had been medicating yourself with jenever. By 1714 the three-syllable foreign name had been abbreviated to the convenient *gin*. The English took to gin in a big way—it was cheap and highly intoxicating, and the lower classes found it a handy anodyne for their miserable lives. Soon the ruling classes, and the middle classes, too, became alarmed at the destructive effects of gin. As the poet Alexander Pope said in a footnote to one of his satirical poems, "the exorbitant use (of gin) had almost destroyed the lowest rank of the People till it was restrained by an act of Parliament . . ." Even Parliament could not control the gin plague, as the poor managed to get hold of it illegally. The great caricaturist William Hogarth created a horrifying print called *Gin Lane* to illustrate the evils of gin-bibbing. In the background is a dreadful slum with a building toppling on the drunken crowd beneath. In the center foreground, a drunken, half-naked mother lets her infant fall to its death off a flight of stairs. At the right, a skeletal drunk collapses in his last swoon, while at the left gin addicts wait in line at a pawnshop to hock their last goods for the price of a dram or two.

Gin remained the drink of the lower classes for a long time. It did not really attain respectability until the late 19th century, when bartenders invented upper-class gin drinks like the Ramos Gin Fizz and the Martini. During Prohibition, bootleggers often made gin by mixing cheap grain alcohol with turpentine or other dubious flavorings in any handy large receptacle. It was called "bathtub gin" for obvious reasons.

Eli Whitney's cotton gin had nothing to do with the beverage. In that case, "gin" was short for "engine." But the cotton gin, by making slavery profitable, may have done even more harm than the drink.

Gourmet and Gourmand

Gourmet and *gourmand* stand at opposite ends of the gastronomic spectrum. The gourmet is very fussy and choosy about what he eats and drinks, and how the food is prepared. The gourmand cares mainly that there is plenty to eat and plenty to wash it down with. Both words are borrowed from French, as is so much of our vocabulary dealing with food.

Gourmand, which is actually one of the French words for "glutton," entered English first, toward the end of the 15th century. It was then, as now, a term of reproach, but it was probably a much stronger word then because food was scarce for most people and gluttony was therefore considered a grave sin. No one has been able to trace the origin of *gourmand*, although my own theory is that it has something to do with *gorge*, meaning "throat."

Gourmet became an English word only about 1820, although it had a long history in France. Scholars think it came from an Old French word, *gromet*, which meant a serving boy or a stableboy. Somewhere along the line the meaning was upgraded to a winetaster's assistant, and the *r* changed its position. French wits probably then used the title of *gourmet* to poke fun at people who were excessively fussy about their food, and later being a gourmet became respectable.

A word often used as a synonym for *gourmet* is *epicure*. For a change, here is a word that came to English directly from

Latin instead of sneaking in by way of French. It comes from the name of Epicurus, an Athenian philosopher who lived from 342 to 270 B.C. Epicurus himself preached a very austere philosophy in which he advised his disciples to abstain from sensual pleasures. He founded a community of like-minded idealists, and they lived mainly on barley bread and water. For an occasional treat, the Epicureans indulged in cheese and a half-pint of wine. Epicurus held that the highest good in life was pleasure, which he defined as the pursuit of virtue. Later Epicureans, however, must have given virtue a different definition, for *epicureus* (the Latin form) seems always to have carried the meaning of one who cares excessively for the pleasures of the table. Poor Epicurus would be appalled if he knew what his name had come to stand for, and he really does not deserve this bum rap.

Liquor
Liquor is a Latin word for any liquid, and when it entered the English language in the early 13th century it meant just that. We pronounce it *licker* instead of *lik-wor* because we got the word in an Old French form, *licour* or *likour*. So our spelling is proper Latin, but our pronunciation is pseudo-French. But in a few decades it came to mean a liquid for drinking, particularly one that had been fermented or distilled. And in the late 1500s you could "liquor up" someone to get him drunk. The old, nonalcoholic meaning lasted for centuries, however; as late as 1806 Noah Webster defined coffee as "a liquor." Today, however, *liquor* in the sense of *liquid* is used only in specialized technical applications, such as the "chocolate liquor" that forms when cacao beans are ground to make chocolate, or certain liquids used in cookery. And in the sense of the beverage, *liquor* is generally understood to mean "hard liquor," or distilled spirits, the strong stuff.

Liqueur is a modern French form of *liquor*, and it was adopted into English in the mid-18th century to denote a sweet, aromatic, rather syrupy alcoholic beverage, quite different from the raw brandy and rum and gin that were so popular. Liqueurs, which are usually based on some secret blend of herbs or spices, are the direct descendants of the medicinal preparations that medieval monks and druggists concocted.

The early name for liqueurs was *cordials*, from the Latin *cor*, "heart." The idea was that the cordial medicine cheered, comforted, and restored the heart. This use goes back as far as the late 1300s. Chaucer used it to describe the greedy Doctor in the prologue to *the Canterbury Tales*: "For gold in phisik is a cordial/Therfore lovede he gold in special."

Since liquors and cordials are based on alcohol, it is an interesting point that *alcohol* (from the Arabic *al-kohl*) originally meant a black powder that Middle Eastern women used as eye shadow. Since *kohl* was prepared by a type of distillation, *alcohol* eventually came to mean any distilled essence and finally "alcohol of wine." From there it has been all down the hatch.

Meat

Meat comes from the Old English *mete*, which may stem from an old Germanic root, *med-*, meaning "to be fat." Originally, *meat* meant any kind of food, including bread, cheese, and vegetables. What we call "meat" the Anglo-Saxons called "flesh." It was only in the 15th century that "meat" began to refer to the flesh of animals. The original meaning still lingers on in the phrase "meat and drink" and the obsolete word "sweetmeats," which we now call "candies." For some obscure reason we do not consider the flesh of fish or shellfish to be "meat," and most people do not think of poultry as meat, although the Roman Catholic Church does for fasting purposes.

The British still persist in calling ordinary mammal meat

"butcher's meat," due to their former marketing customs. Chickens, ducks, geese, turkeys, and other poultry were sold at poulterers' shops; game (usually reserved for the gentry) had its special dealers; while the butcher dealt in the flesh of cows, sheep, and swine. *Butcher*, incidentally, originally meant a dealer in goat's meat; the word is derived from the Old French *bochier* or *bouchier*, from *bouc*, "billy-goat."

Most of our modern terms for meat are derived from Norman French, which outranked Old English in the kitchen as it did in government. *Beef*, for instance, comes from the Old French *boef*, meaning "bull," ultimately derived from the Latin *bos, bovis*, "cow." *Veal*, which is the meat of a young calf, comes from the Old French *veel, vael, veal*, and other forms, all from the Latin *vitellus*, "little calf." *Mutton* was the Old French *moton*, "sheep," probably of Celtic origin. *Pork* comes from Old French *porc*, from the Latin *porcus*, "pig."

Two exceptions are *lamb*, from the Old English *lamm* or *lomb*, and *ham*, whose Old English original meant "the hollow of the knee" and only later came to mean the thigh and buttock of an animal or a human.

A shopper would be hard put to it to find a cut of mutton at an American meat counter, although lamb is plentiful. The reason is a bit of gastronomic deception. Young animals have always been tenderer and tastier than old ones; so butchers sold mature "mutton" as young and tender "lamb." The same psychology gave us "chicken" in place of the older word "fowl," for a chicken was originally a very young hen or rooster.

If you had asked a butcher for a *cutlet* before about 1700, the chances are he would have gaped at you in bewilderment, for this word was a latecomer to English. It is a borrowing from the French word *côtelette*, meaning "little rib," from the latin *costa*, "rib." In French, the word *côte* means not only a rib but also a coast and a hill, which can be confusing for a foreigner. The French, however, always seem to know which one they are talking about.

Steak, however, goes back at least as far as the early 1400s. It comes from an old Scandinavian word, *steik*, which may be derived from a very old Germanic verb, *stikan*, and refer to meat stuck on a spit to roast it. Today *steak* always applies to beef unless othewise specified.

Chop is about the same vintage as *steak*, and originally meant a piece of meat chopped off from a larger one. Today it refers to a cut from the rib, loin, or shoulder, with a bone in it.

Primitive man, a hunter and gatherer, depended heavily on meat in his diet. But it takes a great deal of territory to support enough game for a single human to live on. Therefore hunting peoples have always been few in number, although they may have been divided into many tribes. For most of the history of civilization, meat has been a once-a-week luxury (or even less frequent) for the great mass of the people. One of the great attractions of the New World, and one about which immigrants to the United States frequently wrote home, was that even the poorest man could afford meat every day. The quality of the meat may have been wretched, but at last the peasant could feel he was the gastronomic equal of his lord back in the Old Country. And that is food, if not meat, for thought.

Rum
In the 17th and 18th centuries sugar was the chief crop of the West Indian islands, and one of the byproducts of sugar refining was molasses, a thick, dark-colored, strong-flavored syrup. Molasses was hard to market because it made an inferior sweetener. What could be done to dispose of the thousands of gallons of sticky, smelly, fly-attracting mess that each sugar mill turned out every harvest season? Some genius came up with a solution: distill it. The result was rum.

Rum

From the very beginning, rum had a controversial history. Cheap rum from the West Indies could be had for a penny or two a glass, and that was enough to cause serious drunkenness among the lower classes. In New England, colonial legislatures tried to curb the excesses of the working people by imposing a stiff tax on rum sold by the glass, which was all a laborer could afford. But if rum were sold by the barrel, the tax was low. However, only the prosperous could lay out enough money to buy five gallons or more of rum at a clip. As might be expected, a black market sprang up to circumvent the designs of the elite.

In 1657, only a few decades after the first permanent English settlement in New England, the first American rum distillery was opened in Boston. Shrewd Yankee sea captains soon followed a scheme that came to be known as the "triangular trade." They sailed with cargoes of New England rum to West Africa, where the rum was traded for slaves; then to the West Indies, where they sold the slaves and bought molasses; then back to New England, where the molasses was processed into more rum for the next round of trading. A tidy profit was made at each stage.

Rum was also an important item in the fur trade, in which English and French traders competed furiously for the business of the Indians. Both sides dispensed liquor freely, both to put the Indians in a receptive frame of mind and also to reduce their bargaining ability. On their part, the Indians loved the white man's "firewater" and the effects it produced on them. It is tempting to speculate that the Indians enjoyed being drunk because their everyday lives were so strictly ruled by convention, from which the alcohol temporarily freed them. At any rate, they demanded free drinks as an essential precondition of trade. With a misplaced touch of poetic euphemism they called brandy "French milk" and rum "English milk." The traders took advantage of the Indians by watering the liquor and adulterating it with such substances as tobacco juice and vitriol to give it the proper color and fiery taste.

Unlike other kinds of ardent spirits, the origin of rum's name is shrouded in mystery. Its first name seems to have been "kill-devil," but this was soon replaced by "rumbullion" or "rumbustion." These words may have had some connection with tumult or hell-raising behavior, to both of which rum was a generous contributor. Another possibility is that *rum* came from 16th-century thieves' cant, in which *rum* meant "very good" and *rum bowse* meant "good drink."

Rum was, as we mentioned above, one of the favorite drinks of the lower classes. As such, it was one of the first targets of the 19th-century prohibition movement. Prohibitionists personified it as Demon Rum and preached fiery sermons against it. Even gin and whiskey did not get such star billing, although as the 19th century rolled on they surely made just as many people drunk, with equally harmful results. Today, however, rum is no longer considered the bane of the poor. It is associated with exotic tropical drinks at some island vacation paradise.

Salad Not long after the middle of the 15th century, a new word entered the English vocabulary: *salad*. Although the word was new, the dish it described was not, for man has eaten raw vegetables since his earliest days. Strangely enough, the word *salad* did not sprout from some ancient root having to do with vegetables or greens. it comes from the popular Latin *salata*, "that which is salted," from *sal*, "salt." Salt water was one of the earliest salad dressings, although oil, vinegar, and herb flavorings also go back to ancient times. The Romans must have used a lot of vinegar on their salads, because the classical Latin word for "salad" is *acetaria*, from *acetum*, "vinegar."

Salad

Salad was once commonly spelled *sallad* and *sallet*. Literary folk sometimes use the phrase "salad days," as in "Hemingway's salad days in Paris." I always thought this meant a period when the person in question was flourishing like a vigorous head of lettuce, and my astonishment was great when, in researching this book, I learned that it really meant a time of youth and inexperience. "Salad days" goes back to Shakespeare, who served it up in *Antony and Cleopatra*, making Cleopatra say, "My salad days, when I was green in judgement: cold in blood . . ."

Salad has for centuries been an internationally used food term. The French *salade* (from which the English *salad* comes), Spanish *ensalada*, Italian *insalata*, German *Salat*, and Swedish *sallad* are all easily recognizable. So is the Russian *салатб2*, if you can decipher the Cyrillic characters. In formal Dutch, a salad is a *salade*, but a short form was *sla*. Dutch settlers in New Amsterdam ate a great deal of a dish they called *kool sla*, or cabbage salad. With a slight change in spelling, this is our coleslaw.

Only a philologist would connect *sauce* with *salad*, but the fact is that both have to do with salt. *Sauce* comes from the medieval French *sauce*, which comes from *salsa*, another Latin variant on "salted." Sauces in the Middle Ages were heavily salted, and also strong on vinegar and pepper in order to disguise the taste of spoiled meat. Tart and pungent sauces were so standard that the meaning was transferred to "saucy" in the sense of "impertinent."

Salt is vital for people and animals. Until 19th-century technology gave the world cheap, mass-produced salt, salt was a costly necessity. In medieval times, a person's rank determined whether he or she was seated above or below the salt. Above the salt was close to the host and a place of honor. Below the salt was another of the many symbols of low rank in which medieval society delighted. During the Roman Empire, soldiers were given part of their pay in salt; this was called a *salarium* and is the origin of today's *salary*. It also gave us the expression "worth one's salt." Salt is also connected to the modern oil industry, partly because the great oil pools of the world formed beneath underground layers of salt, and partly because the derricks that 19th-century salt producers used to drill for brine inspired a New York lawyer named George Bissell. He hired an obscure ex-railroad conductor named Edwin L. Drake to drill for oil at the petroleum springs of Titusville, Pa., making possible the mass production of oil and giving John D. Rockefeller his start.

Whiskey
Probably no liquor has loomed as large in American folklore as whiskey. Yet whiskey was a relative latecomer to the American scene. The early colonists drank prodigious quantities of rum and brandy. Whiskey was ignored as a tipple fit only for Scotch and Irish barbarians—except in the isolated valleys of the Appalachians, where Scotch-Irish pioneers began to make their way in the early 1700s. (It was not that they had any special desire to become backwoodsmen—it was simply that the better land east of the mountains had already been taken by earlier arrivals.)

Anyone living in the mountains had to be self-sufficient. The mountain settlements were far from the market towns of the lowlands, and there were no roads to reach them—only narrow trails. A trip to town to buy a jug of rum was out of the question. Instead, the Scotch-Irish began to distill the beverage of their homeland, a spirit made from grain, which they called whiskey.

Whiskey is a worn-down form of the Gaelic *uisge beatha*, which means "water of life," a direct translation of the medieval alchemists' *aqua vitae*. The Irish pronounced it "ishkeba-ha"; the Scots apparently called it "usquebaugh." But another form, "whiskybae," must have been more popular, for this gave us "whiskey."

Up through the American Revolution, whiskey was pretty well ignored, except along the frontier where it was made and drunk. But in 1794 it burst upon the consciousness of the newly-fledged United States like a bombshell. The farmers of western Pennsylvania, most of them Scotch-Irish, raised a good deal of corn, and they wanted to sell it for ready cash. However, packing this bulky, low-priced crop on horseback across the mountains to the market centers would have eaten all their profit. But if they turned it into whiskey and shipped it east, they could make enough money to pay their land taxes and have a little left over to spend on their families. In 1791 Alexander Hamilton, then Secretary of the Treasury, persuaded Congress to impose an excise tax on distilled spirits. This hit the Pennsylvanians hard, since it struck at their one cash crop. Americans resented excise taxes anyway—think of the Stamp Act and the Boston Tea Party—and the men of western Pennsylvania reacted violently. There were angry confrontations and riots; in some cases the Federal tax collector was tarred and feathered, an exceedingly unpleasant experience. Finally, in 1794, President Washington was persuaded that the national government could not safely ignore this threat to its authority, and he sent 15,000 militiamen, led by General Henry Lee and Hamilton himself, to quell the uprising. Faced with these odds, the Whiskey Insurrection collapsed without bloodshed. Hamilton's enemies accused him of fomenting the whole affair to demonstrate the power of the Federal Government and, not coincidentally, to aggrandize himself.

As the western lands of the Ohio Valley began to fill up with settlers, the demand for whiskey more than kept pace. As early as 1811 there were more than 2,000 distillers in Kentucky alone. But it was the War of 1812 that gave whiskey its toehold in the East by cutting off the supply of cheap molasses from the West Indies and thus raising the price of rum. By the 1820s whiskey was well-established even in such cosmopolitan ports as New York. It was still a frontiersman's drink *par excellence*, however, and for the rest of the 19th century it served as a kind of national symbol, along with the eagle, the log cabin, and the farm boy who became President. Gin and rum were scorned as effete.

Scotch whiskey is made from barley. Its smoky taste comes from drying the malt over a fire of peat. The first whiskey made in America, however, was rye. Then the backyard distillers tried adding corn, which was easier to raise. They liked the taste, and eventually switched to pure corn whiskey. Bourbon is a corn whiskey (by law it must be at least 51 percent corn) and got its name from Bourbon County, Kentucky, a center of distilling. It is one of history's pleasanter ironies that a drink named for autocratic European kings came to be a democratic beverage.

Wine   Wine was man's second earliest alcoholic beverage. The first was almost certainly mead, which is fermented honey, nature's most concentrated source of sugar. A part-full pot of honey, left out in the rain, ferments easily with the aid of the ever-present wild yeasts, and some experimental Neolithic man or woman, tasting the liquid, found that it was not spoiled, but gave the drinker a pleasant sensation. Later, early farmers found that sweet fruits could also be fermented to make a pleasant drink, and we call the result *wine*.

Wine almost certainly originated in the Near East, the cradle of agriculture. It may have been the Egyptians who first made wine—at any rate, they were making it when they began to record their history. Date wine was the most popular in ancient Egypt, and in Mesopotamia too. It was often flavored with herbs and spices and made even sweeter with honey.

Until quite late in their history, the Egyptians used grape wine only for temple rituals. However, the Hebrews made wine of grapes, as did the Greeks. The Bible credits Noah with the invention of wine, but the Greeks believed that it was given to mankind by the god Dionysos. The Greeks drank a lot of wine, but they drank it diluted with water. At their feasts, a master of ceremonies shouted out the correct ratios, such as three parts water to one part wine, to the guests before each round of drinks. To drink one's wine neat was considered extremely ill-bred. The Greeks stored their wine in huge pottery jars that they coated inside with resin to keep the wine from leaking through (Greek pottery was rather porous), and the wine took on the taste of the resin. Since this was what they were used to, the Greeks came to think that this was the way wine *ought* to taste. The modern Greek wine called Retsina preserves this tradition.

The Romans, who were the great wine-bibbers of antiquity, put grape-growing on an almost scientific basis. They developed a number of varieties of grapes and became every bit as snobbish about wines as the French of later years. For the Romans, the sweeter a wine was, the better. They did not rely solely on nature to provide the sweetness, but added their own in the form of honey or boiled-down grape juice called *defrutum*.

Scholars believe that the Romans learned how to raise grapes and make wine from the Greek colonies in southern Italy, and the Greeks in turn learned about wine from the Near East. In fact, Greek mythology states that the wine-god Dionysos came from Asia Minor, disgusted because the natives there drank only beer. But it was the Romans who spread wine-growing to Spain, France, Germany, and even Britain. It was also the Romans who gave us the proverb *"In vino veritas,"* or "In wine (there is) truth."

Wine

The Greek name for wine, *woinos* or *oinos*, probably came from a Semitic original that sounded much the same. The Roman *vinum* may have come from the Greeks, or it may have come from the Near East by a separate route. *Vinum* gave rise to offspring in many languages, such as the French *vin*, the Spanish and Italian *vino*, Welsh and Breton *gwin*, Old Norse *vin*, German *Wein*, and Old English *win*. *Vinum*, via trade, even entered languages whose homelands the Roman legions had never penetrated, giving us the Irish *fin* and Lithuanian *vynas*.

The downfall of the Western Roman Empire was a setback for Europe's wine-growers, but the vine never died out completely. Monasteries, in particular, kept vineyards going for the sacramental wine that is an essential part of Roman Catholic ritual. During the Middle Ages wine again became the drink of the rich. Poor people drank beer or cider, except around the Mediterranean, where they drank cheap, thin, sour wine. There was no nonsense then about the superiority of dry wines—heavy, sweet wines got the top prices. The preference for dry wines is a 19th-century phenomenon, sparked by the masochistic English snobbery that also exalted cold showers in the morning and tasteless food at any time. Since England at that point was a trend-setter for the rest of the world, this taste prevailed. Anyone for a nice tumbler of Manischewitz Concord wine? (Actually, most people agree that a moderately dry wine goes better with most foods than a sweet one, but it took 19th-century science and technology to produce a dry wine that did not pucker the drinker's mouth.)

DRESS

Brassiere When I was a boy, the word *brassiere* was taboo in mixed company because of its quasi-sexual connotations. Yet the word itself is an outrageous euphemism, having nothing at all to do with the objects it supports. It comes from a medieval French word for a piece of armor: *bracière*, meaning "arm-guard." How a word for military hardware came to be used for a woman's undergarment is a mystery, but it is certainly a triumph for Anglo-American prudery. Actually, the French are pretty prudish about it, too; the French term for a brassiere is *soutien-gorge*, literally "throat supporter." German is more to the point with *Büsten-halter*, or "bust-holder." But then *bust* itself is a euphemism. Appearing around the mid-17th century in various Romance languages, it originally referred to the head, shoulders, and chest of a statue. About 1727 it was used as a euphemism for a woman's bosom, which originally referred to the chest rather than the mammaries. Prudery will go to almost any length to avoid saying "breast."

Breast itself is a reverse example of what we have been discussing. In Anglo-Saxon times it originally referred to the mammary organs; later, by extension, it was used for the entire chest. Still later, it was applied to the corresponding parts of animals and birds, so that we now speak of chicken breasts, breast of veal, and the breast feathers of birds.

Brassiere

The brassiere did not come into use until the early 1900s. Before then, women's breasts were either unsupported or pushed up by a stiff girdle or bodice. For most of the world, they hung loose. At certain times and in certain cultures they were strapped down as flat as possible, as in 16th-century Europe (a fashion started by Spain) and in the "flapper" era of the 1920s in the United States and western Europe. The idea may have been partly to de-emphasize female sexuality, but a more influential factor was probably that large breasts were associated with peasants and wet-nurses and were therefore unfashionable. But in periods when full breasts were in favor, "gay deceivers," or bosom pads, were freely used to make up for nature's lack.

In the 19th century, mass production put girdles within reach of most women in the industrialized nations, a very mixed blessing even if they did support the breasts by means of a shelf at the top. Girdles, made of whalebone or spring steel, constrained the torso into very uncomfortable and unnatural positions and made motion difficult. It is no coincidence, as many writers have pointed out, that the Victorian period was the great age of female weaknesses. The brassiere must have come as a great relief when it replaced the all-confining girdle (girdles survived, but in smaller and more flexible form).

Early brassieres (they weren't called bras until about 1920) were almost a throwback to the original piece-of-armor sense of the word. Stiffly wired or boned, they formed the breasts into artfully designed contours and served as a kind of chastity device, even as they drew attention. The soft, "natural" bra did not come into fashion until the late 1960s, when many young women gave up brassieres entirely. In 1968, a wave of bra-burnings swept the country as furious feminists and their followers demonstrated their contempt for what they said was a symbol of male oppression. Yet the bra never disappeared entirely. Brassieres definitely make life more comfortable for women with large, heavy breasts. On the job, many women found that they preferred not to have their male co-workers staring mesmerized at their braless bosoms. Jogging has taught many women that it is more comfortable to run with breast support than without. Men will watch future developments with interest.

Breeches

Breeches comes from the Old English *brec* or *brych*, which comes from an old Teutonic root, *broc*, referring to a garment that covers the loins and thighs, as the dictionary delicately puts it, or about the same area as a pair of Bermuda shorts. The Greeks and Romans had no word for breeches, or for any kind of pants, since they did not wear them. Trousers were for northern barbarians like the Scythians and Celts and Germans. In fact, trousers were a northern invention, made necessary by the cold. The Mediterranean peoples, however, could get by with nothing but a sheet draped around their torsos. In warmer areas, such as Egypt, poor people and slaves often had no more than a loincloth. Breeches were introduced to Rome in the 4th century A.D. by legionaries returning from the chill northern outposts. They were known by their Celtic name of *braccae*. Even the Romans had to admit they were practical, and in time they were almost universally worn.

For a long time—down to the 17th century, in fact—some people used "breech" as a singular noun, like "shirt" or "jacket." But the plural form was used alongside it from the beginning of the 13th century. Apparently no one spoke of a *pair* of breeches until the 15th century.

About the 16th century, *breech* was extended to the part of the body that is covered by breeches—the rear end. Hence, by analogy, the breech-loading gun.

211

Breeches

Breeches went through many changes of style. Sometimes they barely descended below the groin—but to compensate for this they were fantastically puffed and slashed. At other times they went down to the knee. During the 16th and 17th centuries breeches were so voluminous that a fashionable man could hardly walk. In the 18th century, tight-fitting knee-breeches were the fashion, ornamented with silver buckles at the knee—jeweled, if the owner were wealthy enough. Such fancy pants were *de rigeur* at the courts of Europe, and especially at the court of France. The French called them *culottes* (from *cul*, "backside"), and they became a symbol of the Old Order during the French Revolution. The Revolutionaries called themselves *sans-culottes* ("without breeches") and proudly wore the long trousers of the urban working classes. Breeches made a brief comeback with the end of the French Revolution, but trousers soon conquered them permanently, except at court functions, where they endured along with other deliberately antique sartorial symbols of rank and privilege. In 1938, Joseph Kennedy, then Ambassador to Great Britain, caused a stir by appearing at a royal reception in white tie, tailcoat, and long trousers instead of the hallowed breeches. British conservatives reacted with shock and horror, while Americans generally applauded the gesture. The King and Queen took it in stride and did not send Ambassador Kennedy home in disgrace to change.

A peculiar kind of knee-breeches called "plus-fours" came into fashion in the late 19th century when the game of golf became popular. Originally worn only for golf, they had an elastic band just below the knee and enough extra material to hang down four inches below that. Their looseness made striding around a golf course easy. In the United States they came to be known as knickerbockers, from the knee-breeches worn by the comic Dutchmen in the illustrations of Washington Irving's historical spoof, *Knickerbocker's History of New York*. Knick-

erbocker is a real name, and a few of the early Dutch settlers in New Amsterdam bore it. It is thought to mean a baker of clay marbles, *knickers* in Dutch. Knickerbockers—knickers for short—used to be standard wear for boys who were not exactly little children any longer, but were not yet grown men. It was a proud day for a boy when he graduated from the short pants of childhood to the knickerbockers of near-adolescence. At one time, women wore a briefer form of knickerbockers as under-pants; in England, women's panties are still called "knickers" to the confusion of Americans.

Returning to *breeches*, bibliophiles get a lot of slightly naughty fun over the so-called "Breeches Bible," which tells of Adam and Eve making breeches for themselves from fig leaves. This particular Bible was published in 1560, but the phrasing was nothing new and original. Wycliffe had used it already in 1382.

Coat

Coat comes from the Old French *cote*, which is derived from the medieval Latin word *cotta*, a rough, heavy sort of outer garment. The *cotta* may have originated as a cloak and was later given sleeves. Or it may have begun as a workman's smock that was cut open down the front for convenience in putting it on. Romans of classical times would have had no word for it, since they didn't wear coats. In cold weather, they simply draped an extra cloak around their bodies. It was the northern peoples and the horse-men of the Central Asiatic steppes who wore coats.

In the mid-12th century, knights began to wear a long, sleeveless coat over their armor, probably to keep the sun's rays from overheating it. Some called it a *surcoat* (literally "over-coat"); others called it a *coat of arms* because it went over the armor. The knights were already painting heraldic symbols on their shields to identify themselves in battle and in tournaments, and soon enough they had them embroidered on the coat of arms. Eventually *coat of arms* stopped referring to the actual coat and meant only the heraldic symbols.

Turncoat means a person who changes sides in a dispute for personal advantage, or even a traitor. It dates back to the 16th century, when soldiers of certain regiments were given distinctively colored coats to wear—the first uniforms since the days of the Roman legions. Supposedly some soldiers, when they saw their side was losing a battle, would turn their coats inside out and make their escape as "civilians."

In the Middle Ages, *coat* was also used to translate the Biblical Latin, Greek, and Hebrew words for a tunic, an almost universal ancient Mediterranean garment that resembled an extra-long T-shirt or sweatshirt. Joseph's "coat of many colors" in the Exodus story must have been one such. It would have been costly because it had to be pieced together out of differently dyed strips of material, and thus a clear indication of his father's favoritism. Coupled with Joseph's incessant bragging about his prophetic dreams of glory, who could blame his brothers for wanting to get rid of the insufferable boy?

Cotton

Cotton is the soft fibers surrounding the seeds of the cotton plant, a bush or small tree related to the hibiscus and rose-of-sharon. It was probably originally native to India and spread from there to other regions with frost-free winters or at least a long growing season. Cotton cloth was being made in India as early as 3000 B.C. In the Greco-Roman world, fine cotton textiles from India were prized almost as highly as silk. Greeks and Romans called it *gossypion* or *gossypium*, which is its botanical name today.

During the breakdown of the Roman Empire, cotton disappeared from Europe. But the trade routes were gradually reestablished, and cotton may have reached England as early as the 11th century. Cotton was still an upper-class fiber because it had to be shipped across territories whose rulers exacted tolls, and this kept the price high. It was called by the French name of *coton*, which was derived from the Arabic name *qutun*. Perhaps returning Crusaders brought the Arabic name back from the Near East along with the soft, comfortable, easily washable material. But fine cloth was not the only use for cotton. It was also used for stuffing cushions, mattresses, and a padded garment called the *hacqueton* or *acton* (from the Arabic *al-qutun*, "the cotton") that was worn under chain mail to cushion the blows of swords and spears. It was also used to make candle wicks.

Medieval Europeans knew little about cotton except that it was like a super-soft wool and grew on a "tree." Thus, they fantasized about a "vegetable lamb" that was borne on a tree and was permanently fastened to it by an umbilical cord. The lamb grazed contentedly on the grass around the tree, but when all the grass within the range its cord allowed it was gone, it starved to death. Then its fleece was harvested for the benefit of Man. Some charming pictures of the vegetable lamb, or *barometz* (a Russian word) survive in medieval bestiaries.

It was the spice trade that took Europeans to India in the early 1500s but cotton prints soon became a major item in the East India export trade. European cotton mills were established to keep up with the demand, using cotton grown in Egypt and the Near East. New cotton plantations were established in the Caribbean and South America. Even so, cotton fiber was in short supply. In the late 18th century, American planters in the southern states began to grow cotton—but they had a severe problem: how to separate the cotton fibers from the fuzzy seeds. The kind of cotton that grew in India and the Near East did not present this problem. Its fibers were long and silky, and the seeds were smooth. The seeds could be separated from the fiber simply by pulling a wad of the stuff through a coarse comb. An easier and faster method was to feed the cotton through a device that the Indians called a *churka* but the English called a *gin* (short for "engine"). It resembled an old-fashioned, hand-cranked laundry wringer. The slight pressure of the turning, fluted rollers squeezed the seeds out neatly. But the kind of cotton that grew in the United States—except in a few favored places like Georgia's Sea Islands—had short, curly fibers and fuzz-covered seeds that clung to the fiber like obstinate burrs. A slave picking out the seeds by hand might, on a good day, produce a pound of cleaned cotton—not enough to cover the costs of plowing, planting, weeding, and picking. The cotton planters, on the verge of bankruptcy, were in despair.

Enter now the savior in the person of a Yale-educated Yankee tutor on a Georgia plantation. His name was Eli Whitney. Soon after arriving at his post, Whitney was almost buried alive under the incessant complaints about the cotton-planters' predicament. Although his education had been classical, Whitney had a native flair for things mechanical, and he devised a gin that was able to clean the seeds of the short-fibered upland cotton so efficiently that his basic design is still used today. In essence, it was a roller studded with stiff wire hooks that passed through a slotted plate. As they turned, the hooks grabbed the cotton fibers and pulled them on through the slots, while the seeds, torn free, fell off on the ground. Whitney's first hand-cranked model of 1793 upped the production rate to 50 pounds a day. Using a horse or a water wheel for power, productivity was increased manyfold.

Whitney's gin saved the day for the cotton planters and brought new wealth to the South. It also contributed to the prosperity of the new mill towns of the North. But it had another effect that in the long run far outweighed its benefits: it gave new life to the institution of slavery by making it profitable again. And it was slavery that lay at the root of the conflict that grew into the Civil War and left America with a race problem that still is not solved.

Cravat

The story of the cravat goes back to the Thirty Years' War (1618–1648), a power struggle that ravaged Germany and much of Central Europe. Most of the fighting was done by mercenaries, though most of the suffering was done by civilians, and a notable supplier of mercenaries was the kingdom of Croatia (now a part of Yugoslavia). The Croatian soldiers were renowned, if not notorious, for their fierceness and dash. They wore a kind of long linen scarf around their necks, tied in a big bow with long ends, which was much admired. It was named cravat after them—a French version of "Croat." (The Croats called themselves *Hrvati* or *Khrvati*. Their neighbors, who found all these consonants difficult to pronounce, called them *Chrobati, Chrovati*, and *Horvati*. No doubt during the war they also called them bloodthirsty devils.)

The cravat became the rage all over Europe, especially since Louis XIV of France, the fashion leader of the Western world, favored cravats of lace. Louis even posed for a marble bust in a cravat, along with what looks like an anachronistic Roman toga. The cravat was no doubt far more comfortable and easier to take care of than the great, cartwheel-like starched ruff of the Elizabethan era. (On the other hand, some authorities claim that the ruff served the practical purpose of intercepting spilled food before it fell on one's clothes.)

Not everyone was enamored of the cravat—every fashion has its detractors. In 1676 one English moralist lamented that a man's worth should be judged by how neatly he tied his cravat. A decade or so later, another English writer sneered that a cravat was "nothing but a long towel put around the collar." But

Diaper

these complaints were mere bubbles on the rushing stream of popularity: by the early 1670s the anxious man-about-town could find ready-tied cravats for sale.

And so the cravat continued to encircle men's necks until the early 19th century, when it began to metamorphose into a modest-sized bow tie. Eventually, the modern necktie descended from it. Scarves worn in place of a necktie are still called cravats, but fortunately their wearers no longer behave like violent and rapacious soldiers-of-fortune.

Diaper A diaper is a cloth (or even a disposable hunk of absorbent paper) that is wrapped around a baby's bottom to catch its infantine excretions. This is indeed a comedown for a word that once referred to a fine fabric that once adorned Byzantine bishops and other dignataries.

Diaper comes from the Greek *diaspros*, meaning roughly "white all the way through" (from *dia-*, "through," plus *aspros*, "white"). The original diaper fabric was probably conceived in the 10th century, for we read of a newly invested rector of a Byzantine church being draped in a cloak of diaper. The finest diaper was woven of silk, with a diamond-shaped pattern to the weave that caught the light and made the garment shimmer. Sometimes gold or silver threads were woven in to increase the luster of the cloth. A less fancy grade of diaper was made of linen or cotton. Diaper was not always a diamond weave; it was often woven in a white-on-white floral pattern. The design of diaper so impressed artists that the name was also given to certain decorative architectural patterns.

As usual, the new material reached France before it reached England. The French dropped the s in the middle of the name and turned it into *diapre*. The English then made it *diaper*.

218

Since the late 16th century, Englishmen have used *diaper* to mean a towel or napkin of diaper fabric. Even when Noah Webster dictionarified the American language in the early 19th century, that was all that *diaper* meant. It did not become a baby's bottom-wrapping until the mid-19th century, probably as the same sort of prissy euphemism that referred to a man's trousers as "inexpressibles," a bull as a "gentleman cow," and a piano's legs as its "limbs." By the way, in Britain diapers are known as "nappies."

Galoshes

Could you imagine Julius Caesar in a pair of galoshes? It's not likely that the aristocratic Caesar would have worn such plebeian garb, but the Romans did indeed have galoshes of wood. The popular Latin name for them was *galopia*, a Romanized form of the Greek *kalopous*, which meant "shoemaker's last" but whose component words really meant "foot-logs."

The Roman galosh was a wooden clog or sandal, worn mostly by farmhands. But there was another model for wet weather, a wooden platform several inches high, which was intended to raise the wearer above mud and puddles—at least on the paved streets of the cities. On muddy country lanes it was a different matter.

In the Middle Ages, the Latin *galopia* became the French *galoche*, a name that the English took over. At that period, *galoche*, or *galosh*, as it was later spelled, may have been just another name for a boot or shoe. Chroniclers refer to galoshes made of velvet or fitted with buckles of gold, which hardly sounds like rainwear, even for the privileged classes. But by the late 17th century galoshes began to be defined as overshoes. These overshoes were of leather, heavily waxed or greased to keep out the water. Rubber overshoes had to wait until Charles Goodyear discovered the process of vulcanizing rubber in the 19th century. (Goodyear perfected the process in 1839 but did not patent it until 1845. In the meantime, a clever Britisher had seen a sample of Goodyear's rubber and literally sniffed out the secret. He patented the process in Britain in 1843.)

Another name for galoshes is *arctics*, which were first used in the United States in the late 19th century. Arctics were originally a heavy, warmly lined overshoe for winter wear, hence the name. I have a tantalizing suspicion that they were first designed for Arctic explorers, but I cannot track it down.

Hose

Hose today means stockings or socks, but originally it was a kind of legging, and for a time it meant "pants." *Hose* comes from the Old English *hosa* or *hose* (*hosen* in the plural), and as a garment they go back at least to A.D. 1000.

Originally, hose stretched from the hip to the ankle, though sometimes they covered the foot as well, like a very long stocking. These separate hose were tied to the doublet (a short, jacket-like upper garment) with *points*, which were strong cords with metal tips, rather like shoelaces. They were supposed to overlap at the top to cover certain portions of the anatomy, but often they did not. In the 14th century, skintight hose and short doublets were in fashion. The doublets were so short that when a man bent over, the cleft between his buttocks was exposed. All too often, there was an embarrassing gap in front as well. Obviously, this kind of exposure could not be tolerated in the common folk; so an English law decreed that no one below the rank of gentleman was permitted to wear a coat so short that when he stood erect it failed to cover his buttocks.

A solution for this social problem was found around 1370, when someone hit upon the idea of fastening the two separate hose together at the seat. A movable triangle of cloth closed the frontal gap. Hose were now pants; in German, pants are still called *Hosen*, while a stocking is a *Strumpf*. But hose became stockings in another fashion maneuver.

Some time around 1550, the daring new fad was to divide the hose again, but this time into upper and lower components. The upper hose, which could be anything from baggy shorts to knee-length breeches, were called "trunk hose" or "upper stocks." The lower portions were called "lower hose" or "nether stocks," from which *stockings* is derived.

Meanwhile, the cloth triangle at the front of the united hose blossomed into that curious and rather obscene accessory called the *codpiece*. Its name was derived not from the cod-fish, but from an old meaning of *cod*, in the sense of a bag or pouch, or by analogy, the scrotum. The codpiece in fact began as a simple pouch for the male organs, but soon became the male equivalent of the padded bra. Fantastically padded and boned to exaggerate the size of the wearer's genitals, it assumed the semblance of a permanent erection. The codpiece reached its height of phallic mimicry in the 1560s, but soon thereafter began to detumesce. By 1600 it had disappeared.

Another name for the codpiece, and an apt one, was the French term *braguette*, which means just what one might think. (It comes from the 16th-century French verb *braguer*, "to brag.") But the codpiece was not just a brag-piece; it also had its practical uses. It commonly served as a handy pocket for small items and it was also used as a pincushion, for fashionable men's costumes needed numerous pins to keep them properly draped. Another use, though not a common one, was to support a flagstaff in processions. The codpiece could do this because its stuffing and bone framework made it stiff, and it was tied securely to the doublet and hose.

Hose in the sense of a flexible tube, like a garden hose, is a spin-off from the sense of *hose* as a kind of sheath. It dates back at least to the late 15th century, when writers spoke of hoses for ship's pumps. Hoses then were made of leather, greased to keep it waterproof and flexible, or of tarred canvas. Canvas is still used for fire hoses because of its strength, but for other purposes rubber or plastic is used.

Another spinoff of *hose* in the sense of a sheath was used in botany. Some flowers with a double set of petals were described as "hose-in-hose." I never encountered this term until I researched this entry. Have you?

Jacket

The jacket is descended from a garment worn by French peasants in the 14th century. The French name for it was *jaque* ("jack" in English), and it was almost certainly named so in derision of the peasants who wore it. *Jacques* was the generic French name for a peasant, just as *Hick* (a nickname for Richard) was the contemporary English name for a rustic, and *Rube* (short for Reuben) was the 19th-century American equivalent. *Jacquet* ("jacket" in English) was the diminutive form of *jaque*. The original jack was a short, close-fitting sort of vest, opening down the front and usually without sleeves.

Another form of the jack was worn by common soldiers, who could not afford armor. This was a quilted leather jacket that gave fairly good protection against sword cuts. In later centuries it was made more effective by facing it with plates of horn or steel.

The peasant's jacket was adapted in the 16th century by the German *Landsknechte*, mercenary soldiers who were employed by all the major powers of Europe. (They were also known as *lansquenets*, a French version of their name.) The *Landsknechte* liked the freedom of motion that the jacket gave them, and they disdained the uncomfortable, confining body armor. Boldly defying convention, they slashed their jackets and breeches to give them more freedom, then lined the slits with brightly colored material that gave a fine display for the girls and ended up setting the style for the stylish. The *Landsknechte's* detractors claimed that the reason they slashed their garments was because they stole them from civilians, and they wouldn't fit without the slashing.

The next big mutation of the jacket was to the *justaucorps* (French for "fitting close to the body"), not long after the 1650s. Louis XIV may have set the fashion, as he did in so many things. At any rate, he designed a special *justaucorps*, blue with a red lining and gold embroidery. These were given to favorite members of the court. The King himself wore brown, his favorite color. The *justaucorps*, which reached to the knee, remained the fashion through the 18th century. Young sartorial revolutionaries cut away the lower front portion of the *justaucorps* to create the frock coat, short in front and long in back, which was the standard for decades. Toward the end of the 19th century the hip-length "round jacket," so called because it was the same length all the way around, gained popularity for upper-class sporting wear. Somewhat modified, it is still with us even though the old upper-class way of life is long since vanished.

One relic of the old order is the *tuxedo*. The tuxedo began in the mid-19th century as the "smoking jacket," which was worn by European gentlemen at informal evening get-togethers for men only. It was first worn as formal dress in 1886, at a ball in the wealthy community of Tuxedo Park, New York. The daring man who first wore it was the young tobacco heir Griswold Lorillard, who was so rich that he could easily defy convention and get away with it. In so doing, he started a new convention.

In much of Europe, the tuxedo is still called a "smoking." The British insist that it is a "dinner jacket," as do social climbers over here. Up through the 1950s, men customarily struggled into tuxedo outfits, including the infamous boiled shirt, when they went out to dances. Now they are worn mainly to high-school proms, and not very many men own one any more. It is so easy to rent one.

Jeans

Jeans, now a high-fashion item, began as a sturdy workingman's garment. The name is derived from a medieval English perversion of Genoa, and it was originally "Genoa fustian." Fustian was a coarse, heavy twilled cloth of cotton and linen, used for work clothes; it also came to mean bombastic talk, and Shakespeare used it in that sense. *Fustian* brings in another city, the Egyptian town of al-Fostat, a suburb of Cairo, where it was invented sometime in the Middle Ages. In Britain, jeans fabric has always been called *jean* in the singular, but in America it has always had the plural form.

Levis take their name from Levi Strauss, a merchant who settled in San Francisco during the Gold Rush. Strauss sold jeans of heavy-duty blue denim, sturdy enough to stand up to the hard wear the prospectors gave them, easy to wash, and comfortable to wear. *Denim* is another geography lesson, for it is short for *serge de Nîmes* (Nîmes is a city in southern France and was a noted textile center). *Serge* is a heavy, twilled cotton fabric similar to fustian, and, like fustian, was used for work clothes in the 19th century. But, curiously, serge was originally a costly fabric of silk—its name is derived from the Latin *serica*, meaning "silk"—and it graced the bodies of the elite. So perhaps it is only poetic justice that serge de Nimes, reduced to the humble status of denim, should again become a status symbol in the 1960s, even though *jeans* now seems to describe a certain cut of pants rather than a material. What, me change the oil in my car in my stretch jeans by Calvin Klein? No way!

Pants and Trousers

Pants and *trousers* are two words for the same thing, which hardly needs defining. Of the two, *pants* has the more illustrious ancestry, for it goes all the way back to the 16th-century Italian *commedia dell'arte*. This was a rowdy, traditional comedy with stock characters. One of them was a mean, scrawny, foolish old man named Pantalone, who always wore baggy breeches that were much too large for him. These nether garments came to be named *pantaloons* in his honor. Believe it or not, baggy breeches were once the height of style. In the late 18th century, *pantaloons* referred to a kind of tight-fitting trouser that was fastened by a strap beneath the sole of the footgear, like a child's snow suit. In the next century, *pantaloons* was shortened to *pants*, which is the accepted term in the United States. In Britain, it is considered slangy and vulgar.

Proper Britishers prefer *trousers*, which is actually a corruption of *trouses*, a version of the Scottish and Irish word *trews*. Trews were a kind of tight-fitting long pants worn in lieu of the kilt. Soldiers in Scottish regiments sometimes still wear them. But they were not the direct ancestors of today's long trousers. Those were patterned after a loose-fitting type that sailors from northern Europe had worn for centuries. In the late 18th century, city workmen began to wear them too, and they became part of the uniform of the French Revolutionaries, as opposed to the knee-breeches of the aristocracy.

Pants, trousers, and breeches have been a distinctly masculine prerogative for many centuries, at least in the West. In the last century, women were arrested and fined for wearing pants in public. Asking a man who wore the pants in his house was tantamount to challenging his masculinity. The implication, of course, was that the wife wore the pants and gave the orders. Nowadays that question is irrelevant, since women wear pants all the time.

Robe A robe is a long, loose, flowing garment, worn by royalty and nobles on state occasions, by bishops and popes of the Roman Catholic Church, and by solemn academics. So it is a bit surprising to learn that *robe* is derived from a Late Latin word meaning "plunder" or "booty." (The Latin word is *roba* or *raupa*, and it probably comes from a Germanic root, *rauben*, "to rob." The Latin term also survives in the Spanish word for clothing, *ropa*.) Clothing was apparently a big item in the spoils from a raid. In English, *robe*—a French import—dates back to the late 13th century. But the garment itself is far more ancient.

Archaeologists have found that the Sumerians wore robes about 3000 B.C. In fact, the robe may well be a Near Eastern invention. Enveloping the body from neck to ankle, it provides protection against the burning sun, while its looseness makes it comfortable to wear. It is still the traditional garb for Arabs.

Egyptians, Cretans, Greeks, and Romans all wore robes on occasion. They were definitely upper-class garments, made of rich stuffs and magnificently embellished with precious metals and gemstones. Byzantium carried robes to new heights of luxury, especially those worn by the rulers and the high clergy. Even in the barbarian-overrun West the robe had taken firm root. A 6th-century Frankish queen named Arnegonde (her husband was a rough, tough nonentity of a warrior that only specialized historians have heard of today) was buried in a beautiful robe of dark-red silk, lined with blue linen and with the cuffs embroidered with gold. (The detail that most excited the archaelogists who exhumed her was that the robe was cut away in front to show off her legs.)

At one point, robes were the sort of thing that potentates presented to other important people. In 1248, for example, the Pope gave a present of scarlet, fur-trimmed robes to a group of Tatar envoys. Since earliest times, robes have been a badge of rank or official function. The parliamentary robes worn by members of the British House of Lords and the magnificent garments worn by royalty for their coronations, and by Catholic and Eastern Orthodox bishops are examples. There are also informal robes, such as the bathrobe and the beach robe, but these are modern innovations.

Jesus and the Apostles are always depicted as wearing long, robes, white for purity but otherwise the standard Near Eastern garb of their day. In Christian lore, those souls who enter paradise are also envisaged in white robes for eternity. Mohammed also commanded his followers to wear white robes as a sign of virtue. But black robes, too, have played a part in history. Much of North America was explored—and won for France—by black-robed Jesuit missionaries. In fact, the Indians took to calling all the Jesuits "Black Robes." One particularly successful Black Robe was Father Pierre Jean de Smet, who set off in 1841 to convert the Flatheads and neighboring tribes of the Rocky Mountains. A town in South Dakota today commemorates his name.

The French used to distinguish between "nobility of the sword"—those who had won noble rank by their exploits in war—and "nobility of the robe"—men who had been ennobled for services to the king. Lawyers as a group are called *gens de robe*, "people of the robe," in France. It was not only in France that the legal fraternity had a taste for robes. English judges, and later, lawyers, wore special robes for court sessions. Judges in the United States continued this tradition and wear black robes to impress everyone with the solemnity of the courtroom.

Satin
Satin appeared in English in the 14th century, taken over from French. Before that, its ancestry is mysterious. Satin was originally a smooth, glossy

silk fabric produced by a special weave, and the name was probably introduced to Europe by Arab merchants, who in the Middle Ages had a trading post at a city in southern China name Zaiton. *Satin* may have been a corruption of Zaiton, or it may be derived from the Mandarin Chinese name for the material, *ssu-tuan*. The Arabs may have been just as inept as Europeans at decoding the inscrutable Chinese language.

Satin's smoothness is proverbial; it has given us the expression "satin finish." As long as satin was made of silk only, it remained a luxury fabric for the rich. But as far back as the 16th century a passable imitation was made using a satin weave and thread of other fibers. The invention of rayon and nylon in the 20th century brought cheap satin within the reach of everyone.

In the 17th century, satin clothes were the mark of a dandy. Even into the 19th century (and in the good old homespun United States too!) men wore satin breeches, satin waistcoats, and satin neckcloths to signal their status. Women at times virtually wallowed in satin. Satin is still a standard fabric for dressy women's clothes, but for men it has retreated to such last stands as the lapels of tuxedo jackets and the stripes on waiters' pants.

Silk
Silk is named for the Seres, an unidentified Oriental nation from whom the West obtained its first silken fabrics. The Seres may have been Chinese, or they may have been middlemen. No one knows. The only certain thing is that the Romans called them by that name, and that in Latin the extremely costly fabric was called *sericus*, or "silken." At some point down the centuries, the *r* in *sericus* got turned to an *l*, and the word reached Anglo-Saxon England as *seoloc* or *sioloc*, long since shortened to the luxury-connoting monosyllable *silk*.

Silk

Silk, as most people know, is the thread that the larvae of a particular species of moth spin into their cocoons. Many other insects beside the silk moth also spin silken threads, but none produce a silk so fine and smooth, or one that makes such an exquisite fabric. A silk thread is stronger than a steel wire of the same thickness; that is why silk thread can be woven into cloth that is thin enough to be semi-transparent, yet durable enough for repeated wear. (Spiders also spin a very strong silk for their webs, but there is not enough silk in a web to pay for the labor of collecting it. Besides, spiders bite when disturbed; silkworms in their cocoons don't.)

The silkworm, whose scientific name is *Bombyx mori* (silkworm of the mulberry tree), is native to southeastern Asia. The Chinese were the first to discover how to unravel the silken cocoons by putting them in hot water. This dissolves the natural glue that holds the thread together, and the thread can then be carefully—very carefully—wound up on a reel. It can then be spun into heavier, stronger thread and woven into cloth.

Tradition states that the Chinese learned the secret of silk around 3000 B.C., but it was barely known in the West until Alexander the Great conquered the Persian Empire in the 4th century B.C. This opened up the trade routes; more silk came west when the commerce-minded Han Dynasty took power in China just before 200 B.C. Silk, worth its weight in gold or even more, was all the rage for wealthy Greeks and Romans, especially the women. It was the epitome of imported luxuries (even in China, sumptuary laws had forbidden silk garments to the common people for nearly 2,000 years). Stern moralists in the Roman Senate passed law after law forbidding silk, but it was not only because they disapproved of foreign fripperies or see-through garments. They had a more practical reason, which today we call negative cash flow. The Oriental middlemen through whose hands the silk goods passed on their long and tortuous journey from China were not interested in any of the items the Roman world produced. They demanded gold. And so there was a constant drain of gold from Rome to the merchants of the East. Morality and economics notwithstanding, the Roman ladies of fashion insisted on their diaphanous silken robes, and they got them.

China maintained its monopoly of silk production for almost 4,000 years; to reveal the secret to a foreigner meant death. But the secret did reach the West eventually, in the 6th century A.D. According to tradition, two Byzantine monks, sent as trade spies by the Emperor Justinian, smuggled silkworm eggs home inside their hollow walking staffs. They must have made several stops along the way to feed the newly hatched silkworms on mulberry leaves and raise a new generation of moths that laid another supply of eggs.

Vast acreages of mulberry trees were planted in various Mediterranean lands to feed the voracious silkworms—it takes on the average three to five tons of mulberry leaves to make 50 pounds of raw silk, and it takes an acre of healthy mulberry trees to produce this many leaves. At any rate, a thriving silk industry grew up in the Near East, Spain, Italy, and eventually the south of France. Silk was still a luxury, of course. The silk garments that graced nobles and royalty were thriftily recycled: an outmoded gown was taken apart and restitched into the newest fashion; when the material began to show wear, it could be unraveled and respun and woven.

Few consumers would connect silk with pasteurization or rabies, but a plague that wiped out most of the French silkworms in the 1860s gave an important boost to the career of Louis Pasteur. Pasteur had already won renown by his discovery of the microorganisms that cause wine and beer to turn sour, and how to kill them by gentle, controlled heating—and thereby won the gratitude of his countrymen. So the silkworm growers, faced with disaster, called on the hard-working chemist to find cause and cure for the disease. (It was called *pébrine* because the stricken silkworms were covered with little black spots, like specks of pepper.) Within a year he had identified the causative organism and worked out a method for rearing disease-free stock. This success strengthened Pasteur's position in the competitive world of science; two decades later he crowned his career by discovering rabies vaccine.

It was not only the Old World that engaged in silkworm culture. During the colonial period of the United States there were periodic attempts to start local silkworm industries, and mulberry trees were planted by the thousands. Benjamin Franklin and some associates were on the verge of success in Philadelphia when the American Revolution broke out. After independence, state governments continued these abortive attempts. For one reason or another, all of them failed, but their memory is immortalized by the many Mulberry Streets in our cities and towns.

The attempt to create a native United States silk industry also brought us one of our worst insect pests: the gypsy moth. A French-American scientist in Massachusetts was experimenting with these European insects, which he knew were hardier than the Chinese silkworm, turned out a passable grade of silk, and would eat almost anything. Alas, some of the moths escaped from their breeding cage, and their progeny began devastating the surrounding forests. There is a story that a visitor to this scientist's laboratory released the moths because he was outraged that the innocent little creatures should be imprisoned. But this tale is probably too good (or too bad) to be true.

Skirt

Skirt comes from the Middle English *skirte* or *skyrte*. It is derived from the Old Norse *skyrta*, or "shirt," which probably comes from an old Germanic root meaning "to cut off." Just when English speakers learned that there was a difference between "shirt" and "skirt" is uncertain. The earliest written record of the word *skirt* is from the early 14th century.

Originally, *skirt* simply meant the lower part of a woman's long gown; later it came to mean a skirt in the modern sense. Of course, skirts existed long before the 14th century, but they were called by other names, such as *kirtle*. In time, *skirt* also came to mean the edge or border of anything, from a coat to a city (today we would say "outskirts"). We also have saddle skirts, the leather flaps that hang down from a saddle and protect the rider's legs and the horse's flanks from chafing each other. And we also *skirt* around something we don't want to encounter directly.

Through most of recorded history, skirts have been long and confining. Feminist writers claim that this was a deliberate plan to enforce male dominance by restricting women's mobility. Whatever the facts may be, skirts were a physical restraint. But short skirts came in with a vengeance in the naughty 1920s. Hemlines came down again in the depressed 30s and stayed below the knees for many years. But the 1960s saw a bewildering succession of mini-skirts, midi-skirts, maxi-skirts, and micro-skirts, most of which were not very flattering to the wearer's legs and must have been mighty uncomfortable on a cold winter's day. Even so, they were far less uncomfortable than the voluminous structures of the 19th century, supported by hoops and padded out grotesquely in the rear with immense bustles.

As early as the 16th century, *skirt* was a metaphorical expression for "woman." In the 19th century "the skirt" was a racy way of referring to women collectively. By the early 20th century, it had descended into slang of a very low class, used chiefly by males who wanted to show what he-men they were. Sparked by fiction writers of the tough-guy school, "skirt" increased in popularity up through World War II, only to decline as other faddy slang words took its place. Today it is not only vulgar but dated.

Tweed

Tweed comes from a careless London clerk's misreading of the label on a consignment of cloth from Scotland. It is generally agreed that in or about 1831, a shipment of twill fabric from Scotland arrived in a London shop. It was labeled *tweel*, a Scottish form of "twill." The receiving clerk, however, read it as "tweed," possibly because of the bad handwriting of the person who had written the label or because he was thinking of the River Tweed in Scotland, whose valley had an important textile industry, or both.

The new name caught the public fancy, and by the 1850s it was well established. Tweed also became a popular fabric for clothing, as it was durable and comfortable to wear. It was particularly favored by certain groups of people, academic types for one. The tweedy professor, with wrinkled tweeds and pipe, was long a stereotype of popular fiction. Writers, too, were supposed to favor tweeds. And the English country gentry pretty much lived in tweeds, if writers are to be believed. Tweed was also popular among other folk who wanted to give a sporty, casual impression.

Having nothing at all to do with tweed fabric, but nonetheless celebrated in American history, is William Marcy Tweed, the notorious boss who ruled Tammany Hall from 1863 to 1871. Tweed and the cronies with whom he packed the New York City government bilked the public of a sum estimated at anywhere from 75 million to 200 million dollars (some of the graft was too cleverly concealed to be traced). In 1870, a member of the Tweed Ring, disgruntled because he wasn't getting a big enough cut of the pie, leaked his secrets to the press. A cartoonist for *Harper's Magazine*, Thomas Nast, savagely exposed Tweed with biting caricatures, and *The New York Times* attacked from the other flank. A henchman consolingly pointed out to the beleaguered Boss that all this didn't mean a thing, since most of the people who voted for him couldn't read. "No," snarled Tweed, "but they can see those damned pictures!"

As the law closed in on him, Tweed fled to Spain on his luxurious yacht, but was arrested there by an alert Spanish customs officer who recognized him from the Nast cartoons. Tweed was returned to the States in disgrace, tried, and convicted.

Vest *Vest*, like the *vestments* of a clergyman, comes ultimately from the Latin *vestis*, "garment." It once meant the long robes or gowns worn by Persian men and other Middle Easterners. (It could also refer to similar garments worn by women.) As a waistcoat, which is what the British call it, the vest was pioneered by the Merry Monarch, King Charles II, who announced in 1666 that he wished to establish a new fashion. Charles' waistcoat was a long thing, but waistcoats have generally stopped at the waist (hence their name). In the late 17th and 18th centuries, vests were a major item of a well-dressed man's costume. They were brightly colored and patterned to make a dazzling display in the opening of the coat. That, of course, was before sober, somber clothing became the badge of wealth and respectability. Robespierre, the fanatic who turned the French Revolution into a reign of terror, wore a white vest to symbolize the purity of his motives. In the early 20th century, American cartoonists began portraying the Trusts as potbellied, grinning businessmen wearing vests covered with dollar signs.

In the late 19th century, the term "vested interests" was prominent in the American political vocabulary. It had nothing to do with the garment called a vest, with or without dollar signs; it came from the verb "to vest," one of whose meanings was "to establish." Populist orators fulminated fiercely against the "vested interests"; their opponents sneered back, "Yes, and them without vests, too!"

Bougainvillea

Travel to southern Florida, Mexico, or a hundred other warm-climate places, and your eye will be delighted by the brilliant, papery blossoms of the bougainvillea. Most people probably think that *bougainvillea* is just one more of those cumbersome botanical names that scientists dream up. Actually, it memorializes an 18th-century French soldier, explorer, and scientist, Louis Antoine de Bougainville, who was also something of a boy wonder.

Born in Paris in 1729, Bougainville became a lawyer but escaped this humdrum career by enlisting in the famed regiment of the Black Musketeers. Somehow he also found time to publish a treatise on integral calculus that later won him a membership in Britain's prestigious Royal Society. He was only twenty-five.

In 1755 he was sent to Britain as a junior diplomat, but his diplomatic career was short. The next year, war broke out between England and France, and Bougainville was shipped off to defend Canada against the British. As every Canadian knows, Britain won that contest, but Bougainville went back to Europe and fought for France until the exhausted nations made peace in 1763. His next project was to found a French colony in the Falkland Islands, off the southern tip of present-day Argentina. Spain, outraged by the idea of a foreign colony so close to its own possessions, forced France to scrap the colonizing project, and Bougainville, who had established the colony at his own expense, had to sail halfway round the world to hand it back to the Spanish officials. (Spain did pay him back, though.) As a consolation, the French government commissioned Bougainville to conduct a worldwide voyage of discovery, and as soon as he had turned the Falklands colony over to Spain he set off.

He sailed up to Rio de Janeiro to meet his supply ship, and there he found that the expedition's botanist had collected many tropical plants unknown to French science. One of them was a woody vine with brilliant flowers, which the botanist diplomatically named in honor of his boss. Bougainville went on to explore many of the islands of the Pacific—one still bears his name—and his account of his discoveries was an 18th-century classic. But today his name is best known for that symbol of the tropics, the bougainvillea, which is admired by millions of people who never heard of the French navigator.

The camellia was named for a Jesuit missionary from Czechoslovakia, Georg Joseph Kamel, born in 1661. Kamel, whose name is German for "camel," was sent by his Order to the Philippines, where in addition to his preaching duties he set up a free dispensary for the poor. Since the most reliable medicines at that time were prepared from plants, Kamel had to become an expert on the local flora. Eventually he put his hard-won botanical knowledge into a book, which may well have been the first scientific description of Philippine plant life. The Spanish rulers of the islands had never undertaken such a study, because they were interested chiefly in lucrative commercial crops such as sugar, rice, and tobacco. Years after Kamel's death in 1706, the great Swedish botanist Linnaeus honored him by naming a recently discovered flowering shrub from Asia after him. Kamel probably never saw a camellia in his life, since the plant is native to China and Japan, and he spent his entire career in the Philippines. However, China and the Philippines are both in the Far East, and that was apparently enough of a connection for Linnaeus.

There is an interesting sidelight to the camellia story. The tea plant is one of the nearly 100 species of camellia, and when Europeans began to trade directly with China, instead of through a long chain of Middle Eastern middlemen, they tried to buy tea seeds. In this way, they thought to raise their own tea at home and bring the price down. But the Chinese, not wishing to lose their highly profitable monopoly on tea, sold them seeds from ornamental camellias instead. In this way, it is thought, camellias first reached the gardens of Europe and later the United States. Alabamans, whose state flower is the camellia, might send a thought of thanks to those long-dead Chinese monopolists as well as remembering Kamel.

A few of the other familiar plants that perpetuate the names of otherwise forgotten people are the forsythia, the gardenia, and the poinsettia. William Forsyth (1737–1804) was a humble Scottish boy who worked his way up to the position of superintendent of the Royal Gardens at the palaces of St. James and Kensington. The forsythia was named for him in 1788. But in his own time Forsyth was better known as the author of a famous book on the care of trees. Infatuated by his own theories, he invented a patent remedy for injured trees. A compound of lime, manure, soapsuds, ashes, and urine, this "plaister," as Forsyth called it, was supposed to heal tree wounds, banish rot, and restore sick and dying trees, even those that were completely rotted out inside. The British government, desperate to increase the supply of timber for warships, bought a large order of the "plaister," and Parliament voted Forsyth a reward and a medal. The wonder remedy failed to live up to its claims, however, and a nasty scandal flared up. Forsyth died at its height.

Alexander Garden was an 18th-century society doctor in

Charleston, South Carolina. His search for more effective medicinal plants got him involved in botany, and this led to a passionate interest in every phase of natural history. It was Garden who sent the first specimens of the electric eel (native to South America) to Europe, just as he sent innumerable other specimens of plants and animals to fellow scientists. When the American Revolution broke out, Garden sided with the British; at the end of the war he left the country and never returned. His son fought on the American side, and Garden never forgave him. The gardenia was named in honor of this diehard loyalist.

Joel Poinsett (1779–1851) was another Charlestonian. His career path led him not to science but to politics. After two terms in Congress, he was made ambassador to Mexico in 1825. During his sojourn, he unwisely became involved in a struggle between two Masonic factions for control of the Mexican government. Even more unwisely, Poinsett sided with the losing faction, and the winning clique ordered him out of the country in 1830. Among the souvenirs he brought back to Charleston were specimens of a weedy, wild shrub with brilliant red rosettes that blossomed in winter. Poinsett developed ornamental varieties with bigger flowers. (The rosettes are actually specialized leaves called bracts rather than true flowers, but that makes no difference to their beauty.) This exotic plant became popular as a house plant because it could be made to flower in the dead of winter, when almost every other plant is dormant. Nurserymen knew a good thing when they saw it and promoted it as a Christmas plant. Its name, as the astute reader has probably guessed, is poinsettia.

Ending up our person-to-plant collection is Caspar Wistar, a Philadelphia doctor who lived from 1761 to 1818. A hospitable man, Wistar held open house for scientists one night a week at his large, comfortable house on Fourth Street. One of the scientists he befriended was an eccentric English botanist named

Thomas Nuttall, whose personal quirks kept him permanently and desperately poor. But Nuttall, who had great difficulty in getting along with other people, was always made to feel welcome at Wistar's house. After Wistar died, the grateful Nuttall named a new plant for him. However, Nuttall was as eccentric in his spelling as in other matters. He spelled the plant's name w-i-s-t-*e*-r-i-a instead of w-i-s-t-*a*-r-i-a, and his whimsical error prevailed.

Bowie Knife

The bowie knife, both weapon and tool of the 19th-century frontiersman, was named for James Bowie (1796–1836), who died at the siege of the Alamo. The bowie knife was a heavy hunting knife with a fifteen-inch blade and a curved tip. It was used for skinning animals and a multitude of camp tasks. It was also a fearsome weapon in hand-to-hand combat.

Tradition says that Bowie invented it after a duel in 1827. Bowie killed his opponent, a Major Norris Wright, but during the fight his hand slipped and was gashed on his own knife blade. Bowie took the knife to a local blacksmith and had a cross-guard added just above the blade to keep his hand from slipping. With this addition, the weapon became safer to use.

It is not certain whether Bowie actually did design the bowie knife, but he used it enthusiastically in duels and fights with Indians, and he made it popular, especially along the western frontier, where the *macho* spirit was strong and brawls were frequent. By 1840 the bowie knife was so common in what was then the Southwest that it was nicknamed the "Arkansas toothpick."

Bowie was a typical early 19th-century go-getter. Born in Georgia, he moved with his family to Louisiana as a child. After a number of business ventures (possibly including a lucrative slave-smuggling scheme), he crossed over into Texas to seek a larger fortune. Texas then belonged to Mexico, but Americans felt that they had as much right to be there as the Mexicans, and hundreds of them moved in. To obtain land, they had to become Mexican citizens and Roman Catholics and take an oath of loyalty to Mexico. Most of them did not take it very seriously.

After an abortive search for a lost mine, Bowie became a Mexican citizen in 1830 and the next year married the daughter of the Mexican Vice-Governor. Despite this family connection with the Mexican establishment, he usually sided with the American immigrants in their frequent disputes with the Mexican government. To be fair, the Americans had ample grounds for complaint. The Mexican government was corrupt and ineffectual, and seemed to exist only for the purpose of collecting taxes to support the officials in comfort. Less creditably, the American settlers were angry because Mexico had banned slavery. Many of the native Mexican settlers in Texas were disgruntled, too, and there was much talk of a coup to establish Texas independence.

After some preliminary skirmishing, the Texan Revolution broke out in earnest in the fall of 1835. Thanks partly to the distance of Texas from Mexico proper, and partly to the inefficiency of the Mexican command, the Texans won a string of early victories. In one bold action, they defeated a much larger force of Mexicans at a fortified mission called the Alamo in San Antonio. The Alamo had not been built to resist a modern army with artillery, and the Texan commander-in-chief, Sam Houston, ordered the fortifications dismantled. But a cocky subordinate countermanded his order and sent in additional troops to occupy it.

At this juncture, the self-styled Napoleon of Mexico, General Santa Anna, came up from the south bent on chastising the impudent *gringos*. He had 1,600 troops with plentiful artillery to surround the fort; the defenders of the Alamo had 183 men and a handful of antique cannons, captured from the Mexicans, that were not much more effective than a popgun. At first the Texans were not alarmed—after all, one white man could lick ten, twelve, a hundred of those dark-skinned foreigners. But the dark-skinned foreigners did not go away. They kept on shooting at the jerry-built fort. Supplies and munitions began to run low inside the Alamo. The defenders smuggled out a last desperate plea for help. On the morning of the thirteenth day of the siege, Santa Anna ordered his buglers to sound the "No Quarter" call, and his troops, sustaining frightful casualties, swarmed over the wall. Bowie, gravely ill with pneumonia, fought from his sickbed. The former frontier brawler managed to slay several of his attackers before he died himself. With him died all the other defenders.

"A small matter," commented Santa Anna after the dust had settled and the dead had been counted. He was wrong, for the Alamo gave Texas a battle cry and a symbol of heroism; six weeks later the *gringos* captured him in a surprise attack, and Mexico lost Texas. Bowie is still remembered for his heroic death, more than for the murderous knife he popularized.

Boycott
Until 1880, boycott was nothing more than an unremarkable family name. It became a catchword when former Captain Charles Cunningham Boycott, late of Her Majesty's Army, ran afoul of the Irish Nationalist movement. Boycott had served in the British Army without distinction or disgrace, and had retired early. His pension not being very large, he had taken respectable employment as the estate agent of an Irish aristocrat, the Earl of Erne, who had vast holdings in County Mayo.

In 1880 the Earl's tenants, hard-pressed by a bad crop season, decided to pay a lower rent than the noble Earl demanded. Boycott, following orders, refused to accept the rent cut. This was the opportunity for which the Land League, an Irish nationalist organization, had been waiting. The leader of the Land League, a fiery orator and Irish patriot named Charles Parnell, had advised his followers to treat anyone who threatened to evict tenants "like a leper of old." His plan was put into effect, most devastatingly. No Irishman would speak to Boycott, his servants left, and farm laborers would not work for him. Storekeepers refused to trade with him. His mail was intercepted; nationalist vandals tore down his fences by night. A group of Protestant volunteers from Ulster came to harvest Boycott's crops; it took 900 soldiers to safeguard them. When the luckless Boycott ventured into town, people booed him in the streets. Sometimes they assaulted this hated representative of Britain. He was hanged and burned in effigy.

Seeing how successfully Parnell's plan had worked, the Irish Nationalists applied it on a wider scale. For a time, the boycott campaign produced a virtual reign of terror in every Catholic county of Ireland. The merest suggestion that someone was pro-British meant that he was totally cut off. Even his friends would cross the street to avoid meeting him, and they would make the sign of the cross when they passed, as one would do in the presence of an evil spirit. The boycott was taken up abroad, particularly by labor unions. By the time the unhappy Boycott died in 1897, his name had become an international cliché. Although boycotts have often been banned by law, they are frequently called for today, more than a century after Captain Boycott made his tactical error.

Cadillac
When a couple of Detroit businessmen organized an automobile manufacturing company in 1902, they wanted a distinctive name for their product. They chose *Cadillac*, which offered the slightly racy glamour of France, yet had provable ties with the American past, and in particular with the history of Detroit.

Cadillac

The Sieur Antoine de la Mothe Cadillac, for whom the new company was named, was born in southwestern France in 1656, the son of a minor nobleman. Cadillac was the name of the family estate; De la Mothe was the actual family name. Cadillac, as was the custom for impoverished young noblemen, enlisted in the French army. He was sent to Canada, where he served so well that he gained the favor of the governor, Count Frontenac. (Frontenac has a fine hotel in Quebec City named for him, but he never made it to automobile stardom.) Frontenac put Cadillac in charge of Fort Mackinac, on Mackinac Island. It was an important post, for Mackinac was the strategic key to the upper Great Lakes. But Cadillac was not overjoyed with the honor. He complained of the climate, the food, and the Indians with whom he had to deal while encouraging the all-important fur trade.

The French government found its western outposts expensive to maintain and abandoned them in 1697. Cadillac returned to the fleshly pleasures of Quebec, but he had bigger plans. In 1699 he made a politically useful trip back to France, where he persuaded the King and his ministers that they should found a new outpost at the outlet of Lake St. Clair, where the waters of Lakes Superior, Huron, and Michigan empty into Lake Erie. There they could effectively block off British agents from the western fur trade. The river there was narrow; so they named it Détroit (the French word for "strait").

Cadillac returned to Michigan (then a part of New France) with a charter to found a colony at Detroit; he was to be the proprietor. He also secured the right to a monopoly on trade. Ground was broken for the new fort in 1701. With visions of a grand future as the overlord of the fur country, Cadillac brought his wife and children to the new settlement. But his high-handed rule brought his downfall. He alienated the powerful Jesuit order by transferring the missionary enterprise to a rival order, the Recollects. To make matters worse, he had a running feud with the French Canadian Fur Company, whose monopoly grant conflicted with his. Finally he was transferred to the governorship of the newly created colony of Louisiana.

Cadillac, who had grown fond of Detroit, disliked Louisiana and promptly quarreled with the little group of French who had settled there. He spent most of his term attempting to enrich himself, even traveling as far as Illinois (then part of Louisiana's territory) to look for silver mines. Instead, he found deposits of another heavy metal, lead. Cadillac could not see the potential value of the lead, which could have supplied bullets for all New France, and sulked. The civilian developer who actually owned the colony, a man named Crozat, eventually had all he could endure of Cadillac's constant complaints and quarrels. Using all his influence with the Court, he had Cadillac recalled to France. There Cadillac spent a short time imprisoned in the notorious Bastille; on his release he went back to his native province of Gascony and spent the rest of his life in retirement. He died in 1730, embittered by his fiasco in Louisiana.

The first Cadillac car, a one-cylinder model, appeared in 1903. (A scant eleven years later, the Cadillac Company pioneered the first high-speed V-8 engine.) In 1909 Cadillac was one of the small auto companies that were combined to become General Motors. Cadillac's engineers made several important technical contributions to automobile design, but the one that was most appreciated by the average motorist was the electric self-starter, which came on the market in 1911. Before then, starting the car had been a complex and physically demanding procedure. The driver had to set his choke, spark, and throttle controls very carefully, according to his car's individual peculiarities. Then he left the comfort of his seat, walked around to the front end of the vehicle, inserted a crank into a slot at the end of the crankshaft, and cranked lustily. If he were lucky, the engine would cough into action after only a few revolutions. Then the driver dashed back to his seat to re-set the controls before the engine could choke up and stall. Sometimes the engine would not respond to any treatment, even the mechanically refined approach of a hard kick, and sometimes it would kick back when being cranked, breaking the luckless driver's wrist. No wonder Cadillac quickly gained a reputation for quality! (The electric self-starter did not be-come standard on all cars for many years thereafter, for the American people still had a strong streak of puritanism that could not swallow such a luxury—owning a rich man's toy like a car was sinful enough. Hand-cranking it to start it was a spir-itually wholesome penance. But standards of morality relaxed, and even the die-hards finally accepted the self-starter.) GM's executives decided that the Cadillac was to be their flagship, their luxury, top-of-the-line make, a reputation it has borne down the years. Although the Sieur Cadillac died a disap-pointed man, he would certainly be pleased to know that the car bearing his name has become an international symbol of "class."

Other automobiles (no longer produced) were named for explorers in an attempt to cash in on the appeal of "Cadillac." The LaSalle was named for Robert Cavelier, Sieur de la Salle (1643–87), who explored the Great Lakes, the Ohio Valley, and much of the upper Mississippi region. La Salle also sailed down the Mississippi to its mouth and claimed its vast drainage basin, which he called Louisiana, for France.

The De Soto was named for the bold and cruel Spanish aris-tocrat Hernan de Soto (1500?–1542), who had taken part in the conquest of Peru. High in favor with the King of Spain, De Soto was given a contract to conquer Florida. From his Florida base he ranged far afield in search of gold, exploring as far as North Carolina and western Arkansas. On his last expedition, he and his soldiers became the first Europeans to discover the Mississippi River.

Many more makes of automobile took their names from their original makers. The Buick was named for David Dunbar Buick, a Scottish-born manufacturer of plumbers' supplies who became interested in gasoline engines. The Oldsmobile was named for Ransom E. Olds, one of the successful early tinkerers who combined an internal-combustion engine with a buggy body. John Studebaker had a thriving wagon-making business before he branched out into making horseless carriages. Walter Chrysler was a former locomotive mechanic who went into the auto business and eventually produced his own line of cars. Horace and John Dodge were skilled machinists who got their start building engines and chassis for Henry Ford. Louis Chevrolet was a French-born designer and racing driver for Buick; his innovative idea was to build a light, attractive, powerful car and sell it at a moderate price. It is hardly necessary to mention Henry Ford, except to point out that he invented neither the automobile nor the assembly line. However, Ford, a shrewd if crotchety mechanic, made maximum use of the assembly line (apparently copied from the overhead tracks that carried carcasses of cattle and pigs through the great Chicago meat-packing houses as they were systematically disassembled.) Ford's goal was to produce a cheap but reliable, no-frills car for the mass market, so simple that almost anyone could do his own repairs. How the auto business has changed!

Cardigan

Cardigan A cardigan is nothing more than a sweater that buttons up the front, a popular leisure garment. No one would connect it with a bungled European war. Yet the cardigan's story involves the Crimean War, a long-festering feud between two high-born, haughty British officers who were also brothers-in-law, and the futile heroics of the ill-fated Charge of the Light Brigade.

The two brothers-in-law were James Brudenell, seventh Earl of Cardigan, and George Bingham, third Earl of Lucan. Both men were born to rich and powerful aristocratic families with excellent connections at court and elsewhere. Both were handsome and dashing, with unfulfilled ambitions for military glory. Both were arrogant and autocratic, flying into a fury if crossed or contradicted. But Cardigan was intensely stupid, whereas Lucan was highly intelligent.

Each of the earls purchased the command of a crack cavalry regiment when in his twenties. This was the way things were done in most European countries in the early 1800s. It kept power in the hands of the rich and well-connected, and prevented the rise of popular military dictators like Napoleon, or so the British thought. It was true that ability and competence at the soldier's trade were ignored while rank and connections were excessively rewarded. But somehow Britain always managed to muddle through.

As commanders, Cardigan and Lucan both proved to be martinets, obsessed with such trivia as the placement of epaulets and the length of a horse's coat. But Cardigan was a luxury-loving dandy, while Lucan worked himself even harder than he drove his unhappy troops, rising before dawn and sharing all the discomforts of military life.

Although Lucan and Cardigan both yearned to win distinction on the battlefield, they were too young to have fought against Napoleon (Cardigan was born in 1797 and Lucan in 1800), and the ensuing decades were peaceful. The would-be heroes had to wait until the outbreak of the Crimean War in 1853 at last gave them their longed-for opportunity.

In the interim, Cardigan won notoriety for his monomaniac obsession with having the smartest cavalry regiment in Britain and for his persecution of his officers. His aim was to force the resignation of all but those who cut the most fashionable figure in society, and in this he largely succeeded. True, he lost his most able officers in this fashion, but this was unimportant to Cardigan, a thorough snob. Severely reprimanded on several occasions for mismanagement, Cardigan was saved by aristocratic solidarity. Once Cardigan fought a duel with one of his aggrieved subordinates, gravely wounding the man, but was acquitted by the House of Lords on a ridiculuous technicality. Once again aristocratic connections had paid off. But all agreed that Cardigan's regiment, the 11th Hussars, were the most smartly drilled and most gorgeously turned-out of any. Officers and men rode in tight, cherry-red trousers, jackets of royal blue trimmed with gold, tall fur hats adorned with brilliant plumes, and furred capes gleaming with gold lace. Most of the costly adornments were paid for by Cardigan himself from his huge fortune.

Lucan, unlike Cardigan, had actually had a taste of combat. As a young man he had served as a volunteer officer with the Russian army in one of the frequent Russo-Turkish wars, distinguishing himself for reckless bravery. Returning in triumph from this glorious adventure, he married one of Cardigan's seven sisters. It was a brilliant match; society applauded loudly. The two brothers-in-law detested each other immediately.

Lucan spent some years drilling his regiment and quarreling with various personages, then retired to administer his vast estates in the west of Ireland. There he earned the bitter hatred of his tenants by his harshness, particularly during the dreadful years of the potato famine of the 1840s. However, Lucan was convinced that he was doing right: to improve the living standards of his overcrowded and impoverished tenants, he had to get rid of most of them. Their future fate did not concern him.

The immediate cause of the Crimean War was the Russian invasion of Turkish provinces in southeast Europe. The Turkish Empire, a huge and sprawling collection of resentful nationalities, was corrupt and weak. Russia was an awakening giant. Britain and France, each with its own reasons for fearing Russian expansion, joined the Turks in early 1854. Glory-greedy aristocrats flocked to the colors, naively afraid that the war would be over before they had a chance to show their stuff.

In overall command of the British force was Lord Raglan, a hero of the Napoleonic wars who had lost his right arm at Waterloo and bravely undergone amputation without the customary anesthetics—opium and alcohol. Raglan had been the revered Duke of Wellington's chief administrative assistant for forty years, and the Duke's reputation—but not his ability as a commander—had rubbed off on Raglan, whose great talent was as a conciliator. Now, at sixty-five, Raglan was an old man who could not quite grasp that in this campaign the French were his allies, not his enemies. He was a close friend of Cardigan's and on reasonably good terms with Lucan.

As the campaign got under way, Cardigan was promoted to brigadier general and put in charge of the Light Brigade of cavalry. An elderly man of fifty-seven, he had at last achieved the recognition he had always considered his due—except that the Earl of Lucan was his divisional commander. However, Cardigan convinced himself that Raglan had authorized him to operate independently of Lucan, and acted accordingly. Raglan, placed in a difficult position between the feuding commanders, was at length compelled to support Lucan.

The Crimean campaign went wretchedly, marked by horrendous mismanagement on both sides. At length, the Anglo-French force settled down to starve out the great Russian naval base at Sebastopol. The British base was at the nearby harbor of Balaclava, and here it was that the Russians struck back.

The British and French troops were holding two steep ridges and a deep valley between them, which ran from the coast to the edge of the Russian position. The massive Russian counterattack surged down the ridges, throwing back the defenders. Raglan, standing on a height at the mouth of the valley, had a superb view of the action, but the commanders on the hilly valley floor could see little.

Raglan issued a stream of orders from the heights, commanding the cavalry to pull back to a defensive position. Then the Heavy Brigade were ordered to charge the Russian lines while the Light Brigade remained in reserve—much to the fury of Cardigan, who assumed that he was being deliberately deprived of glory. At last an aide galloped down from the heights bearing an order for Lucan to advance rapidly up the valley and prevent the Russians from removing some British cannon they had captured.

The order was obviously ridiculous, an invitation to annihilation, since there were Russian cannons and riflemen on both ridges now as well as at the end of the valley. Unfortunately Lucan was convinced that Raglan and Cardigan were plotting to have him removed from command, and to deprive them of pretexts he obeyed each order from Raglan literally. After a feeble remonstrance, he trotted over to Cardigan and delivered the order.

Cardigan, for once showing sense, pointed out the dangers of such a charge. But the two men could not bring themselves to talk together and figure out just what Raglan's order had meant. Lucan replied that he was aware of the danger but that this what Raglan wanted, and they had no choice but to obey.

In beautiful order the Light Brigade advanced down the mile-and-a-quarter-long valley, Cardigan five horselengths ahead of his men. The sun glittered off Cardigan's gold lace as he rode ahead, saber upraised and never looking back or to the side. Russian bullets and cannonballs took a terrible toll of the six hundred cavalrymen, but as fast as one fell, his comrades would close in to fill the gap. When the first line came within eighty yards of the Russian cannon, a salvo annihilated them and nearly got Cardigan. But he regained control of his horse and, saber in hand, galloped in among the Russian guns and then out beyond them. He did not fight himself—his duty as he saw it was merely to lead his troops. And, since he did not look back, he was unaware of the carnage among his men. But only 195 men of the original 700 who made the charge returned, including wounded. Cardigan himself, satisfied, went back to the yacht on which he lived and toasted his victory with a bottle of champagne.

War correspondents sped the story of the Light Brigade back to England, where the bravery of the men caused a national sensation. Lucan was blamed for the disaster, and Cardigan, once so hated by the public that it was not safe for him to go to the theater, returned a hero. A knitted woolen jacket or sweater, such as Cardigan had worn in the harsh Crimean winter, was named for him and has kept the name ever since.

The facts about Cardigan's callous disregard of his men eventually came out, and the hero fell into well-deserved disgrace. But the garment named after him is still popular.

Colt One of the most enduring symbols of the Old West is the Colt revolver, trusty weapon of cowboy and cavalryman, and not a few villains as well. Samuel Colt, the inventor of this redoubtable handgun, was born in Hartford, Connecticut, in 1814. Even as a boy he was interested in guns and explosives. When only fourteen, he devised a submarine mine with an electric detonator. He proudly posted signs announcing that he would demonstrate his invention by blowing up a raft in a local pond on July 4. What better day for fireworks? A crowd gathered to witness the demonstration, and the young inventor closed his electrical circuit. The mine went off perfectly. But the raft had drifted close to shore, and the angry spectators were showered with mud and water. Thinking the whole thing was a practical joke, a group of indignant men were about to heave young Colt into the pond, but he was rescued by a fellow enthusiast.

Colt was not popular around his home town, and his father packed him off to a boarding school. There, he managed to set one of the school buildings on fire with another of his experiments. That ended his formal education. At sixteen, he was sent to sea as a deckhand on a trading ship, going to Calcutta by way of London. It was probably in London that he saw his first revolver, the product of a transplanted Boston gunsmith named Collier. We should note here that the revolver itself is an old idea, going back at least to the 1500s, but problems of design kept the early revolvers from becoming more than curiosities. The revolver's day came with the invention of the percussion cap in the early 1800s.

Some of the early revolvers had multiple barrels, each charged with a single load of powder and ball. Others used a cylinder with several chambers, as did Collier's and Colt's. All the latter type suffered from the problem of how to align the cylinder with the barrel of the gun so that the bullet would not jam, blowing up the gun and the shooter's hand as well.

The story goes that Colt was whiling away an idle afternoon on the Indian Ocean when he was struck by the working of the ship's big steering wheel. No matter which way the helmsman turned it, or how far, a pawl and ratchet mechanism would hold it firmly in position if the helmsman wished to rest his arms. Colt saw that this idea could be applied to a revolving firearm, and began to whittle out a wooden model. It was a long voyage, and he had plenty of time to work out his design, but he was not yet ready for production.

For a year he worked in his father's bleaching and dyeing plant and then went on a three-year tour as a lecturer to raise money. Presenting himself as "Dr. Coult, late of New York, London, and Calcutta," he entertained his audiences with lectures on the young science of chemistry, with demonstrations of laughing gas. (In small doses, the gas would produce the effects of intoxication without the disgrace of actually getting drunk. Inhaling laughing gas was a popular party pastime for a while.) In 1835 he made prototype models of a revolving pistol and rifle. While waiting for the Patent Office to respond, he went to France and England and secured patents there. The American patent came through in 1836.

Colt manufactured three models of pistols, with rifles, carbines, and shotguns as a sideline. However, it took some time for his design to catch the favor of the public. The Army and Navy turned him down flat, although some civilians bought Colt pistols. Colt's business failed in 1843, and he went back to fiddling with electrically detonated mines. But rescue came from the West. Some of Colt's pistols had found their way to Texas, where they proved to be excellent weapons for horsemen. Armed with Colt revolvers, the famed Texas Rangers held their own against marauding Comanches. The Texas Navy used its own model of the Colt. Then came the Mexican War, and Texan soldiers convinced the War Department to give Colt a big order. Incidentally, the United States thus became the first nation to issue revolvers to its troops. And "Colt" became to revolvers what "Xerox" later became to the photocopying machine.

One early competitor of Colt's was the pepperbox pistol, which was essentially nothing but a big cylinder with five to seven barrels bored in it. It had the great advantage of being double-acting, that is, pulling the trigger cocked and released the hammer in a single motion, whereas the Colt was single-acting—you had to cock the hammer by hand before every shot. The pepperbox was thus a faster-firing weapon. The pepperbox was not an accurate weapon—it was meant for close-quarter use—but at close range it was very effective, and when the ammunition was used up, the heavy cylinder made a dandy bludgeon. However, the pepperbox had the distressing trait of sometimes firing off all its barrels at once, which could sprain the shooter's wrist, and the even worse one of going off accidentally, causing unintended injuries and deaths. By the Civil War it was obsolete.

Another historic pistol of the 19th century was the derringer, designed to be carried in the pocket for emergency use. It was a single-shot weapon (sometimes it was made with two barrels for security), usually of medium to heavy caliber. It was inaccurate beyond a few paces, but at close range it was deadly. This forerunner of the "Saturday night special" was first made by a Philadelphia gunsmith named Henry Deringer, with a single *r* in the middle of his name. Deringer could not patent the single-shot pistol, of course, as the idea had been in use for centuries. But his well-made pocket pistols were so popular that imitators cashed in on his reputation. To avoid lawsuits, they stamped the guns with the name "Derringer," thus safely skirting the edges of infringement. It was a derringer that John Wilkes Booth used to assassinate President Lincoln, which cast something of a shadow on the gun, but its popularity was already waning as pocket-sized revolvers took its place.

Derby
The Earls of Derby trace their ancestry back to 1485, and the family has produced notable warriors and politicians. Edward Stanley, the twelfth Earl of Derby, won no distinction in either of these fields, but he is remembered for founding the original Derby horse race, in 1780. The English Derby is run not in Derbyshire, the family seat—the fashionable set would never have traveled to that provincial backwater—but at Epsom Downs on the outskirts of London. Some whim no doubt prompted the Earl to specify that the course should be not a convenient, even length like a

mile or a mile and a half, but a mile and a half plus twenty-nine yards. The date is linked to the Church calendar, the first Wednesday after Whitsunday, which falls either at the end of May or the beginning of June.

Derby Day is a national institution in England: Parliament adjourns so that the members may attend; the royal family never misses it, and the crowd is always full of aristocrats and celebrities for the ordinary racegoer to marvel at. Rich men and potentates from all over the world enter their specially trained three-year-old horses in the race, which is one of the most prestigious in the world of horse-racing. The glory of the Derby was such that the Kentucky Derby was named for it when it was founded in 1875, and the name has spread to other contests of a racing nature, such as snowshoe derbies and roller derbies.

The derby hat, a hard, round hat with a stiff brim, was devised in the mid-19th century to protect riders from head injuries. In England it is known as a bowler, supposedly because the original manufacturer was the hatmaking firm of Beaulieu. In the United States, it was introduced in the 1870s, and it was the Earl of Derby (a later one) who made it popular.

From its racy beginnings, the derby became part of the uniform of the most respectable English financiers and businessmen. In fact, all classes wore it. In the United States, it was particularly associated with machine politicians and men involved with prize-fighting; at least, they were among the last to cling to it when it went out of style. The derby also had its day of glory on the European mainland, but the jealous French and Germans refused to give credit to the British; they called it a "melon hat" because its shape was like that of half a melon upside down on a plate.

Diesel Rudolf Diesel was a

man with an idea: to invent a better internal-combustion engine. When Diesel was a young engineering student in Germany, in the 1870s, one of his professors told the class how inefficient the steam engine was. At best, only about one tenth of the energy contained in the fuel could be captured and put to useful work; the rest went up the smokestack and was lost. In theory, the professor reasoned, it should be possible to design an engine that would utilize almost all the energy in its fuel. It would be an internal-combustion engine, since it was inherently more efficient to burn the fuel directly inside the engine's cylinders than to burn it under a boiler to make steam, which then drove the pistons. The idea remained with Diesel.

After graduation, Diesel went to work for the professor who had sparked his interest in a more efficient source of power. He worked in neither laboratory nor classroom, for the professor also owned a firm that made refrigerating machines. One day Diesel was checking on the compressors at an ice factory and observed that they became very hot. He knew why, as every engineer did: compressing a gas increases its temperature. Suddenly he realized that the heat produced by compression could be used to ignite the fuel in an internal-combustion engine.

Now, internal-combustion engines were not new. Inventors had been tinkering with them since the end of the 18th century, when a French mechanic named LeBon built a single-cylinder engine fueled by the newly invented street-lighting gas. For ignition, he used another recently popularized marvel of science, the electric spark. LeBon's engine was ahead of its time, for the tools to make an engine that required such precisely fitting parts had not yet been invented. But in 1859 another Frenchman, an engineer named Etienne Lenoir, built the first practical internal-combustion engine. It, too, ran on street gas and was ignited by an electric spark. It was a failure at propelling a road vehicle, since it ran best at constant speed, but it was satisfactory for running factory machines via belts and pulleys.

Not all the early internal-combustion engines ran on street gas. Some burned alcohol; others burned gasoline or kerosene. One experimental model of the 1820s was powered by lycopodium powder, the spores of the plant we call club moss. This powder burns with explosive force and was then used in fireworks. The French inventor intended to use the engine to drive boats, but the cautious French banker whom he approached turned him down. The disappointed inventor, whose name was Nièpce, turned his talents elsewhere and became one of the pioneers of photography.

A major problem of the liquid-fuel engines was igniting their fuel. It had to be atomized to allow it to burn explosively, or it would merely have made the engine hot without pushing the piston an inch, and it had to be ignited when the piston was just beginning its downward stroke. The early ignition systems were temperamental and unreliable. Some used an electric spark. Others relied on an open flame that was caged safely behind a heat-diffusing metal screen; at just the right instant a mechanical device would flick the screen aside, and the flame would ignite the fuel. One of the most dependable systems used a red-hot steel ball as its igniting element (the ball had to be heated up first with a blowtorch). The engine ran at a slow, fairly steady thunk-thunk-thunk and burned a lot of fuel to generate a little power.

Germany had no oil to speak of, but it had lots of coal, and Diesel first intended to use coal dust as his fuel. However, when the engine stood ready for its trial run and the inventor started it, it blew up with a violent roar, nearly killing Diesel. He redesigned the engine to burn liquid fuel, which he squirted into the cylinder with a little pump he called an injector, and he strengthened the weak parts. The piston of the engine came up in the cylinder, squeezing the air to a red-hot temperature. At the top of the stroke, the injector squirted in a mist of oil, which burned explosively just as Diesel had predicted. The engine worked.

By 1896, Diesel was ready to market his engine. It quickly became a success, and Diesel became a millionaire. His career was cut short by tragedy. On a September night in 1913, he fell from the deck of a passenger steamer in the English Channel and was drowned. His body was never recovered. Suspicious people whispered that the German government had had him assassinated, since he was on his way to England to advise the British Navy on installing his engines in their ships. (Relations between the two great powers were very tense then, and World War I was only a year off.) But it turned out that Diesel, although a brilliant engineer, was an inept businessman and faced financial ruin. In addition, claims had been made for his engines that they could not live up to. Diesel's sense of honor compelled him to take this drastic way of atoning for his failures. Had he lived today, he would probably have hired a public-relations firm to gloss over the non-performance of his engines and passed his cost overruns on to the government.

Galvanized

"The unknown object on his radar screen galvanized the weary pilot into action."

"This ought to last you for twenty years. It's made of galvanized steel."

Both these examples of the word *galvanized*, so different in meaning, are derived from the name of an 18th-century Italian physician, Luigi Galvani, who, through a chance observation, became one of the pioneers of electrical science.

Galvani was born in Bologna in 1737. He wanted to become a priest, but his parents pushed him into medical school—Bologna's was one of the finest in Europe. At only twenty-five, Galvani was appointed lecturer in anatomy. His students considered him brilliant if uninspiring. His research on the hearing organs and the genito-urinary system of birds soon brought him renown as an anatomist.

Electrical experiments were then all the rage with scientists and science buffs. The nature of electricity was not yet understood, although Franklin's experiments had proved that lightning was a huge electrical spark. But a machine had been invented that produced a fairly strong charge of static electricity, and this was used in experiments both serious and playful. It was a globe of sulfur or glass, spun at high speed by a hand-cranked set of pulley wheels. When a person's hands were placed on the spinning globe, quite a powerful charge could be built up, and it could be led off by a metal chain and stored in a condenser called a Leyden jar. A common prank was to send an electrical discharge through a circle of people with linked hands and watch them jump involuntarily. In one demonstration in Paris, a line of 180 guardsmen was sent leaping into the air.

Galvani, like many another scientist, was fascinated with electricity and its effects on the body. One day in 1786, he was dissecting the legs of a skinned and very dead frog when his assistant idly spun an electrical friction machine that stood close by on the same table. A spark jumped from the machine to Galvani's steel dissecting knife, and the frog's legs kicked just as if it had been alive. Galvani, intrigued by this hint that electricity was somehow connected with life, did more experiments. Once, during a thunderstorm, he hung a pair of frog's legs by a brass hook off an iron fence outdoors to see if the lightning could make them twitch. He found that the legs twitched each time they touched the iron, whether there was a lightning flash or not. In another famous experiment, Galvani touched a zinc rod to one end of a frog's leg and a copper rod to the other, then brought the free ends of the two rods together. Again, the leg kicked! Galvani was convinced that animals were full of electricity, like living Leyden jars, and that the frog's leg had kicked because it was so fresh that it still contained a substantial charge.

At this point, another Italian scientist, Alessandro Volta, became interested. He also experimented with electricity and frog's legs, and became convinced that Galvani was wrong. It was the contact of two different metals in the presence of moisture that created the electric current, not the frog itself, said Volta. To back up his claim, he created the world's first known electric battery in 1799 or 1800. Volta's "pile," as he called it, was a multi-layered sandwich of silver coins alternating with disks of zinc, with pieces of cloth soaked in salt water in between. It was the first device capable of producing a steady electric current rather than a series of sparks. This made it possible for later scientists to develop electric motors and generators, on which our modern way of life depends so heavily. So we are indirectly indebted to Galvani and his frog's legs for much that makes our lives convenient and pleasant.

In the late 18th century, Galvani's name was applied to the spasmodic reflex motions that his experiments involved; hence the expression "galvanized into action." Galvanized iron or steel has been dipped in molten zinc to protect it from corrosion. It is so called because of an early confusion between the discoveries of Galvani and those of Volta. Chemically speaking, we might say that galvanized iron has been galvanized into *inaction*.

Watt The watt, a unit for measuring electricity, is named for the man who made steam power practical, James Watt (1736–1819). Contrary to the nonsense that is often taught in schools, Watt did not invent *the* steam engine. He invented a better one. Let us explode another cherished bit of nonsense: Watt was not inspired as a boy to build a steam engine by watching steam joggle the lid of a teakettle. That story was fantasized for the benefit of a biographer by an elderly aunt of Watt's when he was a middle-aged man, rich and famous.

Watt's inspiration came when he was a young man working at the University of Glasgow as the official maker and repairer of scientific instruments. A gifted, self-taught mathematician, Watt was on friendly terms with many of the professors. The Department of Natural Philosophy (an old name for the sciences) owned a little model of a Newcomen steam engine, which was not working properly, and Watt was asked to put it in order.

Thomas Newcomen had built the first reciprocating (piston-and-cylinder) steam engine in 1712. It pumped water from a coal mine in Staffordshire, in the midlands of England. Pumping water was all that Newcomen's engine was good for, but it was desperately needed for that. All over Europe, mines were threatened by flooding, and some had been forced to close down. Men could not work the pumps fast enough to keep up with the encroaching water, and horses cost far too much to feed. Besides, a horse could work only so long before it was exhausted. The time was ripe for mechanical power.

Newcomen's engine was an ungainly monster. It had a huge, open-topped cylinder, usually six feet in diameter and two to three times that in height. The cylinder had to be open-topped because the force that drove the piston was not steam, but the weight of the atmosphere; the greater the surface of the piston, the more push it received from the air above it. The piston was linked by a long chain to a big wooden rocker beam whose other end was connected to a pump rod. The engine worked like this: the weight of the pump rod dragged the piston to the top of the cylinder. A workman then opened a cock that let steam into the cylinder from a crude boiler. When the cylinder was filled (probably announced by steam leaking out around the piston), the steam cock was closed, and another cock was opened to spray cold water into the cylinder, making the steam condense. This formed a rather imperfect vacuum, and atmospheric pressure then slowly pushed the piston down, operating the pump. It was a slow process—under the best conditions, the engine might make twelve strokes a minute, accompanied by a mighty creaking and groaning and hissing of steam. It burned immense quantities of fuel. Still, it worked more effectively than men or horses, and coal was cheap and plentiful at the coal mines. In fact, the engine could burn low-grade waste coal that would otherwise have been thrown away or used to fill holes in the roads. By the time Newcomen died, in 1729, his engines were keeping mines dry in France, Belgium, Czechoslovakia, and Hungary. Other men made improvements in Newcomen's engine over the years, such as a mechanical rod for operating the steam and water valves, but in essence this was the kind of engine that Watt had been asked to repair.

The trouble with the University's model was that after two or three strokes it would run out of steam from its little model boiler. (This did not happen with the real mine engines because they each had several boilers to keep them supplied.) Watt was puzzled, but he conducted experiments for several months. At last he identified the problem. Each time the steam was condensed to make a vacuum, the cylinder was cooled down. Then, when new steam was let in, almost four fifths of it was wasted in simply heating up the cylinder to the point where the incoming steam did not condense. That was why the little model ran out of steam so fast, and why the big engines required so much fuel.

Watt saw clearly what the trouble was, but it took him several more months to find the solution. The idea came to him while he was taking a stroll on a fine Sunday afternoon: condense the steam outside the cylinder! The next morning (Scottish law forbade work on the Sabbath), Watt began to work on a model, borrowing a brass syringe from the University's medical department for his piston and cylinder. It ran so well that he built a full-sized engine. This engine, unlike Newcomen's, was closed at the top. The piston's rod passed through a hole in the cylinder cover, packed with greased rope fibers to make it airtight. The space above the piston was kept filled with steam at low pressure, which drove the piston down in the power stroke. A valve let the waste steam below the piston into a second, smaller cylinder that served as the condensing chamber. A small pump kept the condenser clear of condensed steam and trapped air.

Watt had to overcome many difficulties before he could bring his engine on the market. He had to get his parts from commercial suppliers, but their mechanics were not used to doing such accurate work as Watt's engine required. Machines for boring an accurate cylinder did not exist. The metal parts often had hidden flaws that made them break under stress. Above all, there was the problem of money, for Watt was a poor man. It was 1769 before he was able to offer an engine for sale. There were more financial reverses, for his customer went bankrupt, and Watt had to work as a surveyor to support his family. At last he joined forces with a wealthy and progressive businessman named Matthew Boulton, and the road to success was open.

Watt made another important contribution. All the early steam engines, including his own, were single-acting. That is, they produced power only on the downstroke. This was not suitable for rotary motion, as it was too jerky. In 1782 Watt designed a double-acting engine, which produced power on every stroke and incidentally doubled the engine's power output. He intended this engine to produce rotary motion that could drive mills and factory machines, but he could not use a crank. A competitor had taken out a patent on all uses of that venerable device in steam engines. Rather than pay the man a royalty, Watt worked out an ingenious sun-and-planet gear system that produced the same effect. This engine also embodied another idea that Watt had long cherished: to cut off the steam automatically part way through the stroke and let it drive the piston the rest of the way by its own expansion. This saved a good deal of steam and consequently fuel.

Watt did more. He invented one of the earliest examples of automation, the governor, a device that all by itself kept the engine running at a constant speed. Earlier, he had invented the horsepower as a unit of measurement to enable him to rate the power of his engines accurately.

Watt's discoveries won him such a reputation among scientists and engineers that in the late 1800s his name was chosen for the basic unit of electrical power. Other names of electrical units honor pioneers of electricity. The *volt* is named for Alessandro Volta, who invented the battery and discovered direct current. It measures electrical force, corresponding to the pressure of steam or water. The *ampere* is named for the French physicist Andre Marie Ampère (1775–1836), who was a botanist and poet before he made his classic discoveries of electromagnetism. The ampere is a measure of quantity, and it has been calculated as equivalent to 6,242,000,000,000,000,000 electrons. The *ohm* is named for the German physicist Georg Simon Ohm (1787–1854), whose discoveries are much too complicated to explain here. The ohm is a unit of resistance, and since the reader may be developing some resistance at this point, we'll pull the switch here.

Fahrenheit There is a reason

why the Fahrenheit scale of temperature has such strange

freezing and boiling points, and that reason is a strange experimental quirk on the part of its inventor, the German scientist Gabriel Daniel Fahrenheit (1686–1736). Fahrenheit devoted his life to the study of physics, but this brought him only fame. To support himself, he made meteorological instruments, and this may well have led to his interest in measuring temperatures accurately.

An accurate temperature scale must have reliable and unvarying fixed reference points. Fahrenheit chose for his two fixed reference points the boiling point and freezing point of water, a very reasonable decision. He then subdivided this temperature range into 180 degrees. Again, this was a perfectly sound choice. Astronomical measurements were based on a circle divided into 360 degrees (of which 180 is precisely half), and so were geometry, trigonometry, cartography, and navigation. There were then, as there are now, 60 seconds to a minute and 60 minutes to an hour. Enough said.

Instead of using the freezing point of water as his zero mark, Fahrenheit chose to determine zero by the lowest temperature he could attain by stirring a mixture of ice and salt. On this arbitrary scale, the freezing point of water was a balmy 32 degrees. Add 180 to this, and you have water boiling at 212 degrees.

Actually, the story is not quite this simple. It begins with Galileo, who invented a thermometer in 1612 and was apparently the first person to attempt to measure temperature with precision. Galileo proposed a temperature scale of 1,000 degrees, each degree being one thousandth of the volume of the fluid in the thermometer's bulb. It was a very precise scale in theory, but far beyond the technology of the times to accomplish. Next came the famous English mathematician Isaac Newton, who in 1701 proposed a simplified scale in which the freezing point of water was zero. His upper reference point was the temperature of a healthy human body, to which he assigned the value of 12, a number much used in English reckoning.

Fahrenheit began his work with the same reference points, in 1714, but soon found that twelve subdivisions were not precise enough. He multiplied the degrees by eight, which made body temperature 96. The choice of the boiling point of water for the upper reference point and the lowering of the zero point were later refinements. Quirky as it was, the Fahrenheit scale was the best available, and it was quickly adopted by Europe's scientists and governments.

Hardly had Fahrenheit's scale won general acceptance than a Swedish astronomer named Anders Celsius (1701–44) became aware of the shortcomings of its cumbersome reference points. He devised a new temperature scale in which the reference points were again the boiling and freezing points of water, but on his scale zero and the freezing point were the same, eliminating the silly business with 32. Celsius also divided his scale into 100 degrees rather than 180, reasoning that the decimal system made most calculations vastly easier.

Celsius' scale, which he announced in 1742, was originally called the centigrade scale (*centigrade* is Latin for "hundred steps"), and it became one of the bases of the metric system. In this century the name was changed to Celsius to honor him. Today the Celsius scale is universally used for scientific purposes, and virtually every country except the United States uses it in everyday life.

Gatling Gun
Ever since the first crude firearm was invented, men had tried to find a way to increase the rate of fire. None really succeeded until Dr. Richard Gatling perfected the first machine-gun in 1862. It is true that the revolvers invented by Samuel Colt and others could fire off six or seven shots without reloading, but then you

had to reload them with paper cartridges and put a percussion cap on each nipple of the gun's cylinder, and all that took time. The Gatling gun, however, even in its crudest form, could fire off 250 rounds a minute.

It was a beautifully simple device, a cluster of ten breech-loading rifle barrels mounted around a central spindle. The gunner turned a hand crank to make the barrels revolve; as they turned, a bullet dropped into the topmost one from a hopper on top of the gun. Gears, also powered by the hand crank, closed the breech and cocked and fired the hammer as each barrel came round in sequence. One factor in the success of the Gatling gun was that it used self-contained metal cartridges, which held the bullet, the powder to send it on its way, and the primer to ignite the powder. Such cartridges were not widely manufactured in 1862, and they were often defective, but their quality, and the Gatling gun, improved rapidly as the Civil War went on. The hopper was replaced by a drum that could be changed in seconds. Eventually the rate of fire rose to 1,200 rounds a minute.

Official foot-dragging kept Gatling's rapid-fire gun from actual combat use until the end of the Civil War, but improved models saw use in many armies until the end of the 19th century. The U.S. Cavalry used them against the Indians. Both French and Germans fired them at each other to a limited extent in the Franco-Prussian War. British troops used them in their wars with the Zulus in South Africa, and against the holy warriors of the Mahdi in the Sudan. Gatlings saw service against the Spanish in 1898, and Theodore Roosevelt, who loved playing soldier, praised them highly for their reliability.

The Gatling gun was big and heavy; mounted on wheels, it was pulled into position by horses or mules. For some reason, the underworld took a fancy to the name and used it for pistols. They also cut the name down to *gat*. From there it passed into the vocabularies of writers of cheap thrillers and so into the general language. It is now obsolete, but the detective stories of my youth bristled with the short, ugly word.

Gatling himself was an interesting man. Born in 1818 to a slave-owning North Carolina family, he moved north and was a strong Union supporter during the Civil War. Gatling was a talented inventor; at the age of twenty he devised a screw propeller for ships. But when he found that another inventor had beaten him to the patent by a few months, he turned instead to farm machinery. Then came a traumatic interlude. On a business trip in 1845, he came down with smallpox. He could get no medical aid because the riverboat on which he was traveling was stuck in the ice, far from any town, for two weeks. On his recovery, Gatling enrolled in medical school simply to learn how to take care of himself and his family. Although he never practiced medicine, he always liked to be addressed as "Doctor."

Gatling's patents for farm machines continued to keep him prosperous, and he invented new ones, including a steam-powered plow. The outbreak of the Civil War turned his mind to weapons for the Union, and the Gatling gun was the result. Later, he experimented with heavy artillery but that venture ended in failure when his test model blew up. At the age of eighty-two, he invented a gasoline-driven plow, one of the forerunners of today's mammoth farm tractors.

Neanderthal
In 1856, workmen quarrying for limestone near Düsseldorf, Germany, blasted open a small cave in a picturesque, steep-sided river gorge. Inside the cave they found some strange-looking bones. No scientists, the workmen casually tossed the bones out of the mouth of the cave to get them out of the way. They happened to fall at the feet of the quarry owner, who had come to inspect the work. Thinking that they were the remains of a cave

bear, he sent a message to the natural-history teacher at a local high school to come and fetch them.

The delighted pedagogue came post-haste. The bones had suffered badly from their 60-foot drop from the cave mouth to the rocky valley floor. The largest pieces left were part of a skull, some arm and leg bones, and a few ribs. But these were enough to tell the astonished schoolmaster that it was no cave bear's bones he was looking at, but those of a totally new species. A little more study convinced him that they were the fossils of a strange kind of beast-man, as he put it, somewhere between a gorilla and mankind. The gorge where the bones were discovered was called the Neanderthal (German for Neander Valley), and the remains were eventually dubbed Neanderthal Man.

The bones showed some apelike features, such as heavy brow ridges on the skull. Scientists did not know what to make of them. In 1856, Darwin had not yet published his epochal work *On the Origin of Species by Means of Natural Selection*, and his even more shocking *The Descent of Man* was years in the future. Most people were not prepared for the idea of primitive man. The very concept seemed preposterous. It conflicted with Biblical chronology and the myth of the Garden of Eden, so scholars came up with some interesting theories to explain away the embarrassing find.

"A primitive savage," sniffed one savant. "A degenerate of brutish type," cried another. "A pathological idiot," was a third opinion. The most ingenious theory offered was that the bones belonged to a Mongolian cavalryman in the Russian army who had died while his unit was pursuing the fleeing army of Napoleon four decades earlier. The soldier had suffered severely from an advanced case of rickets, said the professor, and the pain of the disease had forced him to take shelter in the cave, where he perished.

None of the above were true, and later finds revealed that

the bones came from an extinct race of humans that had lived in Europe and the Near East during the great Ice Age, from 100,000 to 35,000 years ago. But Neanderthal man had a bad press from the start. When he was accepted as a genuine, if primitive, human, he was depicted as a hulking, apelike brute who walked with a stoop. His muscles might have been massive, but his low brow with its projecting ridges obviously concealed an undersized, inferior brain. (Actually, skull measurements show that Neanderthal man had a larger brain than modern man.) Late-19th-century racial theorists, intoxicated by a perversion of Darwin's ideas, insisted that savage, brutish Neanderthal man had been exterminated in a deadly war by Cro-Magnon man, the intelligent and highly cultured ancestor of modern man.

Twentieth-century discoveries exploded this view. Neanderthal skeletons found in Shanidar Cave in Iraq were buried with carefully arranged bouquets of flowers, showing that the Neanderthals cared about their dead, had burial rituals, and apparently believed in a future life. Some of the skeletons had belonged to elderly people, crippled by old injuries; the Neanderthals took care of their disabled members instead of leaving them to die. Skillfully made Neanderthal tools have been found, demolishing the myth that these ancient men were ham-fisted savages. Even the ape-like stoop was a deliberate misinterpretation of a skeleton found in the south of France. The skeleton was one of an elderly person who was so crippled by arthritis that he could not stand up straight. A modern anthropologist has said that if you dressed a Neanderthal man or woman in modern clothes and put him in a rush-hour crowd, he would pass unnoticed.

Neanderthal man disappeared about 35,000 years ago, and his place was taken by modern man's direct ancestors. The sudden disappearance lends some credibility to the theory that the more advanced Cro-Magnon man wiped out his more

primitive cousin. But current theory holds that the Neanderthals died out when the great ice sheets melted away and the
giant animals that they hunted—mammoth, woolly rhino,
giant bison, horses, and cave bears, disappeared. Superbly
adapted to the life of an arctic hunter, Neanderthal could not
cope with the changing conditions. Some Neanderthals were
undoubtedly slain in battles with Cro-Magnon men, as man
has a distressing predilection for fighting his own kind. But
there is also fossil evidence that some Neanderthals interbred
with the newer men, and both are now classified as members
of the same species, *Homo sapiens*.

Let us return now to the Neander Valley, which gave its
name to Neanderthal Man. It was named in honor of a 17th-
century German hymn writer, Joachim Neander. His family's
name had originally been Neumann, but they had changed it
to the Greek equivalent, Neander (both mean New Man).
Neander, in addition to writing numerous hymns, was the
headmaster of a school in Düsseldorf. He loved to take his pu-
pils on strolls in the gorge, and when he died at the age of
thirty, they apparently kept reminiscing about their excursions
in Neander's Valley, until the name became permanent. The
devout Neander might well have been horrified to know that
his name was linked with a kind of man not mentioned in the
Creation myth; on the other hand, he might have looked upon
that 19th-century find as further proof of the infinite variety
of God's creations.

Nicotine

Nicotine is the alka-
loid that gives tobacco its narcotic properties. It is also a strong
poison, used in insecticides. Its name comes indirectly from a
16th-century French diplomat, Jean Nicot (1530–1600). A
bright young man, Nicot was appointed French consul at Lisbon before he was thirty. This position was a real plum, for

Nicotine

Portugal was then one of the wealthiest nations in Europe. It had colonies in Brazil, Africa, India, China, and the East Indies, with a huge merchant fleet to carry precious goods back to the homeland, and a powerful navy to protect them. For a time, Portugal pretty much controlled the lucrative Oriental spice trade. The envious King of France privately sneered at the Portuguese sovereign, calling him "that grocer king," but only in private, for he wanted to stay on good terms with his wealthy confrère. As consul, Nicot's main job was to keep the King of Portugal friendly to France and secure favorable trade terms.

There was great interest in Europe in the exotic plants of the New World, and in 1559 a Belgian merchant in Lisbon, with whom Nicot was friendly, gave him a sample of tobacco. Tobacco itself was no novelty, for Columbus had seen natives of the West Indies "drinking the smoke" by inhaling it through a forked tube they inserted into their nostrils. Columbus and his men tried it and liked it. They called the plant *tobaco*, which was actually the Indians' name for the inhaler. But tobacco had still not caught on in Europe.

Another friend of Nicot's, a doctor named Nicolas Monardes, investigated the medicinal properties of tobacco. From men returning from the New World, he learned that the Indians chewed the dried leaves of tobacco to numb the pain of toothache and relieve hunger pangs. Chewed tobacco leaves were used as poultices on cuts and bruises and skin diseases. Smoking the leaves was believed to cure colds.

Nicot presented some tobacco to the King and Queen of Portugal, who were delighted with it. When he returned to France in 1560, he took along some tobacco as a gift for his sovereign, the notorious Catherine de Medici. According to one story, the Queen one day suffered a violent headache. Nicot offered her some snuff—finely ground tobacco—to inhale. The Queen sniffed, sneezed, and, presto!, her headache was gone. From that moment Catherine was a tobacco enthusiast. Her courtiers, anxious to follow the royal example, sedulously imitated her, and snuff-taking and smoking were soon all the rage in France. Since France was the center of fashion, the tobacco fad spread rapidly. Rulers tried to eradicate it, but even the harshest measures could not prevail against the "sotweed," as King James I of England later called it.

Monardes published a book in which he did his utmost to promote the use of tobacco as a drug, and he mentioned Nicot prominently. The French named the tobacco plant *nicotiane* in Nicot's honor, and botanists later Latinized the name to *Nicotiana* to make it scientific. When chemists investigated the composition of tobacco in the 19th century, they named the active compound *nicotine* from the plant. Nicot's diplomatic accomplishments are long since forgotten, but men and women around the globe honor him daily each time they smoke.

Sideburns

The 19th century —most of it—was a glorious time for beards. Men cultivated them in the most fantastic variety of shapes and lengths. There was the Vandyke, a small, neatly trimmed, pointed beard; it was named for the renowned 17th-century Flemish artist Anthony Vandyke, who painted many portraits of men wearing that style of mandibular adornment. The imperial, a 16th-century style, was revived by the Emperor Napoleon III of France. It was a mere tuft running down the middle of the lower lip and chin, but it was counterbalanced by a magnificent waxed mustache. Another popular beard was the goatee, which strictly speaking grew under the chin, where a real goat's beard grows. In the United States it was associated with old-fashioned farmers. The journalist Horace Greeley cultivated a curious set of chin-whiskers that surrounded his lower jaw like a ruff while leaving his cheeks, chin, and lips bare. The top of his head was bare, too, which added to the effect.

However, the focus of this essay is the style known as sideburns, which are, logically enough, whiskers on each side of the face. They were named for the Civil War hero, General Ambrose Burnside, who wore a luxuriant set of these side whiskers. A playful inversion gave birth to "sideburns." Burnside was a pretty inept general, but he was well-liked and handsome, which was no doubt a reason for the popularity of sideburns.

Side whiskers, however, reached their apogee before the Civil War, thanks in part to a British playwright named Tom Taylor. In 1858 Taylor, who wrote over a hundred plays all told, came out with a popular comedy titled *Our American Cousin*. One of the minor comic characters was a stuffy, pompous old nobleman called Lord Dundreary, who wore the longest, bushiest set of side whiskers yet seen in public. They resembled a pair of enormous spaniel's ears propped out from the sides of the head.

The play was popular in England, and it was a smash hit in the United States. The actor who played the role of Dundreary in the New York production stole the show, making Dundreary the center of attention. The actor, Edward A. Sothern, became a popular idol, and his male admirers by the thousands cultivated Dundrearies in imitation. It was *Our American Cousin* that President Lincoln was watching at Ford's Theater when he was assassinated.

To Orthodox Jews, Amish, Muslims, and Sikhs, beards are badges of piety and devotion. In the turbulent 1960s, beards were associated with youthful radicals and rebels (this was also the case in Europe in the 1830s). But, for most of history, they have been a symbol of maturity. There was one notable exception, ancient Rome. In Rome, it was the proper young men who grew beards, while the older men went clean-shaven.

Pompadour

That recurrently popular hairstyle, the pompadour, was named for a woman who controlled French politics, and thus the politics of most of Europe, in the mid-18th century. Madame de Pompadour possessed this power by virtue of being the mistress of the reigning king Louis XV.

Madame de Pompadour was not born to power or wealth. She began life as plain Jeanne-Antoinette Poisson, the daughter of a government contractor who had prospered by supplying provisions to the royal troops. At least, she was baptized as such. It was generally believed, however, that her real father was an extremely wealthy financier and tax-farmer, Le Normant de Tournehem. (A tax-farmer was an official who collected taxes for the government on contract. He was allowed to keep a certain percentage of all he collected for his own profit. Needless to say, tax-farmers were among the most hated people in France.)

When Toinette was only three, her father was caught in a scheme to defraud the government by phony sales and had to flee to Germany to escape the gallows. Le Normant took upon himself the costs of Jeanne's education, lending credence to the story of his paternity. She was an unusually bright and pretty child, and Le Normant had her brought up to be a king's mistress, with the goal of ingratiating himself further with the monarch. "*Un morceau de roi*—a morsel for a king," he described her to his friends. She was taught singing, ballet, acting, engraving, the harpsichord, and other accomplishments.

But becoming a royal mistress was not a casual matter. A certain procedure had to be followed. So at the age of nineteen she was married off to a nephew of her patron, a young nobleman named Le Normant d'Etioles. Her husband fell passionately in love with her—a rare thing in those days of arranged marriages—and spent his money freely to gratify her. She became a leader of Paris fashion and the reigning belle of the financial community, but she still had not met her destined royal paramour.

The king's current mistress, on guard against the ambitious young beauty, refused to give her an introduction to the court, thus effectively blocking her access to the king. For four years she tried to catch the king's eye while he was out hunting, all in vain. Then the current mistress died, and the king accepted an invitation to a public ball in honor of his infant son. There, at last, the fair Madame d'Etioles met her prey and instantly subdued him. She left her husband and moved to Versailles, where in 1745 she was proclaimed *maîtresse en titre*, or official mistress. The poor husband accepted this with as good grace as he could muster. This sort of thing happened frequently on every social level but the poorest, and the cuckolded husband customarily received a generous compensation from the higher-ranking man who took over his wife. Indeed, many an ambitious courtier schemed and plotted to push his wife into the king's bed in the hopes of advancement.

Louis XV was no prize. It was not altogether his fault. Both his parents (the Duke of Burgundy and the Princess of Savoy) had died when he was only five, and the orphaned princeling was brought up by the regent, the debauched Duke of Orleans. Louis' tutor, Bishop Fleury, was unable to counteract the bad influence of the licentious regent. When Louis came of age and took the crown, at thirteen, there was no way of restraining him. In statecraft he was an utter failure. Louis aspired to be a powerful, autocratic ruler like his illustrious great-grandfather, Louis XIV. His ministers and the great nobles conspired to maintain this illusion, but behind the polished and elegant facade there was nothing but a savage jockeying for power. Louis' royal mind could not quite grasp this. At the council table, one of his ministers confided to his diary, the king "opened his mouth, said little, and thought not at all." He was easy prey for an ambitious and unscrupulous woman.

Head over heels in love with Mme. d'Etioles, the king bought her a manor called Pompadour. This carried with it the title of marquise. At last she was noble in her own right! But this was only the beginning for the adventuress who was now called Madame de Pompadour. Quickly, she made herself friends with intellectuals and politicians. Voltaire was her chief poet. A doctor named Quesnay, who was also an influential economic theorist, was her personal physician. Herself a talented amateur, she encouraged artists. She organized a court theater with a repertory troupe of high-ranking nobles and noblesses. They entertained the king with operas, dramas, and ballets, in all of which Pompadour often took the starring role.

As the reigning mistress, Pompadour was a trend-setter in many areas of fashion. A shade of pink was named for her; so were clothing styles, furniture, parasols, and a new kind of rose. She—or more likely her hairdresser—devised a flattering coiffure in which the hair was brushed back from the forehead in an upsweep. Men copied it, too.

But all was not rosy for the Marquise de Pompadour. She had many enemies at the court, and they composed vast numbers of maliciously witty poems at her expense, often making plays on her maiden name. (*Poisson* is French for "fish.") They also plotted to replace her in the King's bed with a younger, prettier woman.

Louis was fickle, and within a few years he tired of Pompadour's amatory talents. It was necessary to do something more to keep her hold on him and her place at court. So she made herself politically indispensable to the king. Within a short time, she had the cabinet ministers conferring with her before they met with the king, and together they prepared the king's agenda. Together with the royal postmaster, she daily screened the king's mail. It was she who decided what appeals should or should not reach his eye. The lazy king was properly grateful for her assistance, and for a time she was the most influential woman in Europe.

But Pompadour overreached herself, and in so doing changed the maps of Europe and of North America. France had been allied with Prussia, counterbalancing the might of the great Austrian Empire. But King Frederick of Prussia had written some nasty poems about Madame de Pompadour, and she was mortally offended. About that time, the Empress Maria Theresa of Austria wrote her a sympathetic letter. (Maria Theresa had a bone of her own to pick with Frederick, for he had stolen the rich province of Silesia from her.) Pompadour, determined to avenge her insults, used her influence to break the French alliance with Prussia and make a new one with Austria. This alliance upset the balance of power, and Britain rushed to the support of Prussia. Russia, Saxony, and Sweden weighed in on the side of France and Austria, seeing advantages for themselves. After a good deal of posturing and bluster on all sides, war broke out in earnest. The result of the Seven Years' War (1756–63) was that France lost all of Canada to her hated rival, Britain, and sold Louisiana to Spain to avoid that territory's also falling into British hands. In 1764 Mme. Pompadour, exhausted by her intrigues, died at the age of 42, dressed in full court costume.

Even after her death, she was not safe from the sneers of her enemies. During her funeral ceremonies, a princess was heard to remark that the noble family whose vault she had purchased would have a real surprise when they found Fish bones beside them. A final spate of nasty poems poured out from titled pens. But Pompadour was soon forgotten for the newest excitements of the moment. Her most enduring monument was the hairstyle named for her, which is still with us. In this country, popular entertainers who have worn it include Elvis Presley and Ronald Reagan, the actor-President.

Occupational names

Many names that come from occupations are pretty obvious. Baker, Butcher, Carpenter, Mason, Smith, and Weaver are a few of the examples. But there are a number that are derived from specialties that no longer exist and have been long forgotten.

For instance, a Fletcher (from the French *flèche*, "arrow") was one who put the feathers on arrows to guide them in their flight. An Archer (from the French *arc*, "bow") was a professional bowman. The ancestors of the Jocelyns (a corruption of *gosling*, a young goose) supplied goose feathers to the fletchers.

Some names come from farming. A Calvert was a calf-herder; the original Cowards were cow-herds. The Hayward or Heyward was a local official who inspected the hedges and fences that kept the farm animals off the croplands—the Old English form was *hege-weard*, from *hege*, "hedge" and *weard*, "guard." Curiously enough, the name Farmer does not refer to the one who worked the land, but to a tax-farmer, a man who paid the authorities for the right to collect taxes in a given area. Anything he collected over the amount for which he had contracted was his to keep—and he usually collected enough to make it well worth his while. Alternatively, the Farmer might be a capitalist who leased an entire manor or estate to run for his own profit. The former editor of the *Oxford English Dictionary* was named Onions, but this, too, had nothing to do with the farm. Apparently it is derived from a Welsh word, *einion*, or "anvil," and once connoted steadiness and reliability.

A Collier was a "coal-man," which in medieval times meant one who burned wood to make charcoal, the preferred fuel. A

Cooper made barrels and tubs. Lorimer meant a harness-maker. Cordwainer meant a man who worked in cordovan leather, named for the Spanish city of Cordova, where it presumably originated. The field of music yields Harper, Fidler, Piper, and Taber (one who played a little drum called a tabor, which was held under the arm; it could be played while the player danced and sang).

Such names as these were usually inherited from one's father, while Pope, Bishop, or Priest (titles that could not be passed on from parent to child because the Church required celibacy) probably came from the popular mystery plays and pageants, in which common people would play these roles. If someone always played a Priest or a Bishop, this became his nickname and eventually his recognized surname. From the plays, too, came names like King, Prince, and Knight. Real knights were aristocrats and already had family names, usually derived from the family estate.

The names Brewster and Baxter are actually feminine. The ending *-ster* was an Old English way of showing that the bearer of the name was a woman. Both brewing and baking were originally carried on by women, but later on men got into the trade as well, and by then the names were so well established that they were applied to men without anyone making bad jokes about it. Webster, as in the maker of dictionaries, was a female weaver.

Many of the non-English names in the United States also came from occupations or professions. Schultz and Schultheiss are German terms for a judge. Kaufman is German for "merchant," and Kramer is German for a petty shopkeeper. Spengler is German for a tinsmith, and Schmidt for an ironsmith. Smiths must once have been very important in the rural economy, for Smith is said to be the most common English surname, despite the fact that the majority of people were unskilled farm laborers. The French equivalent is LeFèvre (lit-

erally, the iron worker), the Spanish, Herrero. The late come-
dian Ernie Kovacs' name is the Hungarian for Smith. In the
Slavic languages, the equivalent is Koval or Kowal or one of
the many other variants. In Hebrew and Arabic it is Haddad.

In the army, I had a friend named Forriter who told me that
a remote ancestor had been a German cavalryman named
Vorreiter, or outrider, one who rode ahead of the troop to
scout out the enemy. In European armies of the 17th and 18th
centuries, the soldiers were often given martial-sounding
names that they passed on to their descendants. Another soldier in my unit was PFC Frimodig, whose name is Swedish for
"courageous." Poor fellow, the other GIs usually perverted his
name to "Frimidog" or "Free-my-dog."

My own name, Limburg, comes by a very roundabout way
from the Roman army of occupation in western Europe. The
Romans established a *limes*, or boundary line, between themselves on the one side and the barbarian Germans, Gauls, etc.,
on the other. Along this line at intervals they built forts, which
they called *burgus*, from an old Germanic word for a fort or
fortified town. So the fort on the boundary was *limis burgus*,
which eventually was shortened to *Limburg*. Limburg was the
name of a good-sized duchy in the Low Countries. It is now
divided into two provinces, one in Belgium, one in the Nether-
lands. There is also a picturesque fortified city named Limburg on the Lahn River in West Germany, from which my
German-Jewish ancestors probably came. Like many Jews,
they took a place name for their surname. When they came to
America in the 1870s, the name was Limburger, like the
cheese. A family story goes that one day my grandfather was
lunching at his favorite German (pre-World War I) restaurant
and ordered a Swiss-cheese sandwich. The waiter yelled out,
"Schweizer für Limburger!" ("Swiss for Limburger.") The
chef shouted back, "You know we don't make any changes
once the order's in!" That decided my grandfather to ampu-

tate the final syllable of his name. Even so, when I was in grade school, my classmates loved to call me "Cheese" and hold their noses when I went by, even though I was forced to take a bath every day.

Lynch

The word "lynch," with all its unpleasant connotations, is derived from Charles Lynch (1736–96), a planter and justice of the peace in back-country Virginia. Lynch was born and spent most of his life near the site of present-day Lynchburg. This man whose name has come to stand for mob violence was brought up as a peaceable Quaker and a strong upholder of the law. He became a justice of the peace in 1766 and a member of the Virginia House of Burgesses three years later. In 1776 he served on the committee that drafted Virginia's new constitution, and later became a colonel of militia. He served under General Greene (whose widow later hired Eli Whitney to tutor her children) from 1781 down to the final British surrender at Yorktown, when he returned to the law and politics.

How did this eminently respectable man come to be associated with brutal mobs? The answer lies in the fact that during the Revolutionary War his area of Virginia was a battleground between Patriots and Tories, and the constituted court system could not function. Into the breach stepped Judge Lynch, establishing an extra-legal court where malefactors of all kinds were quickly tried and usually sentenced to a whipping. In 1780, a Tory conspiracy was discovered in Bedford County, where Lynch lived and held court. It caused great alarm because the British general Cornwallis appeared close to scoring a victory over the Americans, and that meant that the Patriots stood a good chance of being hanged, or at the very least losing all their property. So Lynch and his associates held a summary trial of the conspirators and sentenced them to death. They were sufficiently disturbed by this to want vindication, and two years later the Virginia Assembly exonerated them on the grounds of the imminent danger posed by the conspiracy.

By then, however, "Lynch's law" had passed into the language, and mob leaders invoked it against their victims. Lynching became something of a frontier institution, and it remained strong in the South, where the frontier mentality lingered. After the Civil War, the usual victims of lynch mobs were "uppity" Negroes—"uppity" meaning anyone who didn't choose to go on behaving like a slave after slavery was abolished. Lynching remained a part of Southern life, even though decent people condemned it, until after the Civil Rights acts of the 1960s. It is to be hoped that this national disgrace has died out, but there is always a chance that it will flare up again as long as there are angry and ignorant people who believe that violence is the best solution to all of life's frustrations.

Sandwich

Tradition has it that the sandwich was named for an English nobleman, James Montagu, fourth Earl of Sandwich (1718–92), who had it created for him. The earl, an inveterate gambler, was enjoying a winning streak at the card table and would not leave it for twenty-four hours. To sustain himself, he ordered slices of meat between two slices of bread.

In fact, although the earl may well have ordered this snack, he did not invent the sandwich. The Romans ate sandwiches, and so did medieval peasants of Europe, although the peasants had cheese rather than meat as the filler. Nevertheless, the earl did start a vogue, and Englishmen were using the word "sandwich" as early as 1765.

Gastronomy aside, the fourth Earl of Sandwich was a colorful and rather unsavory character. He was a member of the Hellfire Club, a group of naughty sophisticates who, dressed as monks, held orgies at the ruined abbey of Medmenham, outside London. When the club was exposed, Sandwich turned against his companions; after that, the public called him Jemmy Twitcher, after a despicable character in *The Beggar's Opera*, a bitingly satirical musical comedy. Sandwich, probably due to political connections, had been First Lord of the Admiralty until the king dismissed him for incompetence. Somehow, he got himself reappointed to that post in 1771. He went down in history as the most corrupt and incompetent First Lord of the Admiralty ever. Under his administration, navy supplies were stolen on a grand scale, positions were bought and sold, and unseaworthy, inadequately equipped ships were sent into battle. His retirement in 1782 was an occasion of rejoicing for the entire British Navy.

This Earl of Sandwich is notable for one other thing: Captain James Cook, the first European to reach the Hawaiian Islands, named them the Sandwich Islands in honor of the earl, who was at that time misruling the British Navy.

Index

287

Index